# THE EARTHQUAKE NEVER WENT AWAY

STEWART & KNOX

D0851458

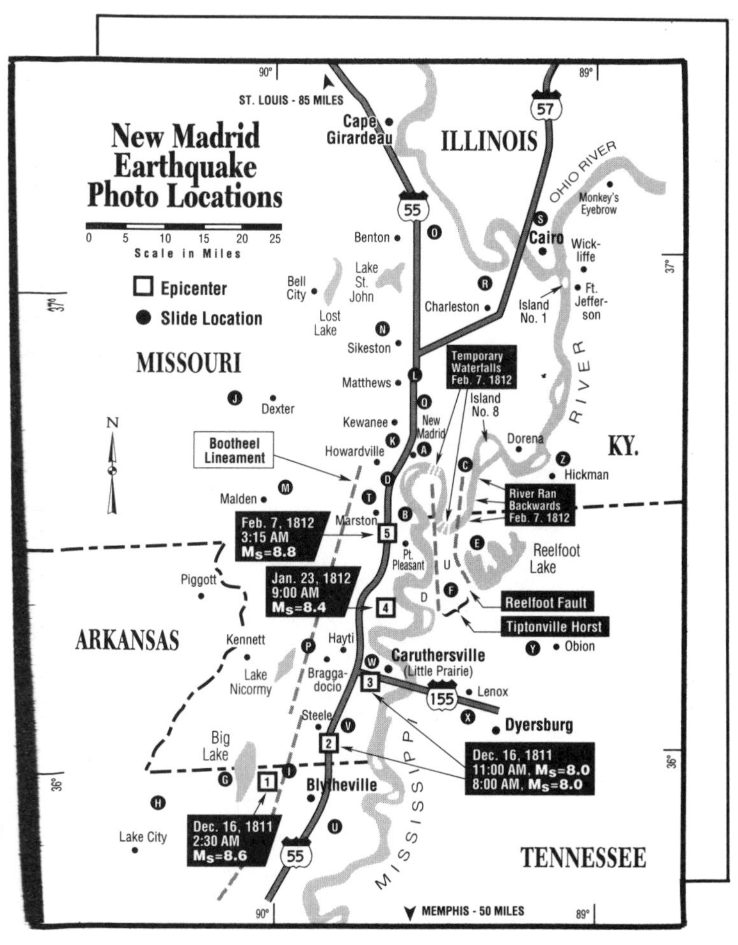

New Madrid Earthquake Photo Locations
0 5 10 15 20 25
Scale in Miles
Epicenter
Slide Location
ST. LOUIS - 85 MILES
MEMPHIS - 50 MILES
90°
89°
37°
36°
MISSOURI
ILLINOIS
KY.
ARKANSAS
TENNESSEE
OHIO RIVER
RIVER
MISSISSIPPI
Cape Girardeau
Benton
Bell City
Lake St. John
Lost Lake
Charleston
Sikeston
Matthews
Dexter
Kewanee
Howardville
New Madrid
Malden
Marston
Pt. Pleasant
Piggott
Kennett
Lake Nicormy
Hayti
Braggadocio
Caruthersville (Little Prairie)
Steele
Big Lake
Blytheville
Lake City
Cairo
Wickliffe
Ft. Jefferson
Monkey's Eyebrow
Island No. 1
Island No. 8
Dorena
Hickman
Reelfoot Lake
Obion
Lenox
Dyersburg
Bootheel Lineament
Temporary Waterfalls Feb. 7, 1812
River Ran Backwards Feb. 7, 1812
Reelfoot Fault
Tiptonville Horst
Feb. 7, 1812 3:15 AM Ms=8.8
Jan. 23, 1812 9:00 AM Ms=8.4
Dec. 16, 1811 11:00 AM, Ms=8.0 8:00 AM, Ms=8.0
Dec. 16, 1811 2:30 AM Ms=8.6
55
57
155
N

## LIVING ON THE NEW MADRID FAULT LINE

My Home's on the Mississippi River
Between St. Louis and Memphis, Tennessee.
I reside in Southeast Missouri.
The "Show Me" State's a great place to be.

Lately I feel a little nervous
About my section of the land of the free,
Living on the New Madrid fault line,
Something's shakin', Lord, I hope it's just me.

They had the big one here back in 1812,
But no one's around to tell the tale.
The old Mississippi ran backwards,
The earth sank, and lakes began to swell.

The good Lord, he put us all here
And only He's gonna take us away.
Living on the New Madrid fault line,
You gotta live it day by day.

People, you've got to be ready.
You've got to treat your neighbor right.
Got to live each day like it could be your last.
You've got to fight your brothers' fight.

You've got to put your trust in the Good Lord above.
That Solid Rock will put your fears at ease.
Living on the New Madrid fault line,
Something's shakin', Lord, I hope it's just me.

Song Lyrics by Lou Hobbs
Released in 1990 by:
Evergreen Records
Sixteenth Avenue
Nashville, TN 37203

# THE EARTHQUAKE THAT NEVER WENT AWAY

## The Shaking Stopped in 1812 . . .
## . . . But the Impact Goes On

**Dr. David Stewart**
**& Dr. Ray Knox**

**150 Original Photos, Figures & Tables**
**On the New Madrid Seismic Zone**
**Of Faults, Fissures & Scars in the Landscape**
**Still Visible from the Great Earthquakes of 1811-12**
**and How They Still Affect You Today**

**NOTE: This Book and all other GR Publications Carry an Exclusive**

***Earthquake Hazard Warranty***

If it is damaged in an earthquake you can receive a replacement from the publisher
**FREE OF CHARGE**
(See page 221 for details)

(*This book is also available with a complete set of 150 color slides corresponding to every photo, table and figure. See page 217 for details.)

**Second Printing**
**1996**

Cover Design by Kate Schaefer and David Stewart.
Photos & Figures by David Stewart.
First Printing 1993, 2200 copies
Second Printing 1996, 2200 copies



**Published by:**

**Route 1, Box 646**
**Marble Hill, MO 63764**
**United States of America**
**Call Toll Free: 1-800-758-8629**

*See Back of this Book for Information on Books, Slides, Services, and Free Literature Available from Gutenberg-Richter.

Publishers Cataloguing in Publication
(Prepared by Quality Books Inc.)

Stewart, David M., 1937-
The earthquake that never went away : the shaking stopped in 1812--but the impact goes on / by David Stewart & Ray Knox.
p. cm.
Includes bibliographical references and index.
Preassigned LCCN: 92-75133.
ISBN 0-934426-54-6

1. Earthquakes--Missouri--New Madrid Region. I. Knox, Ray (Burnel Ray), 1931- II. Title.

QE535.2.U6S84 1993 551.2'2'09778985
QBI93-176

## DEDICATION

We dedicate this book to the residents of the New Madrid Seismic Zone. Thanks folks! You are the nicest people around! The field work we have done in creating this book is enjoyable in and of itself, but you have helped make our field investigations even more enjoyable. We appreciate your interest in our research and the time you have so freely given to us. Many of you have helped us locate features described in this book, and filled us in on interesting things that have happened to them. Many of you have enriched our visits with fascinating stories about the history and folklore and some of the real old time characters of the area. We hope you like what we have done. Again, thanks, and God bless!

## DISCLAIMER

Amost all of the features described and/or photographed in this book can be seen from an automobile, from the air, or from a boat on the Mississippi River, and do not require you to enter private property. Some shown in this book are actually found on public lands to which everyone has access within the regulations and visiting time schedule pertaining to that preserve or park. Should you desire to investigate any of these features closer, where you must enter private property, you should obtain permission first. THIS BOOK IN NO WAY GIVES ANYONE AUTHORITY TO TRESPASS.

We have encountered scores of landowners while researching for this book. We have yet to have our request to enter their property denied. In every case they have been friendly, cordial, cooperative and helpful. This is all the more reason to stop, talk to these nice folks, and get their permission before entering their property. They will be very friendly and will volunteer many interesting historical details, greatly enriching your experiences. Visit with them awhile. You'll be glad you did.

# TABLE OF CONTENTS

# THE EARTHQUAKE THAT NEVER WENT AWAY

## KEY TO APPROXIMATE PHOTO LOCATIONS*

| MAP KEY | GENERAL AREA OF PICTURE | PHOTO NOS. | NO. OF PHOTOS | TEXT PAGES |
|---|---|---|---|---|
| A | New Madrid, MO | 12-26 | 15 | 54-68 |
| B | Marston, MO-Bessie, TN | 27-31 | 5 | 69-73 |
| C | Stump Hole-Island #8 | 32-35 | 4 | 74-77 |
| D | Howardville-New Madrid, MO | 36-43 | 8 | 78-85 |
| E | Reelfoot Fault-Donaldson Point | 44-48 | 5 | 86-90 |
| F | Reelfoot Lake, TN | 49-56 | 8 | 91-98 |
| G | Big Lake, AR-Hornersville, MO | 57-67 | 11 | 99-109 |
| H | Monette, AR | 68-69 | 2 | 110-111 |
| I | Gosnell-Big Lake, AR | 70-73 | 4 | 112-115 |
| J | Dexter-Dudley, MO | 74-77 | 4 | 116-119 |
| K | Kewanee, MO | 78-82 | 5 | 120-124 |
| L | Matthews, MO | 83-89 | 7 | 125-131 |
| M | Malden, MO | 90 | 1 | 132 |
| N | Sikeston, MO | 91-95 | 5 | 133-137 |
| O | Benton-Scott City, MO | 96-101 | 6 | 138-143 |
| P | Hayti-Braggadocio, MO | 102-109 | 8 | 144-151 |
| Q | LaForge, MO | 110-115 | 6 | 152-157 |
| R | Charleston, MO | 116-117 | 2 | 158-159 |
| S | Cairo, IL | 118-122 | 5 | 160-164 |
| T | Marston, MO | 123-125 | 3 | 165-167 |
| U | Blytheville, AR | 126 | 1 | 168 |
| V | Steele-Holland-Cooter, MO | 127-129 | 3 | 169-171 |
| W | Caruthersville, MO | 130-133 | 4 | 172-175 |
| X | Lenox, TN | 134-137 | 4 | 176-179 |
| Y | Obion, TN | 138-140 | 3 | 180-182 |
| Z | Hickman, KY | 141-149 | 9 | 183-191 |

*All of these photos are available in full color as 35mm slides. For details on how you can obtain your own set of New Madrid Earthquake Slides, see back of book for details.

# 1

# Acknowledgements

## OUR THANKS TO A WHOLE LOT OF GOOD PEOPLE

This book, *The Earthquake that Never Went Away,* is the first of a trilogy of books we have been writing about the Great New Madrid Earthquakes of 1811-12. It only takes three years to gestate a baby elephant, but will have taken six to produce these three books and their accompanying set of 150 color slides. Since 1988, when the idea was first conceived, and during the years of pregnancy and labor that followed to complete their birthing, innumerable people have assisted and contributed toward making one or more of these publications possible. Since their contributions to one of these related works cannot always be separated from the others, we shall try to acknowledge everyone here who had something to do with any of the three books, even if it was not specifically this one.

Without the enthusiastic encouragement of hundreds of friends and supporters during these years of work, these tomes would never have made it. So, first of all, thanks to all of you, too numerous to name, who expressed to us your support during this lengthy labor. Send or bring us your copy of this book. We would would be honored and would appreciate the opportunity to autograph our personal thanks to you.

As for specific people, we have to begin with Virginia LaValle Carlson, Director of the New Madrid Historical Museum, whose picture appears on this page. We wish to thank Virginia as well as all of the staff who work in the Museum, especially Margaret Goza, Virginia Howell, and Lorene Higgerson, whose unwavering enthusiasm, encouragement, and moral support for our work has helped us in many difficult times, as well as given us numerous invaluable leads for our research. A particularly enlightening source of information was Virginia Carlson's father, Ed LaValle, born in New Madrid in 1906, whose incredible memory provided us with facts and locations that we were unable to find by any other means. The LaValle family was one of the first two families to occupy the New Madrid town site in the late 1700's and were among those who survived the great earthquakes.

**Virginia Carlson, Director**
**New Madrid Historical Museum**

We wish to express our gratitude to the current and former staff of the Center for Earthquake Studies at Southeast Missouri State University who were helpful in many ways on many occasions in the field and in the office. These include Mike Coe, Karen Coe, Mark Winkler, and Linda Dillman. Linda was one of the editors of the manuscript. Mark Winkler, Southeast Missouri Coordinator for the State Emergency Management Agency, is also a trained forester whose assistance enabled us to establish the age of the living "Witness Tree" (See in Slides #78 and #79).

Besides Linda Dillman, other editors of our works have been Ed Williams, Professor of Geoscience at Southeast Missouri State University, and Steve Owen, a Student at Southeast. Their genuine interest and careful reading of our manuscripts has resulted in many improvements for which we are grateful. Karen Knox and Lee Stewart, wives of the authors, have also helped in innumerable ways. Their many constructive suggestions have considerably improved the quality of this work, as well as that of the other two books of this trilogy.

We appreciate the assistance and encouragement the Friends of the New Madrid Historical Museum as well as the New Madrid Chamber of Commerce. Angie Holtzhouser, who works for the Chamber, was particularly helpful in obtaining some historical information for us. Individually, there are more people in New Madrid than we can list who have personally helped and encouraged us. Particularly, the loyal encouragement and assistance of Dr. Charles Baker and Mr. Jim Bradley of the New Madrid County Health Department has been greatly appreciated, as was the genealogical assistance of Mrs. Lilbourn Lewis "Libba" Hunter Crisler, from whose porch the New Madrid Museum is seen in Slide #14. Also from New Madrid is Mr. Charles Hatley, an attorney, who kindly flew David Stewart in his airplane for some of the photos in this book, as well as Mr. Lynn Bock, another New Madrid attorney, who piloted his boat on two occasions to carry the authors to the site of the cypress stumps shattered by the earthquakes of 1811-12 opposite Island #8 on the Mississippi River (see Slides #32-#35). Lynn has been helpful in some of the historical research, as well as a continual source of encouragement through the years, as has his wife, Marian Bock, who works for the City of New Madrid and who has assisted us in many ways. We also wish to thank Mr. Charles Ice, New Madrid County Surveyor, and Father David Hulshof of the Immaculate Conception Church and Parochial School in New Madrid. Yvonne Morgan, City Collector at Lilbourn, Missouri, was also very helpful in tracking down the Lilbourn Lewis saga told in "The Earthquake America Forgot."

During our dozens of trips to the field to locate and identify these seismic features, we crossed the lands of many property owners and found them to be universally friendly and cooperative. The New Madrid Seismic Zone is very much a part of Southern culture and the practice of "Southern Hospitality" is alive and well down there. We want to thank all of the property owners who not only gave us permission to enter their lands but often led us to seismic features we did not even know about until they showed them to us.

In particular, we want to thank land owners Ernest Carpenter who showed us "The Grinnel Hole" in a sand slough; William and Floy Campbell of Lenox, Tennessee, who have always been most cordial in allowing us and our groups of students to regularly visit the Seismic Earthflow Landslide at the Campbell & Campbell Gravel Works; Ferg Hunter who kindly showed us around his acreage and permitted us to visit the Chartreau explosion crater; Mr. N.J. Nowell, who farms in the Des Cyprie area and whose recollections of how the great floods of 1912-13 modified the land were helpful to us; Mr. J.K. Swilley, landowner of Swilley Pond (an earthquake feature) where two boys drowned in the 1940's; Frank and Bob Stetson (father and son) who leveled a seismic sand ridge and exposed the underlying fissure for us to see on their land near Pascola; Phil Kelley of Sikeston who took the time to drive down to Dry Bayou and show us this unusual polygenetic feature; Robert Riley, landowner of the Sinclair Sand Boil, the largest in the city limits of New Madrid and who has given his kind permission for visitors to enter and explore; Andy Jenkins, landowner of of a compound sand fissure on Bootheel Lineament west of Steele: Fannie Langdon (mother) and Jean Langdon (son), owners of an Indian Temple Mound near Big Lake north of Hornersville, who shared stories with us of the "good ol' days".

In the Benton, Missouri, area, we wish to thank Roy and Elaine Proctor whose hospitality has allowed us to regularly visit the Proctor Landslide, Proctor Sunk Land, and the Proctor Sand Boil, and whose recollections of the past helped us to better understand these features. Mike Lomax, Keith Koepp, Leroy & Nancy Holmes own three parcels of land in the Benton Hills between Benton and Oran, Missouri, in the northern fringe of the NMSZ. All three suffered seismically related landslides on their respective properties from the September 26, 1990, earthquake near New Hamburg, Missouri. Their willingness to help Ray Knox and David Stewart explore and photograph these features has been appreciated. We especially appreciate Mr. Lomax's willingness to allow groups of students to visit his landslide on early Saturday mornings during University field trips.

We wish to acknowledge the professional assistance and encouragement of Dave Hoffman, a geologist with the Missouri Division of Geology & Land Survey (DGLS) who accompanied us to the field on more than one occasion as well as Jim Vaughn, geologist and soil scientist with DGLS whose excavations of seismic features in the Dexter-Dudley area of Missouri are seen in Slides #74-#77. Norman Brown, a surveyor and historian with the DGLS, was also very helpful in providing access to original 18th century survey notes (in French) of the New Madrid region in the archives of the DGLS. These notes, which predate the earthquakes of 1811-12, helped us establish whether or not certain topographic features found there today were caused by the earthquakes.

Steve Obermeier of the U.S. Geological Survey, and noted authority on earthquake liquefaction, lent his encouragement and brought to our attention some excellent aerial photographs taken in the 1950's showing hundreds of sand boils and sand fissures in the New Madrid Seismic Zone. We also relied heavily on Steve's excellent publications which are cited in the bibliography at the end of this book.

We also wish to acknowledge the wealth of information received during a NMSZ weekend field trip conducted in November, 1989, sponsored by the Geological Society of America. Leaders of that trip were Buddy Schweig from the Center for Earthquake Research and Information at Memphis State University and Randy Jipson with the U.S. Geological Survey, Reston, Virginia. David Russ, also with the U.S. Geological Survey, also accompanied us on that trip and provided additional insights. Several of the NMSZ publications of these three scientists are cited in the bibliography and have been very useful in carrying out our work.

Dennis Keely, geological engineer from California who participated in one of our New Madrid field trips, shared with us his Western interpretations of some of these Midwestern features and also provided us with documentation from California earthquakes that helped to explain some of the dynamic seismic processes we had suspected in the NMSZ. Thanks, Dennis.

To U.S. Congressman Bill Emerson, we also extend our appreciation for his continued encouragement, interest and support which has not wavered through the years. We also wish to thank him and his staff for the provision of a copy of a fourteen page report dated February 20, 1850, from the U.S. House of Representatives that described in detail the swampy conditions of southeast Missouri and northeast Arkansas as being due to the New Madrid Earthquakes of 1811-12. The House document presents a case before Congress to provide the funds for a major drainage project in the NMSZ so that the region could be reclaimed for agriculture and other beneficial uses. They argued that the cost to the government would be recouped by the additional taxes that could be levied on land, then unuseable, that drainage would put into agriculture production. (The actual drainage of this area did not take place until 1918-1922.)

We want to acknowledge Bob McEowen, photojournalist for the publication *Rural Missouri,* who took several of the black & white photos used in several of our books.

Karin Fischer of Water Technologies, Inc., working with Phyllis Steckel, shared data on the Mississippi River that confirms the location of a temporary waterfall near New Madrid formed February 7, 1812, during the greatest of the shocks.

Mike Aide, an authority on soils and a Professor of Agriculture at Southeast Missouri State University, gave us insights on some of the "sand boils" that were not "sandy," as well as other insights during informal discussions. We also wish to thank Shamsher Prakash, an authority on soil mechanics and a Professor of Civil Engineering at the University of Missouri, Rolla, without whose persistent encouragement to produce a set of "New Madrid Slides," the resultant set might never have been published.

We also wish to thank Mr. Ken Riddle and others at the Sikeston Power Plant for enabling us to take photographs of the fissure from the top of their 410-foot-tall smokestack.

Several students at Southeast were helpful in producing these books. Principle among them were Phyllis Steckel, a graduate student who earned a Masters of Natural Science degree in

1992 relating to the New Madrid Seismic Zone, and Scott Readnour, whose field work in the Sikeston area first discovered the numerous earthquake features in and around that town, including the Sikeston Power Plant Fissure and the two big sand boils the city uses to drain off their excess storm water (See Slides #91-#95). Mr. John Thompson, a graduate student in the Geoscience department, has also been encouraging and helpful in many ways during the last three years of this project and collaborated with David Stewart on a publication concerning earthquake landslides in the Benton Hills.

There were many other students we wish to thank, too numerous to name, including the annual group of class members in the University Studies Course on earthquakes taught by Dr. Stewart. Many of these students read portions of the manuscripts and critiqued them for a grade. (You will see some of these students in the photographs found in this book taken during class field trips.) Bring or send us your personal copies of this book, class, and we'll gladly autograph our appreciation to you.

We wish to thank Betty Black, head of the Graphics Department at Southeast Missouri State University, as well as the staff of that department, who processed hundreds of our slides and helped in the reproduction of several of the figures.

Kate Schaefer, artist at Concord Publishing Company in Cape Girardeau, spent months working in close cooperation with author David Stewart to produce the cover art, the colored maps, and some of the figures. Her patience, talent and skill are greatly appreciated. The beautiful and striking original art work on the cover of the book, *The Earthquake America Forgot* is by Cape Girardeau artist Don Greenwood, who carefully researched every detail for historic authenticity. This dramatic and colorful drawing is available not only on the book but on T-shirts, as well.

The photographs of the authors on the cover and in the back are the work of Steve Robertson of Robertson's Creative Photography Studio in Cape Girardeau. But the contribution to this book of Steve and his wife, Mary, is much more than that. All of the photographs taken by the authors were color slides. Steve reshot them onto black and white film and then kindly permitted David Stewart access to his darkroom facilities to do the printing and enlarging of hundreds of these photographs. Thanks, Steve, for your confidence and cooperation. Thanks to you, Mary, for keeping Dave supplied with fresh coffee during those many days in the darkroom. And thanks to you both for your ongoing enthusiasm and encouragement to complete these books.

We also want to thank Dave Stewart's son, Keith Stewart, college student, aviation major, and pilot who flew his father all over the New Madrid Seismic Zone to take many of the photos included here. Keith, a computer adept, helped train his father in the use of several programs necessary for the word processing and typesetting of these books. Without Keith's availability and willingness to be called when his dad was stumped, the publishing of these books would have been delayed.

David's wife, Lee Stewart, also deserves a lot of credit. She assisted in the editing and the typesetting. She is also a computer adept who helped train and coach Dave, formerly a computer illiterate, in the use of various computer programs necessary to complete these books. She is also a partner in the business/production side of this enterprise. For this, her patience, her faith in her husband and business partner, and much more, Dave thanks her, because without her courage and support these books would probably have not come to be.

### The Late Dr. Iben Browning

And last of all, no list of acknowledgements for these works on the New Madrid Fault Zone would be complete at this time without thanking Dr. Iben Browning for the attention he brought to the New Madrid Seismic Zone in 1990.

Dr. Browning was an inventor, climatologist, and business consultant from Albuquerque, New Mexico. He specialized in relating upcoming events of nature (weather, volcanic eruptions, major earthquakes, etc.) to future trends in world economics.

In late October of 1989 his projection of the probability of a major earthquake on the New

Madrid Fault became public via an Associated Press news release reprinted by papers throughout the United States. He stated that, in his opinion, there would be a 50% chance of a New Madrid event in excess of 7.0 magnitude on or about the date of December 3, 1990.

Considerable credibility was accorded to Browning's statement by the press inasmuch as he was believed by many to have successfully predicted the California earthquake of October 17, 1989, within 24 hours. He was also believed to have predicted other major earthquakes, including one that hit Mexico City in September of 1985, as well as major volcanic eruptions, including Mt. St. Helens, in May of 1980. These alleged successes were a matter of public debate and many doubted them to be true. However, the point is this: Thousands believed Browning had been right before.

Browning's credibility was also supported by his resume. He was a man whose accomplishments in engineering, aviation, military science, biophysics, climatology, world economics, and several other fields had earned him a high level of respect from a broad spectrum of people. Many corporations and business leaders had found his global economic trend forecasts reliable enough to have been repeatedly profitable. He was a man of repute, listed in the International Edition of *Who's Who*, and a highly successful career consultant to both government and private sector agencies. He was not, however, recognized by seismologists and geologists as an authority on earthquakes.

During the 14 months following his public disclosure in October of 1989, the news media repeatedly publicized and elaborated on his projection. On September 26, 1990, a 4.7 earthquake occurred centered near the northern edge of the New Madrid Seismic Zone. It was felt in five states and did over $500,000 in damages. It was the largest quake to rattle the New Madrid area in over a decade. This added additional fuel to an already growing concern over Browning's projection. The media went into a virtual frenzy, hyping the situation into international proportions. Thus, the New Madrid Fault, which seismologists agree does have the potential for a major quake, became one of the most well publicized earthquake zones in the world.

Browning's hypothesis was based upon an assessment of tectonic instability in specific fault zones combined with calculations of times for maximum vector magnitudes of the gravitational forces from the sun and moon at specific latitudes. The attraction between sun, moon, and the earth's oceans results in a daily rise and fall of sea tides. Undetected by people, but measurable by instruments, there are also "earth tides," an ever so slight daily rise and fall of the upper crust. This places an additional strain on the already strained rocks of an active fault zone. Every day there are regular small strains, but some days, when the forces of the sun and moon are at a maximum, these strains can be relatively strong.

Browning's hypothesis is not difficult to understand, as a concept, but is difficult to carry out if all the relevant details were taken into consideration as he specified. When an active fault has built up enough strain energy that it is about to produce a large earthquake a most likely time for a specific fault to rupture should be when the tidal forces on the earth's crust are at a maximum at that fault's latitude and pulling in a direction that favors that particular fault's tendency for movement. In other words, according to Browning, not all faults in a given latitude of a maximum tidal force would be triggered to move, but only those with an orientation and relative fault motion in a direction to be augmented by the direction of the earth tide.

Solar/lunar earth tides cannot cause earthquakes. Earthquakes are caused by stresses originating within the earth. But the external forces of sun and moon could be the trigger to determine when the quake is most likely to occur. To think of it another way, an unusually high earth tide pulling in the right direction at the location of an already overloaded fault zone could be "the straw that broke the camel's back."

Dates and latitudes of future peak earth tide forces can be calculated by astronomical formulas decades, even centuries, in advance. According to Browning's methodology these dates would mark periods of "enhanced probabilities" for strong earthquake activity in seismically active zones at the affected latitudes. Browning said his theory did not apply to the triggering of quakes of magnitudes smaller than 5.0. The great series of New Madrid earthquakes began on December 16, 1811, which was one of those dates of maximum vector earth tide forces for the latitude of New Madrid. December 3, 1990, was another such date of maximum force for New Madrid, one of the strongest since 1812. While Browning's theory may not have been adequate to pinpoint the exact date of another major earthquake on the New Madrid Fault, history will some day thank him for several reasons.

For one, at some future time, when scientists figure out a way to accurately predict earthquakes, you can be sure that part of the formula will include some of the ideas of Dr. Browning, whether or not he is given credit. He may not have had all of the right pieces to the puzzle, but he did have some of the right ones. A correlation between maximum tidal forces and the timing of earthquakes has been reported in the studies of a number of scientists in several countries. For example, see Heaton (1975A); Heaton (1975B); Kilston & Knopoff (1983); Kokus (1990); Mikumo et al. (1977); Palumbo (1989); Roosen et al. (1976); Tamrazyan (1967); Weems & Perry (1989); and Zetler (1966).

Japanese, Soviets, and especially Chinese scientists have had some success in earthquake prediction. More than once they have evacuated large metropolitan areas prior to major earthquakes, saving thousands of lives. American seismologists, by contrast, have yet to make even one successful public prediction, even though tens of millions of taxpayers' dollars have been spent by U.S. government scientists in attempts to do so. In the early 1980's the U.S. Geological Survey (USGS) publicly announced their first prediction, the occurrence of a magnitude 6.0-7.0 quake near Parkfield, California, to occur between 1984 and 1992. The timing of their pronouncement was not very precise. They gave themselves an eight-year window. They would have counted their prediction a success if any quake of magnitude 6.0 or larger had occurred at any time during that long span of almost a decade. Untold amounts of federal money have been spent to study and instrument the anticipated quake zone, but the eight years came and passed with no strong quake.

As of the publication of this book (Spring 1993), every earthquake prediction publicly announced by the U.S. Geological Survey (USGS) has been wrong. Even so, government seismologists have stated to the newspapers that "False alarms are a good thing because they cause people to get ready for earthquakes."(Associated Press Release, November, 1992) Dr. Browning's apparent failure to pick the right date (within a five-day window) for a strong New Madrid earthquake could also be said to have been "a good thing." Certainly, it brought to attention a problem we in the Midwest must face.

The California Earthquake of October 17, 1989, occurred during the opening of a baseball game of the World Series. It was the first live television broadcast of a major earthquake in history. Tens of millions of viewers were watching, coast to coast, as the drama of devastation and destruction unfolded during the next 48 hours. The World Series Quake brought earthquake awareness into the consciousness of every American. But it was Browning who directed that awareness to the real potential of the New Madrid Fault.

Before Browning's 1990 projection, less than 10% of the population of the Midwest realized they lived in an area threatened by significant earthquakes in the near future. Outside the Midwest, most people had never even heard of the New Madrid Fault. Now virtually everyone in the Central U.S. knows of the risk. Millions have taken appropriate actions to prepare. Not only that, legislators were also galvanized into action by Dr. Browning's pronouncement so that today we have several new laws in several Midwestern states that will make schools, hospitals, and other public facilities safer in future earthquakes. More beneficial earthquake preparation and education took place in the Midwest during 1990 than in all previous years combined. Browning deserves at least some of the credit for this.

Another lasting benefit of the "earthquake scare" of 1990 was the stimulation of an incredible amount of networking between medical people, firemen, policemen, emergency managers, national guard units, public utilities, schools, businesses, government officials, the Red Cross, and others. Several emergency management authorities have pointed out that Browning's warning made the entire Midwest better prepared to deal with a variety of potential future disasters, not just earthquakes. This includes fires, floods, tornados, blizzards, and even riots, warfare and nuclear attack. Emergency professionals and government officials had been saying for years that better communications and more coordinated disaster planning needed to be accomplished between all concerned agencies and institutions, but it took a Browning to make it happen.

Even the seismologists and geologists who disagreed with Browning's methodology received benefits from his pronouncement. Because of the publicity, legislators in Washington, D.C., became more concerned about the earthquake risk in the central United States than they had ever been before. In 1990 the New Madrid Region became the first earthquake zone east of the Rocky Mountains to be designated a priority research area within the National Earthquake Hazard Reduction Program (NEHRP) which is the vehicle by which the U.S. Congress funnels money to scientists engaged in earthquake studies. As a result, many of the researchers in the New Madrid Seismic Zone, including the USGS, who were so critical of Browning in 1990, have since enjoyed greater levels of funding. See Johnston & Shedlock (1992).

Browning's projection for December 3, 1990, was that of a 50-50 chance of a major earthquake on the New Madrid Fault within a five day period surrounding that date. Some threw "earthquake" parties in New Madrid that day. Some residents of the area left town. Many people came expecting to experience an earthquake. Hundreds of curiosity seekers, as well as droves of newspeople and television cameras from all over the world, were in New Madrid that day, waiting. Even Missouri's Governor John Ashcroft and U.S. Senator Kit Bond dropped by. It was the most outside attention ever received by the New Madrid community since the great shocks of 1811-12.

Lou Hobbs was there with his guitar. Lou is a singer and song writer with his own TV show on Channel 12, Cape Girardeau. He had composed a new song. *Living on the New Madrid Fault Line* is the title. "I sang the song about 150 times over a two-day period," he said, "for practically every major news organization in the world." Evergreen Records of Nashville had released a recording of it 10 days before "E-Day," December 3, 1990. It wasn't expected to be popular for long. But since then Lou's song has grown into an international hit. "Living on the New Madrid Fault Line" has now been heard in shows, concerts, films, radio and TV in 90 countries around the globe. In December, 1992, Lou received a royalty check and a commemorative plaque from the BMI Songwriters Guild for the song's worldwide sales. We wish to thank Lou for his permission to let us reprint his lyrics in the Frontispiece of this book.

December 3, 1990, came and went. No quake occurred. Some were glad. Some were mad. Some blamed Browning. Some blamed the scientific establishment for not denouncing Browning soon enough. (See Ad Hoc, 1990, and Spence et al., 1992.) Others blamed the media for hyping the whole thing in the first place. The general public was mostly appreciative of Browning's warning because it had inspired them to take appropriate precautions before the next big one hits, whenever that may be. Besides, who can say whether Browning was right or wrong? A 50% probability of an event happening or not happening could be considered right regardless of the outcome.

The truth is that some day there will be another major earthquake on the New Madrid fault. There is no 50-50 chance on that. It is a certainty. The only uncertainty is when. Whenever it does happen, many Americans will be better prepared to deal with it. Even if it does not happen for another 20 or 30 years, there will be many who will be saved from injury and loss by the education they received years before in 1990 because Dr. Browning was willing to put his reputation on the line to express a concern for others.

The first anniversary date, December 3, 1991, was declared "Iben Browning Day" in New Madrid when the community dedicated a new wing of the New Madrid Museum. (See Slide #14.) The wing has been structurally designed to resist earthquakes. Some of the funds donated to build the annex were in response to interest in Dr. Browning's projection. The City of New Madrid had hoped to invite him to the grand opening. Unfortunately, Dr. Browning did not live to see it. He had died in the summer of 1991 after a prolonged illness. Creative to the end, he had received his 67th patent only a few weeks before. He is survived by his wife, Florence, and his daughter, Dr. Evelyn Garriss, who continues to carry on his work in climatology, volcanology and global economics. Although Dr. Browning was unable to visit New Madrid in 1991, Dr. Garriss was there to graciously accept the honor on behalf of her late father. To Mrs. Browning and Dr. Garriss we wish to express our appreciation for their encouragement in the writing of these books.

# Preface

## HOW TO USE & ENJOY THIS BOOK AND HOW YOU CAN MAKE A GREAT EARTHQUAKE PRESENTATION

Open this book to any page with a photograph and you will be rewarded with an amazing story, an incredible fact, or an astonishing tidbit of new information you can use. You can also enjoy this book by reading it straight through, from beginning to end. But you can also receive much pleasure, and acquire a whole lot of useful knowledge, by sampling it in pieces in almost any order, like a box of chocolates. Once you start, you won't want to stop until the whole box has been eaten.

There has never been a book like this. We hope you will find it exciting, entertaining and informative, as well as an eye-opener to things you have never seen nor thought of before. But we hope you will find some practical value in it as well, something that will save you money, prevent you a loss, or make your life safer from earthquakes. At the very least, it will change your perception of the landscape around you, causing you to notice things you never noticed before, making your travels and vacation trips more interesting and enjoyable.

This book serves many roles. First, it is a picture album of earthquake photos featuring seismically disturbed landscapes which you can still see today, caused 200 years ago (in 1811-12) by a horrendous sequence of major earthquakes that struck the valley of the Central Mississippi River between Illinois and Louisiana.

If you have never been to the area this book will give you a vicarious visual visit, a remote experience of the present-day impact of those historic seismic events. Even though the zone of ruptured rock from which the Great New Madrid Earthquakes originated is buried miles beneath the towns it destroyed, you will see what it did to the landscape above and to its people, then and today.

If you do come to the New Madrid Fault Zone in Arkansas, Kentucky, Missouri and Tennessee, through this book you will already have your eyes trained to see what is there. Millions of motorists pass through this area every year within view of hundreds of seismic faults, fissures, boils and scars and never recognize them as such.

The 101-mile stretch of Interstate Highway 55 from Blytheville, Arkansas, to Benton, Missouri, should be called "Earthquake Alley". How many speed through that troubled passage without realizing the tectonic turmoil seething beneath, despite its many signs and clues in the soils along the way? The area is so seismically active that more than 200 quakes are measured there every year. If you drive there, chances are one in three that a measurable earthquake will occur the day you pass through.

Some day we hope someone will put up two large billboards on the Interstate, one a few miles south of Blytheville, the other at the crest of the Benton Hills near Mile Post #83, saying "YOU ARE ENTERING THE NEW MADRID SEISMIC ZONE." On the other side of each sign it could say, "YOU ARE LEAVING THE NEW MADRID SEISMIC ZONE," with some other appropriate message. This area is a natural national resource, something worth visiting, something to learn from and enjoy, something to travel thousands of miles to see. But you need a guide. This, and the other books we are writing, will serve that purpose.

On the other hand, if you have been there before or are currently in the area, this book will be a keepsake for you, a record of things you may have seen and witnessed, a reference to which you can return when you are back home to remember, relive your visit, and show your friends.

## You Will be the Expert

This book has been written to serve both the technically trained and the untrained. For geotechnical engineers, geologists, seismologists, geographers, or other earth scientists, the information contained herein will be found to be relatively rigorous, accurate, well documented, and complete. In fact, this book can serve as a text for geoscience students and professionals on earthquake landforms. Very little of what you find here can be found in traditional textbooks. In fact, a lot of it is the result of original research by the authors, never before published anywhere. This publication is the most complete and thorough reference on morphoseismology ever written.

On the other hand, you don't have to be a geologist, seismologist or earthquake engineer to understand and benefit from this book. We had the public in mind when we conceived it. You will understand and enjoy this book even if you never had a course in the earth sciences. You will find not only new and fascinating facts, but practical information that will increase your powers of observation and enhance the pleasure you have in traveling, both of which you may use to your benefit. If you understand the simple basics found in this book, you will know more about seismically-induced liquefaction and related phenomena than 90% of geologists or seismologists know, because these topics are not routinely covered in the usual college curriculum, even an advanced degree in geosciences.

Regardless of your background, reading this book will make you quite conversant in the field of morphoseismology—the science of how earthquake forces mold and alter our landscape. Morphoseismology is a combination of seismology, geomorphology, hydrology, and history. Whether formally trained in the geosciences or not, you can become an authority on the subject through this book.

And lastly, not only is the content of this book unique, it carries the exclusive Gutenberg-Richter Earthquake Hazard Warranty. Refer to the back of this book for more details.

## A Trilogy of New Madrid Earthquake Books

This book is part of a trilogy. *The Earthquake That Never Went Away* is the one you want for a visual travelogue or for a set of narrative notes to the set of 150 slides that can be purchased featuring photos of the New Madrid Seismic Zone.

The second book, *The New Madrid Fault Finders Guide* (FFG), has many maps, detailed directions, and road logs by which you can find and see these earthquake features for yourself. It is a field manual of self-guided tours, suitable for anyone desiring to see the seismic features of the New Madrid Seismic Zone. *The Earthquake That Never Went Away* (NWA) gives general locations (within ten miles) for the photographs shown, but not specific maps or instructions on how to actually find and visit what is seen. For actual field location of hundreds of earthquake features, *The Fault Finders Guide* is the book you want. It can be the basis for a short trip around New Madrid of an hour or two, or for a field trip that can last several days or more from which you could make an entire "Fault Finding" vacation for the whole family.

The third book of the trilogy is entitled, *The Earthquake America Forgot* (EAF), subtitled, *2,000 Temblors in Five Months . . . And it will Happen Again*. This profusely illustrated volume is the largest of the three works, the only one in hardback, and details the human history and profound impact on the people living throughout the region at the time. Like the other two books, it stands alone in earthquake literature, being the most complete compilation and account of the social/political/historical/geologic upheavals that simultaneously occurred at that time and place. Once you begin reading this scholarly, meticulously documented, entertaining work, you will not want to put it down. You will identify with the personal lives of the people, and their feelings during the cataclysms that rocked their bodies and their minds. These great quakes forever changed history for Native Americans, black slaves and white folks, alike. You will be swept into a time and place where you will receive your own personal earthquake experience, but from a safe distance in time and space.

In addition to being a part of a trilogy of unique books on the great New Madrid Earthquakes, *The Earthquake That Never Went Away* also provides the narrative notes for a set of 150 full color 35mm slides available to the public. A copy of this book (NWA) is usually included when a full set of slides is purchased. (See back for details.) In the pages that follow are black and white reproductions of each of the 150 slides. Unfortunately, some interesting details are not as visible in shades of gray as they are in a spectrum of hues. Some of the comments under the pictures refer to features barely discernable in the black and white photos but which stand out quite obviously in color. The few comments in this category will be more useful with the slides than with this book (NWA). Perhaps a future edition of NWA can be produced in full color. Details on how to obtain the slides, as well as the other two books (EAF & FFG), are given in the back.

## How To Use This Book with the Slides

The 150 color slides that go along with this book correspond exactly with the 150 numbered maps, tables, figures, and photos published here. By selecting all or a portion of these slides and using the comments from this book as the basis for your narrative, you can present a variety of fascinating programs, both short and long.

There is far more information in this book than can be presented to any group at a single sitting unless you are giving a two-day seminar. So whether you are giving a 15-minute presentation or a two-hour presentation, you can only present a portion of this material. The additional information included is to fill in your background and understanding. When giving a talk or lecture, it always good to know more about your subject than you share with the audience. It will give you confidence to speak before groups and increase your credibility with the audience, who will sense that you know more than you are saying. If your talk is followed by questions from the audience, the additional material found here will help provide the answers.

For a short presentation, you may want to select only a few, perhaps 20 or 30 slides. For an hour's presentation, you may select, perhaps 100 or so, or limit your comments. To make the complete presentation of all 150 slides, 100-120 minutes is required.

The slides and their commentary are ideal for adaptation to a variety of classroom needs, as well as to the needs of professional groups of geologists, geophysicists, geographers or engineers. It is also adaptable to church and/or civic organizations of all types and ages. Many of these slides would be valuable additions to other existing sets of earthquake slides you may have. Hence, as described at the end of this book, the slides are not only available as a complete set of 150, but also a partial set of 80 selected slides. (See back of book for details.)

For public meetings or groups with no special interest in the earth sciences, you may want to omit Slides #4-#11, present the narrative of "What Happened?" with the first three slides, and then jump right into the photographs starting with Slide #12. Each photo has a story to be told. From Slide #12 to Slide #150, you can simply choose as many to present as you have time for, focusing on the ones whose anecdotes you enjoy telling the most. If you visit the NMSZ, your favorites may be the slides of the features you have actually seen, yourself, combined with your own photos.

The narrative, as we have presented it, has a flow, though. If you have a full two hours (or two one hour sessions) you can present the entire slide set of 150. You will find that the story of each slide leads to the next and often refers back to what has been seen earlier.

Don't feel you have to recite the complete commentary given for each slide. That would take considerably more than two hours. A lot of the written commentary is for reading purposes only, not speaking purposes. Present only the tidbits you find most interesting or most applicable to your audience, and skip the rest. You'll have plenty of fascinating material to present even if you only give a fraction of what is here.

If you are shy about public speaking, read a script taken from the comments in this book. In a darkened room with slides on a screen and you standing behind the projector, who can tell if you are speaking extemporaneously or reading your presentation verbatim from notes?

## Literature For Your Groups and Audiences

One of the most unique aspects of the slide set and this book is that the general location of every photograph is identified in Slide #1, "The New Madrid Earthquake Photo Location Map." It is suggested that when you make a slide presentation, you distribute copies of the "New Madrid Earthquake Photo Location Map" for everyone in the audience so that during your talk they can keep track of where each photo has been taken. In fact, we encourage you to make photocopies for your audiences of several, if not all, of the three maps, the four principal figures and the four tables in this book. That would be twelve pages total, or Slides #1 through #11 and Slide #150. This will enable those who hear your presentations to concentrate more on the slides being shown and on what you are saying, instead of on taking notes. In fact, these hand-outs will give them a set of notes to keep. Instead of making your own photocopies Gutenberg-Richter would be glad to supply you with quantities of the maps, tables and figures free, as well as free copies of an earthquake safety brochure. There is a small charge for shipping and handling. (Details given on pages 219-220.)

The comments beneath each slide in this book are ones the authors would probably make during a slide presentation. In some cases, the comments are very brief, only a few words. For some slides, the title heading, alone, is a sufficient verbal comment. In these cases, the slide may be seen by the audience for a few seconds. Rapid panning of selected slides in appropriate places will not detract from your presentation, but will add to it, giving it a sense of motion despite the fact that only still shots are being shown. In movies and on television, a single frozen frame of less than half a second is seen and registered by the viewer. The next time you watch TV, notice how many ads shoot quick pictures by the screen lasting only fractions of a second, yet you still see them and comprehend. You can use this same technique. By varying the lengths of times you hold the slides on the screen from less than one second to a minute or more, your presentations will remain interesting and you will be able to cover an amazing amount of material within a given time. In general, the length of time to hold a slide on the screen for your audience should roughly correspond to the time required for you to say whatever commentary you have chosen to extract from the notes provided below each photo in this book.

On some of the more complex slides, a key or scale has been provided: 1 through 10 across the bottom, A through H vertically along the left side. (For example, see Slide #12.) This makes it possible to identify specific features in the photo. Persons using these keys while reading this book will know what, for instance, "G7" or "B2" means for a specific photo. When showing the actual slide to an audience, you will need a pointer to designate the location of the feature to which you wish to refer.

Don't hesitate to rearrange the order of or delete slides, or to combine the slides of this set with others. The order given here is mostly by geographic location, starting with New Madrid, Missouri, and then wandering around in ever widening circles to take in Reelfoot Lake, Tennessee, just before jumping down to another earthquake lake—Big Lake, Arkansas. After leapfrogging from site to site in Arkansas, Missouri, and Southern Illinois, we go back to Arkansas, again. Working our way north again, and crossing the river on I-155, the slide journey passes back into Tennessee and ends in Hickman, Kentucky. But location is not the only outline by which you could present these slides.

You could, for example, simply pull together all the slides of sand boils, or only the photos of landslides, to suit a particular purpose. In certain classroom applications, or for certain professional groups, you might find that the tables and figures are useful by themselves or can be used in conjunction with other slides not included here.

## Nomenclature Used in this Book

Whenever possible, the names and descriptions of seismic features mentioned here (Slides #4-#11) are the same as those established in existing geologic or engineering literature. However, in some cases, published authorities disagree. For example, some geologists and seismologists refer to all earthquake sand deposits as "sand blows," while some civil and earthquake engineers make distinctions between sand boils, sand blows and other seismic sand features, as we have in this work. The organization and nomenclature adopted here are, to a great extent, original with the authors inasmuch as, prior to our research and field work, several of these features had never been discovered, recognized, described, nor given a name in scientific literature. The classification and description of seismic features given here is the topic of a professional publication by the authors still in the developmental and writing stages at this time. (See Knox & Stewart, 1993.)

At certain points during your presentation, you may want to back up and show certain slides more than once. For example, Slides #147, #148, and #149 show a time sequence on the same landslide that could bear repeating to your audience. Slides #85 and #86 are a "before and after" sequence that also could be viewed twice by your audience.

### Starting and Making Your Presentation

Regardless of the length of your presentation or the nature of your audience, you will probably want to begin with a description of the sequence of earthquakes that brought these landforms into being. Hence, the narration that goes with Slide #1, "The New Madrid Earthquake Photo Location Map," starts on page 1 of the book and is entitled, "The Great New Madrid Earthquakes of 1811-12: What Happened?" The introduction presented in this book is relatively brief but can be abbreviated even more for a very short presentation. On the other hand, by reading the third book of this trilogy, *The Earthquake America Forgot*, (350 pages) one would have enough historical and anecdotal material to make a fascinating full hour's presentation with this single slide as the backdrop. Hence, for those who make long talks on the New Madrid Earthquakes without reference to the visible landforms that can still be seen there today, Slide #1, alone, or Slides #1, #2, and #3 might be a helpful purchase.

Following the three maps (on Slides #1, #2 and #3) is a set of three tables and five figures, that outline and describe the varieties of seismic landforms to be found in the New Madrid Seismic Zone, as well as in many other seismic zones around the world. For non-technical audiences, you may wish to speed through (or omit) the tables and figures, making only a few comments. If you are lecturing a technical audience, such as an earth science, geology, geophysics, hydrology, structural, civil, or geotechnical engineering class, you could spend a full hour or more on these alone. In this case, it would be especially effective to provide copies of those pages as handouts for the students or participants. (See back for details on how you can obtain copies for a small shipping charge.)

The actual photographs begin with Slide #12 and go through Slide #149. They start with an aerial view of seismic sand boils in New Madrid, Missouri, and end with a time sequence of a reactivated earthquake landslide of 1811-12 in Hickman, Kentucky. The narrative notes beneath each of the pictures speak for themselves. The last slide is a table of recurrence intervals for various sizes of earthquakes on the New Madrid Fault.

### Suggested Outline for Your Group Talk

A good outline for giving lectures on the New Madrid Earthquakes or the New Madrid Seismic Zone can be summarized in three parts as follows:

1. What Happened?
2. What's Going to Happen? and
3. What Can You Do About it?

The "What Happened?" part describes the events of 1811-12 so dramatically revealed by the visible scars in the landscape seen in these photos or narrated in the socio/historical account, *The Earthquake America Forgot*. This can be briefly capsulized in 10 minutes or dramatized as a spellbinding story of an hour or more.

The "What's Going to Happen?" part examines the probabilities of future New Madrid earthquakes. That is why Slide #150 is included. One can keep it brief, limited to the information on the slide. One can also elaborate briefly with the short narrative notes given. Or, one can speak at length on this aspect alone. An excellent resource is available free of charge for this. It is a joint publication of the Federal Emergency Management Agency (FEMA) and the Missouri State Emergency Management Agency (SEMA). The title of the book is *Damages and Losses from Future New Madrid Earthquakes* (DAL). This book will enable you to choose any county (including your own) in the Midwest, arbitrarily specify any size of an earthquake on the New Madrid Fault, and then quantitatively calculate, for that county, the numbers of injuries, deaths, displaced persons, collapsed buildings, bridges out, pipeline breaks per mile, and other parameters of interest to anyone desiring to know about or plan for an earthquake disaster. DAL is also an excellent primer on the basic concepts of earthquake seismology. See the back of the book for details about obtaining your own copy. An abbreviated version of DAL can also be found in *The Earthquake America Forgot.*

The last part of the outline, "What Can You Do About It?" can simply be satisfied by handing out earthquake preparedness literature which can be obtained for a small shipping fee by writing the publisher, Gutenberg-Richter, the address and toll-free number for which is given in the back of this book. The awesome events of 1811-12 will most certainly repeat themselves at some future time, though probably not in those magnitudes and intensities for another 200-300 years. The principal 1811-12 events were "Great," which, to a seismologist, means Richter magnitudes of 8.0 or more. Such events are thought to have a 450-650 year repeat interval in the New Madrid Seismic Zone. It has been less than 200 years since the last such episode. However, magnitude 6.0 – 7.9 earthquakes are considered "Strong" or "Major" and would be extremely destructive in the central United States. These have shorter recurrence intervals ranging from 50 to 350 years. The last quake larger than 6.0 on the New Madrid Fault was in 1895. Clearly we are overdue for another 6.0 – 6.9 event, if not for a major quake in the 7.0 range.

The future prospects of major New Madrid earthquakes are discussed in greater detail in the book, *Damages & Losses from Future New Madrid Earthquakes,* by David Stewart, available from Gutenberg-Richter, as described in the back of this book. Persons concerned with future probabilities may also wish to obtain and study copies of the following references listed in the bibliography: Algermissen & Hopper, (1984); Hamilton & Johnston (1990); Johnston & Nava, (1985); Nishenko & Bollinger, (1990); and Wesnousky & Leffler, (1992A), as well as the work of Dr. Liu of Stanford University.

Following the simple three-part outline shown above when giving earthquake talks has the advantage of being adaptable to almost any length of time—from 10 minutes to a full day's workshop. It's all in what you choose to emphasize, de-emphasize or omit.

### Snapshots in Time

It is too bad the science of photography did not exist in the early 1800's. One can only imagine the dramatic images that could have been captured during the actual earthquakes and their immediate aftermath. Think what footage we would be able to view today had television been available then. Unfortunately, we must satisfy ourselves with pictures such as the ones contained here, taken almost 200 years later, using our imaginations to recreate what it really must have been like. Even so, it is awesome to realize that those gargantuan upheavals were so great that photographs of their effects are still possible.

However, the opportunities to take such pictures are diminishing rapidly at this time, due not to the erosive forces of nature, but due to human activities. Some classic earthquake features, preserved for more than a century, have been recently destroyed, removed or filled in. Urbanization, landscaping, and the omnipotent bulldozer are partly to blame, but the principal destroyer of these seismic legacies is agriculture. The new farming technologies and giant earth moving machines, nonexistent two decades ago, are destroying acres of seismic features daily. Some of the pictures published here (taken between 1989 and 1991) now provide the only remaining visible evidence of certain features because of changes in the landscape caused by ongoing land leveling projects to grow rice and other irrigated crops.

Nevertheless, the New Madrid earthquakes of 1811-12 were so numerous and so massive that tens of thousands of features were left strewn over more than 5,000 square miles of real estate in several states. While these seismotectonic blemishes on the face of earth may be covered and modified, most of them will never disappear entirely, even within the eons of geologic time, although their traces will gradually become more difficult to discover. In some cases, the features have only been covered over or filled in and could be restored to their 1811-12 appearance.

The New Madrid earthquakes are a part of our heritage and a part of our history, just as the Revolutionary War and the building of the first transcontinental railway. Without our even realizing it these earthquakes reach down through the decades to touch us in this century, like other important historic events, altering and directing the course of human development, making a difference in what we are, what we do, and where we are going as a culture.

Consider the set of pictures contained here as snapshots not only of places, but also of times, both today and yesterday. A hundred or a thousand years hence, these places will all be different, It is the hope of the authors that many of these outstanding world class features which occur so uniquely here in such massive numbers and sizes will be set aside as sites for historic preservation. Thousands of these natural features have aready been destroyed by agriculture, highway construction, and the channeling of streams and rivers. We have seen many disappear even in the last few years as we worked on these books, scraped off or smeared out beneath the blades of bulldozers and land planers. A number of the features seen in this very book, photographed between 1989 and 1992, no longer exist—including the stumps on the cover which were buried in rock rip rap by the Army U.S. Corps of Engineers in 1993. Other stumps of cypress trees killed in 1811-12 also seen in this book (p. 74) were pulled up and destroyed by the Missouri Department of Natural Resources in the same year. Evidently, they did not realize the significance of these silent victims whose remains had survived the great quakes by almost two-hundred years.

There are practical reasons for preserving at least a representative sample of these remarkable and historic features. What happened in 1811-12 will happen again. Recognizing what happened in the past paves the way for better preparation for the future. A selected set of these features could be parts of a State or National Park system. An "Earthquake Trail" could be established. We hope this trilogy of books will help lead to those ends.

In fact, we have made a specific proposal in *The New Madrid Fault Finders Guide* of just where that earthquake park should begin. There is a grove of more than ten huge oak trees between New Madrid and Kewanee, Missouri, that are all over 200 years old. They were living witnesses to the earthquakes of 1811-12. There are several outstanding earthquake features in and around these trees. It could even be called "Witness Tree State Park."

David Mack Stewart, Marble Hill, MO
Burnal Ray Knox, Cape Girardeau, MO
December 1995

# Introduction

# THE GREAT NEW MADRID EARTHQUAKES OF 1811-12

## WHAT HAPPENED?

### The First Day

At 2:30 on the morning of December 16, 1811, a tremendous earthquake occurred whose epicentral region is thought to have been just west of the location of Blytheville, Arkansas, a city that did not exist at the time. Had it been there, it would have been devastated totally as evidenced by the numerous earthquake boils and fissures that visibly surround the city today. The Richter surface wave magnitude is thought to have been 8.6. Big Lake, a large permanent body of water, was formed in the epicentral area. (See Slide Locations G and I on Photo Location Map.) President James Madison, 800 miles away in the White House in Washington, D.C., was shaken out of bed by the quake.

Many aftershocks immediately followed, some probably magnitude 6.0 or greater. At least two more of the December 16 shocks are thought to have equaled 8.0 on the Richter scale.

According to the testimony of those who were there that day, around 8:00 a.m. another great shock occurred, nearly equal to the first. This time the area of the most intense shaking had moved slightly northward, probably centered at a site near the present-day towns of Steele, Holland and Cooter, Missouri. It is thought to have been an 8.0 in size. More aftershocks followed. (See Location V.)

Then sometime around 11:00 a.m., another great shock occurred in the vicinity of present-day Caruthersville, which to the residents there at the time seemed to be worse than the first. This one is thought to have been another magnitude 8.0. However, present-day Caruthersville wasn't there at the time. It was not founded until 1857. In 1811 another village occupied that site. It was called Little Prairie, Missouri. (See Location W.)

Magnitude 8.0 or greater earthquakes are very rare on earth. On an average, they only occur about once a year. Sometimes the world has gone for three or four years without a single event this large anywhere. So you can immediately begin to appreciate the historic and geologic uniqueness of these events—three "great" magnitude 8.0 quakes in a few hours in one area. And this was only the beginning of what was eventually to become more than 2,000 temblors in five months.

Many phenomenal effects were observed that first day which are discussed in much greater number and detail in the book, *The Earthquake America Forgot*. For purposes of this book, and the set of slides that accompany this publication, we shall mention only a few and omit the names and first person accounts since they appear in the other two books of this trilogy. To learn how Richter magnitudes were assigned to these events, see the postscript at the end of this introduction.

### The River Rampages, and Towns Disappear

The Mississippi River was churned into a virtual maelstrom with miles of banks caving in, boats being swamped and sunk, and even entire islands disappearing along with their human occupants. Island #94, 100 miles south of the first epicenter was one of them. One could call that a case of "divine justice" since it disappeared with a band of river pirates who had been harassing and robbing river boats for some time. Another was Island #32, located southeast of present-day Blytheville near the bottom of the map on Slide #1.

Two towns disappeared at this time. (Three others were to follow before the series of shocks ended.) One settlement to disappear on December 16, 1811, was Big Prairie, Arkansas, just off of the map of Slide #1, whose site was near present-day Helena, Arkansas, at the confluence of the Mississippi and St. Francis Rivers. The

## KEY TO APPROXIMATE PHOTO LOCATIONS*

| MAP KEY | GENERAL AREA OF PICTURE | PHOTO NOS. | NO. OF PHOTOS | TEXT PAGES |
|---|---|---|---|---|
| A | New Madrid, MO | 12-26 | 15 | 54-68 |
| B | Marston, MO-Bessie, TN | 27-31 | 5 | 69-73 |
| C | Stump Hole-Island #8 | 32-35 | 4 | 74-77 |
| D | Howardville-New Madrid, MO | 36-43 | 8 | 78-85 |
| E | Reelfoot Fault-Donaldson Point | 44-48 | 5 | 86-90 |
| F | Reelfoot Lake, TN | 49-56 | 8 | 91-98 |
| G | Big Lake, AR-Hornersville, MO | 57-67 | 11 | 99-109 |
| H | Monette, AR | 68-69 | 2 | 110-111 |
| I | Gosnell-Big Lake, AR | 70-73 | 4 | 112-115 |
| J | Dexter-Dudley, MO | 74-77 | 4 | 116-119 |
| K | Kewanee, MO | 78-82 | 5 | 120-124 |
| L | Matthews, MO | 83-89 | 7 | 125-131 |
| M | Malden, MO | 90 | 1 | 132 |
| N | Sikeston, MO | 91-95 | 5 | 133-137 |
| O | Benton-Scott City, MO | 96-101 | 6 | 138-143 |
| P | Hayti-Braggadocio, MO | 102-109 | 8 | 144-151 |
| Q | LaForge, MO | 110-115 | 6 | 152-157 |
| R | Charleston, MO | 116-117 | 2 | 158-159 |
| S | Cairo, IL | 118-122 | 5 | 160-164 |
| T | Marston, MO | 123-125 | 3 | 165-167 |
| U | Blytheville, AR | 126 | 1 | 168 |
| V | Steele-Holland-Cooter, MO | 127-129 | 3 | 169-171 |
| W | Caruthersville, MO | 130-133 | 4 | 172-175 |
| X | Lenox, TN | 134-137 | 4 | 176-179 |
| Y | Obion, TN | 138-140 | 3 | 180-182 |
| Z | Hickman, KY | 141-149 | 9 | 183-191 |

*All of these photos are available in full color as 35mm slides. For details on how you can obtain your own set of New Madrid Earthquake Slides, see back of book for details.

**SLIDE #1** MAP

**New Madrid Earthquake Photo Location Map**

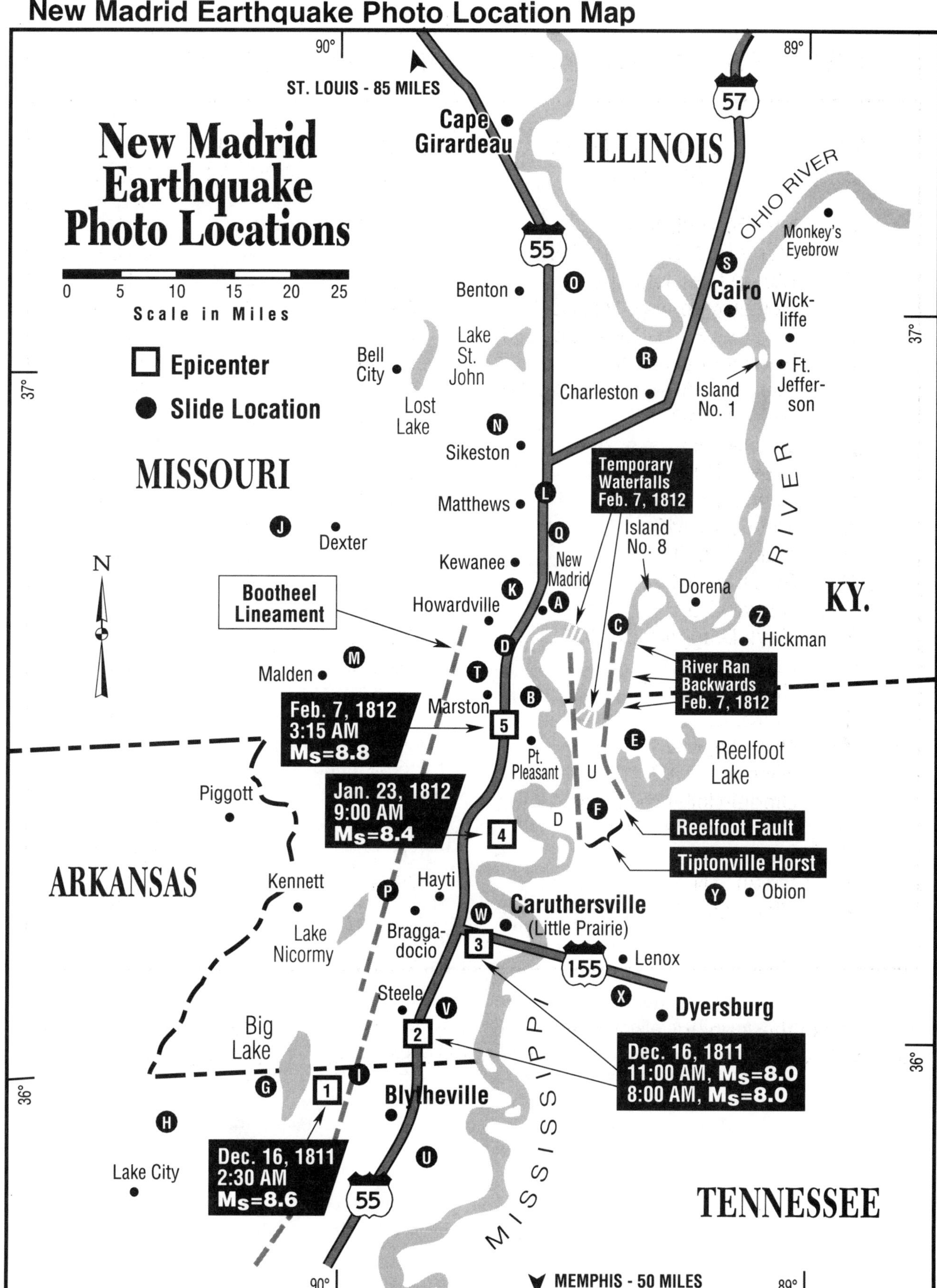

townsite liquefied and sank, but slowly enough for all residents to safely escape. There were about 100 people there at the time. The Mississippi River now occupies that site.

Another community destroyed that day was Little Prairie, Missouri, near present-day Caruthersville (Location W on the map). Eyewitness accounts of the horror tell us of people being violently thrown from their beds in the middle of the night. It had been a bright full moon, but shortly after the shock everything became pitch black. People were injured and bleeding, and some were even knocked temporarily unconscious. The weather had been cool and the hot embers from their fires were strewn across the wooden floors, starting a number of fires. (See Location W.)

The earth continued to jerk and rumble through the darkness until daylight when around 8:00 a.m. the second hard shock hit the area. Throughout the morning more shocks continued with the ground heaving and cracking, sometimes opening and then suddenly slamming shut, spewing groundwater over the tops of tall trees. In some places the ground literally exploded, blasting debris high into the air, raining sand and carbonized wood particles down upon the heads of those nearby, while leaving a deep crater in the ground where smooth land had been before. Sometimes the earth formed spreading crevasses beneath the bases of large trees, splitting their trunks from their roots upwards beyond the levels of their limbs. At one point during the morning a great fissure began to form within the town. The townspeople stood around that pit and watched horrified as dark, viscous fluids gurgled from beneath the earth while gaseous fumes and the smell of sulfur and brimstone filled the air.

Many were thinking that the end of the world was at hand and that the very gates of hell, itself, were opening up to take their village. Amidst the terror, after the third great shock around 11:00 a.m., the soils of their settlement began to turn into quicksand with dark waters oozing from the pores of the earth. As their whole town began to sink, their streets and cabins were flooded, not from the river, but from the ground, itself.

## Escape from Little Prairie

Hastily, the residents of Little Prairie gathered what meager possessions they could hold, lifted small children to their shoulders, and waded westward. Looking ahead of themselves, the rising waters went off the horizon. For eight miles they waded through waist-deep waters, never knowing from one step to the next if they were going to plunge headlong into an unseen crevasse or trip over a buried stump, all the while surrounded by snakes, coyotes, and other wild creatures swimming for their lives in that turgid flood. During their escape, they did not know if they would live through the day or not, but all did survive. Finally the refugees reached high ground near present-day Hayti and camped out for the night.

The next day they decided to head to New Madrid for refuge, not knowing that it, too, had been devastated. It was difficult traveling. What had been 26 miles of passable trail was now a chaotic passageway of tangled trees, fallen trunks, gapping crevasses, sand boils, fissures of quicksand, and whole sections of formerly dry land, now subsided under water. It is features such as these, still visible today, which you will see in the photos that follow in this book.

The weary townspeople arrived at New Madrid on Christmas Eve, only to find a town abandoned and in ruins. Not understanding that earthquakes affect large regions and having no way to communicate with the outside world, the 1000 residents of New Madrid had moved to a temporary campsite two or three miles to the northwest on higher ground. (See Slide #20.) They thought that the earthquakes originated within the city limits of their town and that if they left, they would be safe.

The Little Prairie refugees then learned of the casualties at New Madrid. An uncounted number of injuries and nine reported dead. One lady refused to leave her cabin after the first few shocks and died later in the day on December 16 when it collapsed; Another lady panicked, ran into the street screaming, and died from fright of a heart attack. Six Indians who were camped on the river's edge near town were lost when the bank caved in and was thrown into the Mississippi sweeping them away. And one black man was engulfed in a sand boil and drowned. A boatman passing by New Madrid later in the day said it appeared to him that "all of New Madrid was on fire." (See Slide Location A showing many sand boils in New Madrid, probably including the one in which the man drowned, which was possibly the massive sand boil shown in Slides #24 and #25.)

### The First Day was Over But the Worst Was Yet to Come

What has been described, thusfar, was only the first day of the Great New Madrid Earthquake series. More and bigger tremors were yet to come. At least small tremors were occurring every day with some being moderate to strong. On January 7, 1812, a large shock hit again, this time in the upper sevens on the Richter scale. But then, at about 9:00 a.m. on January 23, 1812, another of the really big ones hit. This was probably centered north of Little Prairie and south of Point Pleasant, a small settlement there at the time. It is thought to have been an 8.4 magnitude earthquake. Like the first great quake of December 16, this one was felt throughout two-thirds of the United States, from the Rockies to the Atlantic seaboard. It was felt in three other countries: Mexico, Canada, and Cuba. Chimneys fell in Cincinnati. Sidewalks buckled in Baltimore. Church bells rang in Boston. And the North Carolina legislature, in session at the time, adjourned in confusion and chaos from what they thought was a "Carolina" earthquake, not realizing the source to be 700 miles to the west.

The Mississippi River bank, on which the village of Point Pleasant was situated, collapsed during the January 23 event. Fortunately, the residents had all evacuated the site prior to that catastrophe so that none were injured. The town, however, was lost forever. Today, a few miles to the west is another community of the same name but safely set back a mile or two from the river. (A photo of that town is in the book, *The Earthquake America Forgot.*)

The January 23 event also caused several huge sand boils in Tennessee that created a dam across Reelfoot Creek. (See Slide #54, Location F.) This was the beginning of the permanent impondment we have since come to call, "Reelfoot Lake." (See Slide Locations E and F.)

The aftershocks continued daily. Then on February 5, the residents noted a change. In addition to the episodic bumps and tremors, the residents of New Madrid noted that the ground began to jerk continuously which they described as being like the random twitches of "a side of freshly killed beef." These spasms continued through the day, through the night, through the next day, and into the night. Then on Friday, February 7, 1812, came the largest quake of all. At about 3:15 in the morning the region was rocked by an 8.8 magnitude shock. Outside of Alaska, that is the largest earthquake in American history and one of the largest in the world. Its center is thought to have been near Marston, Missouri, just southwest of New Madrid. This would place it very near, if not right under, the Interstate 55 Rest Stop between Marston and New Madrid. (See Slides #36 & #37, Location D.)

This is the quake that caused the Mississippi River to run backwards between Islands #9 and #10. It caused such towering waves of water to be thrown over the banks that thousands of acres of trees were shattered into splinters and stumps near Island #8. It threw boats up on dry land along St. John's Bayou at New Madrid. And it created two temporary waterfalls, one 10 miles south of New Madrid near Island #10 and another one only a mile upstream from New Madrid and within sight of people in the town. (See Locations A, B and C.)

The retrograde motion of the river lasted only a few hours, but the waterfalls remained for two or three days. They were described as being similar to the low waterfalls at Louisville, Kentucky, on the Ohio River. These falls have a vertical drop of about six feet followed by a mile or so of shallow rapids. One boat that had been transported upstream by the reversed river motion, later drifted downstream to encounter the first waterfall at Island #10. It survived and made it to New Madrid where the boat tied up for the next few days. The crew watched as 30 other unfortunate vessels came over the second falls at New Madrid. Twenty-eight boats were swamped or capsized with almost total loss of life. The desperate screams of drowning boatmen could be heard in New Madrid where residents could only stand by helplessly watch the tragedy enfold. Nineteen other boats, tied up at New Madrid during that terrifying dark morning of February 7, let loose their moorings to float southward after the 8.8 shock. They were never seen nor heard from again.

During the largest of the New Madrid earthquakes, the river is said to have boiled, whirled and heaved with massive waves bashing from one bank to the other, sweeping boats and debris into oblivion. Some eyewitnesses from the banks said they actually saw the river open up in yawning chasms into which the swirling waters disappeared, drawing hapless flat boats and their passengers into the maelstrom, never to be seen again. Others said water spouts would shoot upwards from the water's surface, like tall fountains. During those five months of tectonic turmoil, hundreds of lives were lost on the river, never to be counted nor accounted for.

## The Quakes Form Lakes and Destroy the Land for Farming

The seismotectonic forces, that caused the river to run backwards and form two waterfalls simultaneously, produced an uplifted region (the Tiptonville Horst on the map on Slide #1) coupled with a downwarping between the Horst the Chickasaw Bluffs. A large empondment had already begun on January 23, 1812, caused by the constrictions in the channel of Reelfoot Creek from massive sand boils. But it was the events of February 7 that permanently locked Reelfoot Lake into the flood plain.

The two earthquake lakes mentioned thusfar still exist. Both are popular fishing areas. Big Lake, on the Missouri-Arkansas line, was formed December 16, 1811, with the first great shock. Reelfoot Lake, in Tennessee, only 15 miles across the river from New Madrid, was finalized on February 7, 1812, with the last great quake. At different times during December, January and February, other lakes formed. The locations of three others are given on the map on slide #1. These are Lake Nicormy, west of Hayti; Lake St. John, south of Benton; and Lost Lake, just east of Bell City.

Other earthquake lakes not shown include Flag Lake, north of Kennett; Lake Tyronza, northeast of Marked Tree, Arkansas; Lake St. Anne, between Howardville and New Madrid, Missouri; and Lake St. Francis, the largest of all. The latter resulted from seismically induced damming of the St. Francis River upstream from Marked Tree creating a huge lake almost 40 miles long extending northward along the Missouri-Arkansas line defining the west boundary of the "Bootheel" between Kennett and Piggott. One boy was reported lost during the quakes where this lake was formed. Present-day Lake City, Arkansas, is situated in the southern portion of the former site of Lake St. Francis.

The lakes were shallow, mostly less than 10 feet deep, 20 feet maximum. Most lasted for a hundred years or more following the quakes that formed them, while Lake St. Francis lasted for little more than a decade. Lake St. Anne is still visible and temporarily fills during heavy rainfall, even today. Several Slides (Location D) show this lake today. The other lakes were drained during the construction of the hundreds of miles of drainage canals between 1918 and 1924. Their only traces remaining today are the fertile flat lands and fine black soils that formed their lake bottoms where abundant crops now grow each year. St. John's Bayou, whose mouth on the Mississippi is just east of New Madrid (see Slide #19), is connected with St. John's Ditch which crosses Interstate 55 near Matthews, Missouri (see Slide #83), and heads up at the site of old Lake St. John north of Sikeston.

The earthquakes had literally destroyed the landscape with sand deposits, crevasses, and permanent flooding. Most residents of the region abandoned their properties and moved away. The Bootheel portion of Missouri was nicknamed "Swampeast Missouri" sometime after the quakes. Most people in this century do not know that prior to the great earthquakes this land had been relatively well drained, although some natural swamps and lakes were there before. The force of the ground motion had so disrupted the natural drainages that many areas, including

**SLIDE #2** MAP

**Intensity Map of Great NM Earthquakes of 1811-12**

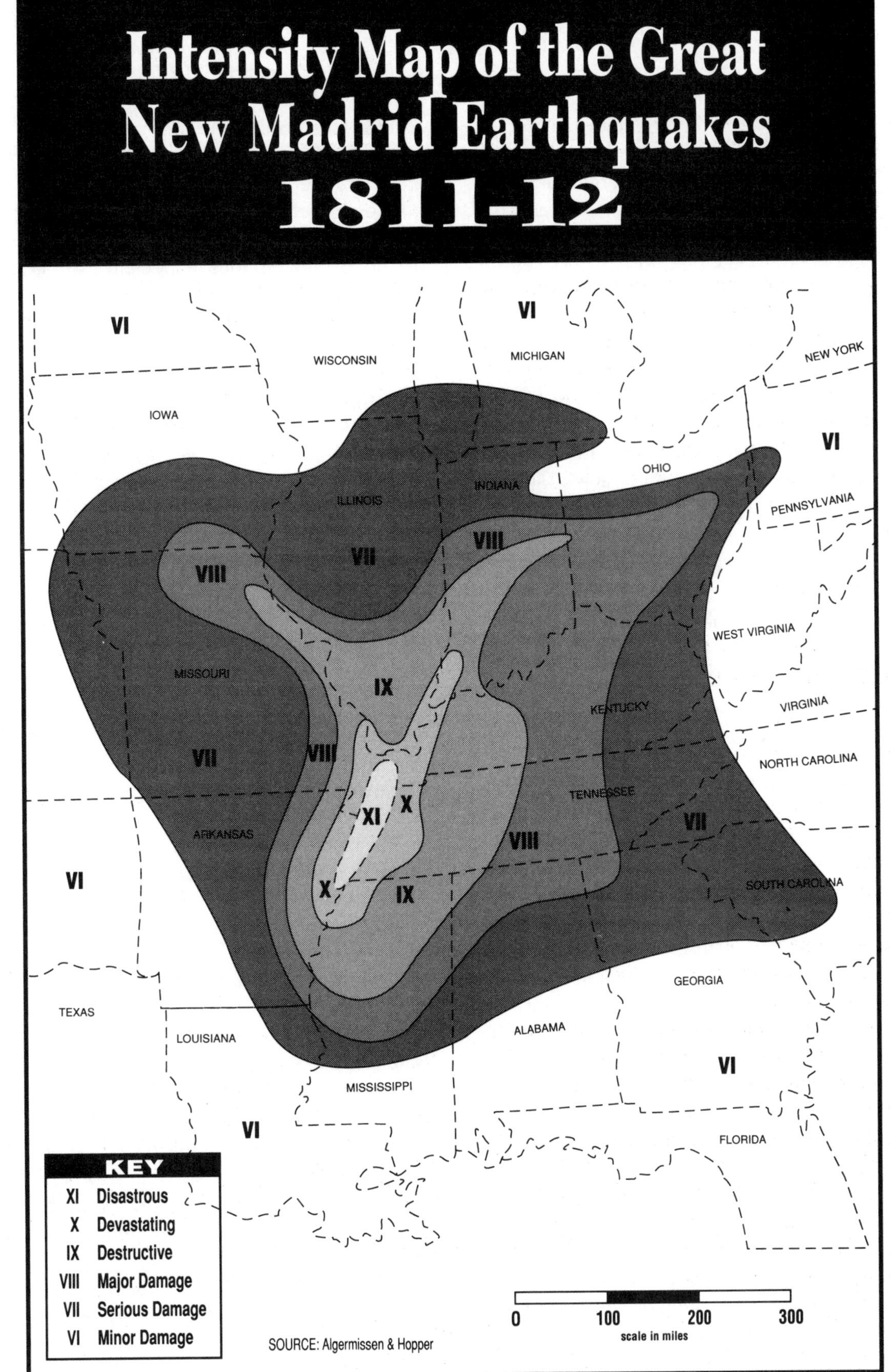

some high ground, became permanent swamp or lake land, destroying the capability for agriculture.

An 1850 document from the archives of the United States House of Representatives contains a report from the U.S. Corps of Engineers that argues in favor of H.R. Bill #44. That bill would have authorized federal monies to drain the swamp lands in Missouri and Arkansas. The report blamed the New Madrid earthquakes for creating the poor drainage and water-logged conditions that had "rendered the land useless." The report argued that unproductive land produced no tax revenues for the government and that if congress would appropriate the money to "reclaim the land and enable it to become productive with agriculture" the tax income generated would eventually pay for the project. Congress never passed that bill. More than half-a-century later the Missouri Legislature authorized the formation of the Little River Drainage District by which the land was finally reclaimed through a major engineering drainage project between 1918 and 1924, more than 100 years after the great ground upheavals that had helped to create the problem.

### Two More Towns Gone Forever

The February 7 quake destroyed two other towns, wiping them forever from the face of the earth. One was Fort Jefferson, Kentucky, swept away by landslides. These slumps are still visible today along Highway 51 leading into Wickliffe. The other lost town was New Madrid, itself. What was left of the settlement slumped downward 15-20 feet into the water's edge and was washed away by the spring floods of 1812. The river has migrated northward about a mile since then. Today you can stand on the Mississippi River Observation Deck just outside the New Madrid Historical Museum and look south toward the Kentucky shoreline. The river is a mile wide there. At a point about halfway across the river is the original site of New Madrid, forever gone. (See Slide #17.)

From that same deck you can look upstream to St. John's Bayou where it meets the Mississippi, the site where the boats were thrown up on land and where the second waterfall took so many lives during that cold winter almost 200 years ago. (See Slide #18.) You can also stand on that same deck and look six miles to the southwest where the 812-foot-tall smoke stack of the Associated Electric Company is plainly visible. This convenient landmark, which can be seen up to 30 miles away, marks the approximate epicentral region of the 8.8 magnitude earthquake of February 7, 1812. (You will see this huge smoke stack in several of the photographs on the following pages, especially from Locations A, B and E.)

In the weeks following February 7 and the great magnitude 8.8 quake, a number of powerful shocks in the range of 6.0-7.6. The sequence then tapered off over the next few months into occasional tremors of 4.0 or less. Perceptible aftershocks continued, however, for several years.

So that's what happened. Those were the Great New Madrid Earthquakes of 1811-12. Two thousand temblors in five months . . . and it will happen again. (But probably not soon.) A map of how far those damaging ground motions of 1811-12 reached, as well as how far they could reach again, is shown in Slide #2. The astonishing reach of the New Madrid Fault is graphically illustrated in this Intensity Map. A level of VII represents serious damage and, as you can see, that level touches 22 states. An intensity level of VIII representing major damage, including some collapsed buildings, would occur in some part of 11 states. The amazing thing is that no place on the Map of Slide #2 escapes entirely unscathed. All 27 states shown there would receive at least level VI intensities which means at least minor damages like broken windows, items thrown from shelves, or cracked brick.

The region remains seismically active. Approximately 200 measurable quakes occur in the New Madrid Seismic Zone every year. Slide #3 shows the epicentral locations of present-day seismicity. About 200 quakes are recorded each year within the region of this map. By comparison with Slide #1, you can see how closely the locations of several thousand current events relate to those of the five greatest quakes of 1811-12.

The throbs and throes of terra firma wrought by the Great New Madrid Earthquakes of 1811-12 trouble us no more. Only the echos of their aftershocks continue. Though the motions of these gargantuan ground vibrations ceased in 1812, their impact goes on. Permanent traces of their violence lie scattered over a 5,000 square mile area spanning five states. The rest of this book (and set of slides) is a photo-essay on the thousands of fissures, landslides, sand boils, surface faults, and other scars in the landscape still visible today from those cataclysms of so long ago.

## POSTSCRIPT:

### How Epicenters & Richter Magnitudes Were Assigned to These Events

It should be mentioned that many seismologists consider the three largest earthquakes of December 16, 1811, as a single great event with aftershocks. Others count only two great (8.0 or larger) events that first day. Therefore, you may encounter publications that classify the events of that day as only one or two quakes of magnitude 8.0 or greater, instead of three as we have done here. The reason for the apparent discrepancy lies in the ways authorities choose to describe the events of that time and place. Dr. Otto Nuttli, leading authority on the New Madrid Earthquakes in his lifetime, counted three great events on December 16. We have elected to follow his lead. (See the booklet entitled, *Effects of Earthquakes in the Central U.S.* by Nuttli, 1990.)

Another apparent discrepancy between accounts of the magnitudes of the New Madrid earthquakes has to do with the difference between surface wave magnitudes and body wave magnitudes. There is a mathematical relationship whereby one can be converted into the other. We have chosen to use surface wave magnitudes here. Surface wave magnitudes in the range of 8.0 – 8.8 convert to body wave magnitudes in the range of 6.9 – 7.4. (See Nuttli, 1990, for conversion table.) Hence, if you read somewhere that the principal 1811-12 New Madrid quakes were 7.0 – 7.4 on the Richter scale, they are using the body wave formula. If you read that the principal magnitudes were in the 8.0 – 8.8 range, then the surface wave formula has been used. Nuttli quoted the surface wave values in his 1990 publication, and so have we in this book.

It should be kept in mind that the numerical Richter magnitudes quoted in this book were not determined by instrumental measurements as they are today because these events predated the invention of the seismograph. Instead, they are sophisticated estimates based on ground shaking intensities reported in the media of the time. Also taken into consideration is the abundance of surviving visible evidence such as sand boils, fissures, landslides, and other seismic features seen throughout the New Madrid Seismic Zone.

Dr. Otto Nuttli's magnitude values for the principal 1811-12 New Madrid shocks, first published in 1973, are now universally accepted by the community of professional seismologists. One could question their accuracy, but considering the thoroughness by which these were derived, better estimates are not likely to be forthcoming. Besides, even today, with the most sophisticated multi-million dollar seismographic instrumentation, Richter magnitudes are still only obtainable to within 0.2 units, at best.

Sometimes, when an earthquake occurs, different stations measuring the same event can report values ranging almost as much as a whole unit of magnitude. This is a significant error. Every full unit on the Richter scale represents a 32 times difference in energy released by the quake, while every two tenths (0.2) of a unit represents a doubling of the energy released. A magnitude 5.2 event is 32 times the size of a 4.2 event and twice the size of a 5.0 event. The fact that the best of current technology is only capable of plus or minus 0.2 units is an indication of the imprecision of today's earthquake science.

Seismology is an infant field of research. It has yet to learn such basics as how to accurately measure the size of an earthquake. For many quakes, there is considerable uncertainty even in the measurement of their exact depths and locations.

Seismic events of truly major proportions are rare enough that a seismologist, geologist or engineer focusing on a specific area may not have a single opportunity to directly study even one great event in his or her lifetime. The late Dr. Otto Nuttli faced this problem. He was the world authority on the New Madrid earthquakes in his lifetime but never lived to experience anything larger than a moderate magnitude 5.0 on that fault. That was a 1976 tremor near Marked Tree, Arkansas, at the southern end of the seismic zone.

It has been almost 200 years since the last great New Madrid quake. It will probably be at least 200 years more before the next magnitude 8.0 will occur. It will take centuries of observations and generations of seismologists before the New Madrid Seismic Zone will be well understood. Even so, we know a lot more now than we did two decades ago. In fact, most of the scientific understanding we now have on the New Madrid fault has been derived since 1970. But much much more remains to be discovered and be made known. Mother earth knows how to keep her secrets.

To learn more about the methodology and the data base by which the magnitudes of the Great New Madrid Earthquakes were estimated, see Nuttli (1973). To learn more about how the approximate epicentral locations were determined, see Obermeier, et al., (1989). To acquaint yourself with the most up-to-date scientific understanding of the New Madrid Seismic Zone, see Johnston, Shedlock, Hermann & Hopper (1992).

# The Featured Text

# RECOGNIZING EARTHQUAKE FEATURES FOR FUN AND PROFIT

Recognizing seismic features when you travel through earthquake zones is fun. It can also be profitable. If you live in a seismically active zone, failing to recognize an earthquake feature and later building your house on it could prove to be expensive. Recognizing such unstable ground and avoiding it can save you a lot of money.

As you will discover in the following photos and text, soils that have been disturbed by previous earthquakes and which bear the scars of liquefaction, fissuring, lateral spreading, landsliding, and other forms of seismic ground failure remain permanently unstable. Not only are such sites more prone than others to move and fail again in future earthquakes, but meteorologic and cultural activities can also lead to future damages and losses even without more quakes. The impact of a major earthquake is not necessarily over when the shaking stops. Some impacts are permanent.

Hillsides with old earthquake landslides are very likely to slide again with future shocks. They can also creep and slip again with prolonged or heavy rains. Old earthquake landslides that have become stabilized by well-rooted vegetation can become unstable again if deforested or developed for urban purposes. Old earthquake sand boils are likely to liquefy again in the next large shake, but can become quicksand again even without a quake when nearby rivers rise high on their levees. You don't want to be driving your tractor across one of these sand boils at the wrong time.

The best course of action is to be able to recognize seismically disturbed earth when you see it and avoid such locations for building and development. If you are planning to farm such land, recognizing the nature of the seismically sensitive portions of your land can save you much trouble and money. This book and slide set will help you to do this.

## Defining the "NMSZ"

The definitions and descriptions of seismic landforms that follow are applicable anywhere in the world where seismically induced liquefaction, lateral spreading and landsliding has occurred. However, all of the photos and examples given in this book are from the New Madrid Seismic Zone, or "NMSZ". The region is shown in a general way on Slide #3. Some clarification is in order when using the term, "NMSZ."

The expression "New Madrid Seismic Zone" has been in use among earth scientists since the early 1970's. At that time, seismic instrumentation in the Midwest was very sparse and unsophisticated. Hence, the boundaries of this active earthquake zone were not known with any degree of precision. Although it had been clear for more than 100 years that active faulting was taking place at some depth beneath the region, by 1970 no visual, instrumental or seismographic evidence of an actual primary fault had yet been obtained. Stearns and Wilson published a map in 1972 in which they simply shaded in an area from eastern Arkansas to southern Illinois and called it the "Reelfoot Tectonic Structure" or "New Madrid Faulted Belt." (See Figure 1 from Johnston & Shedlock, 1992, reproduced on the next page. ) Figures 1a, 1b, and 1c show how the delineation of the boundaries of the "NMSZ" developed as more and more data became available from 1972 to 1980.

We now know that more than 200 small tremors occur every year within the NMSZ but until adequate instrumentation was installed only those large enough to be felt by area residents were noted. This meant that, generally speaking, any quake less than 3.0 on the Richter scale went unnoticed and unrecorded.

A regional seismographic network of modern sensors was first established in 1974. These seismic stations were funded by the U.S. Geologi-

**FIGURE 1.** Evolution of interpretations of the crustal structure of the upper Mississippi embayment and definition of what comprises the "NMSZ." (a) The Reelfoot "tectonic structure" and New Madrid "faulted belt" of Stearns and Wilson (1972). The dashed line they have noted as the western edge of the tectonic structure is from Myron Fuller (1912) who had postulated that the epicenters of the 1811-12 New Madrid series were along this line based upon the abundance of liquefaction features found here. Earthquake scientists now believe the "epicentral line" of 1811-12 was more to the east as given by Obermeier (1989). (b) Based on analysis of the subsurface from borehole data and other sources, Ervin and McGinnis (1975) identify a line (AX) between the Ouachita Tectonic belt in eastern Arkansas and the Ste. Genevieve Fault in southern Illinois as the "probable rift axis" of the NMSZ. (c) Zoback et al. (1980), using aeromagnetic data from Hildenbrand et al. (1977) shows well-defined boundaries (dark lines) of an "inferred subsurface rift". Note small circles plotted to represent epicenters of current seismicity superimposed on the inferred rift zone or NMSZ.

cal Survey. The initial net was telemetered to recorders at St. Louis University. As more and more stations were added, the southern locations were telemetered to Memphis State University. With a large number of seismic stations in place, the magnitudes, frequencies, epicenters and depths of small earthquakes in the New Madrid Seismic Zone could be determined with ever increasing certainty. Even tiny quakes, less than 1.0 on the Richter scale, could be recorded and compiled on a regular basis. Figures 2a, 2b, and 2c (from Johnston & Shedlock, 1992) show the evolution in quality and quantity of seismicity data for the NMSZ region. By 1991 the exact locations and orientations of earthquake foci had been defined so well as to delineate the currently active portion of the New Madrid Seismic Zone into several clear lines of fault motion. (See Figure 2c.) Figure 3 (from Schweig & Marple, 1991) shows another highly resolved plot of current epicenters in the NMSZ and also plots the Bootheel Lineament on the map.

It would be tempting to say that the NMSZ has now been so well defined that we can restrict its boundaries to the most concentrated alignments of epicentral locations as shown in Figures 2c & 3, thus reducing the original area of the zone as postulated in Figure 1 and Slide #3. However, the well defined active fault zones delineated by Figures 2c & 3 only speak to seismic activity during the 17-year period between 1974 and 1991. This is probably only a part of the New Madrid Tectonic System, not its entirety. The indications are that the zone of fractured rock that makes up the NMSZ is much larger, a vast complex of faults. Some portions are active now. Other parts are currently quiescent but were very active in the historic or geologic past and which could become active again in the future. (See Narrative with Slides

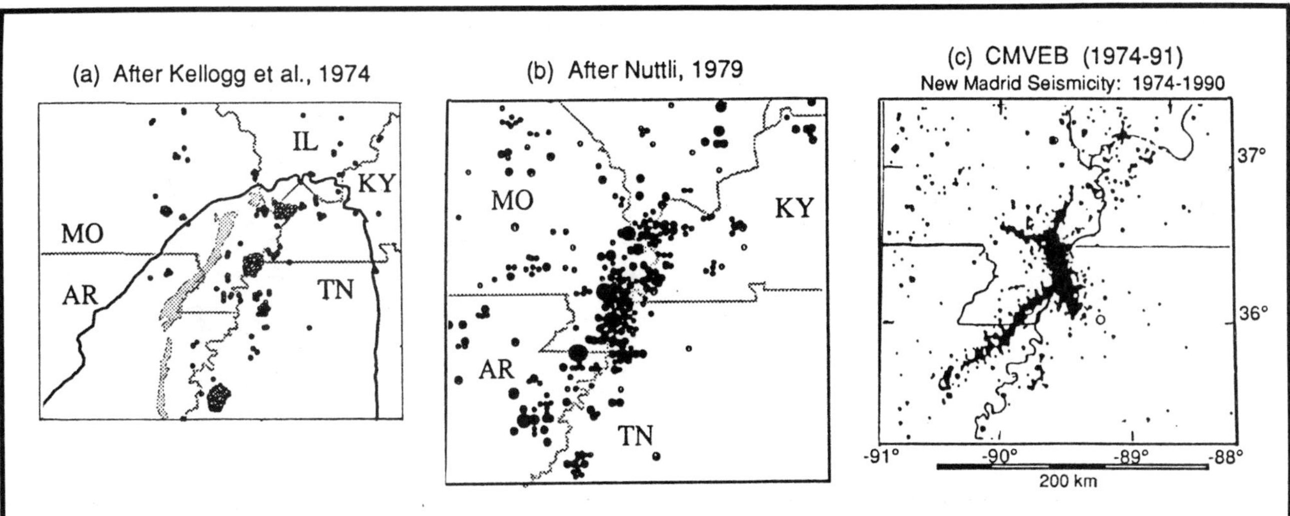


**FIGURE 2.** Evolution in quality and quantity of seismicity data for the NMSZ region. As more and better instrumentation was installed after 1974, more and more earthquakes were recorded with better determinations of their exact depths epicentral locations, thus transforming the scientific understanding of the NMSZ from one of diffuse and scattered earthquake activity into one with well focused lines where most of the seismicity currently occurs. (a) A plot of known seismicity prior to 1970 from Kellogg et al. (1974). It depicts approximately 300 postulated "epicenters" for events between 1871 and 1971 which are probably a better reflection of population centers where people reported the quakes than the actual locations of the quakes, themselves. (b) Epicenters of 488 earthquakes of magnitudes 3.0 or greater occurring between 1811 and 1974 from Stauder (1982) using Nuttli (1979) data base. Although still diffuse, the data are beginning to manifest some patterns of possible lineation with this publication. (c) Epicenters of several thousand earthquakes occurring between 1974 and 1990, including small quakes less than 2.5 that were not felt but which were recorded and located by seismographs of the permanent regional seismic network as reported in the *Central Mississippi Valley Earthquake Bulletin* (CMVEB, 1974-1991). With increased quantity and quality of data, the currently active fault lines of the NMSZ become quite clear. However, even with the instrumentation that provided these data, epicentral locations can still be in error by as much as 10 miles, depths to the zone of rupture can be off by as much as 5 miles, magnitudes can be as much as half a Richter unit too high or too low, and an unknown number of the smallest tremors still remain unrecorded. As of December 1992, a NMSZ seismicity plot of even greater resolution, published in 3-D and full color, has been made available. (See Johnston, Shedlock, Herrmann, & Hopper, 1992.)

#74-#77.) It is not certain that the zones of today's highest activity were the sources of the great quakes of 1811-12. (See Schweig & Marple, 1991; and Schweig, Marple & Li, 1992.) Nor has it been proven that the most active zones today will be sources of tomorrow's quakes.

Furthermore, it is unclear the extent to which the tectonic zone we currently call "The New Madrid" connects with other faults. For example, the Ste. Genevieve Fault runs in a southeastern direction for 100 miles from near Bloomsdale, Missouri, to Metropolis, Illinois. But Metropolis is where seismologists place the northern end of the New Madrid Fault and some believe the two faults are connected. Some scientists also believe that the "Wabash Fault" is a 100-mile northeastern extension of the New Madrid extending from Metropolis and up the Wabash River Valley along the Indiana-Illinois state line. The Wabash Fault has produced the two largest Midwestern quakes in the 20th century, a 5.4 quake in 1968 and a 5.2 quake in 1987. The largest 20th century quake on the New Madrid, so far, was a 5.0 magnitude event in 1976.

## Seismologists, Geologists & Engineers Different Perspectives on the NMSZ

If you read technical works on the NMSZ by professionals with different backgrounds, you will find differences in definitions for the Zone. The variations are due to the time frames by which different disciplines view the world.

Seismologists generally focus on the present (plus or minus a few centuries). They want to know what is happening now and relate the past and future to the present. Geologists tend to focus on the distant past (what happened thousands and millions of years ago) and relate that to the present and future. Engineers typically focus on the near future (what's going to happen in the next 50-100 years) so they can devise measures to minimize damages and losses. An engineer is interested in the past and present, too, but mainly as a guide to what can be expected in the next few decades and how to deal with it.

Seismologists monitor earthquake activity in the NMSZ on a daily basis. They tend to draw the boundaries of the NMSZ according to recent seismic activity. As the the currently active portions of the fault become better defined with the increasing body of seismographic data, this tendency leads seismologists to draw the boundaries of the NMSZ around an increasingly smaller area, tightly constrained to the lines of presently known seismicity.

Geologists are interested in the connections of the New Madrid Fault with other faults throughout a wide region as found today, as well as the relationships of the NMSZ with these faults for hundreds of millions of years into the geologic past. They tend to draw the boundaries of the NMSZ around a larger area than seismologists, including some fault branches not currently active.

Engineers must deal with the hazards posed by earthquakes today and in the near future. They tend to think of the NMSZ in terms of the region that would receive the most intense ground shaking from a major quake originating anywhere within the NMSZ. Hence, their interest in the 1811-12 sequence of shocks is to learn what areas were most severely affected then so they can postulate which areas will at the greatest risk of future damages.

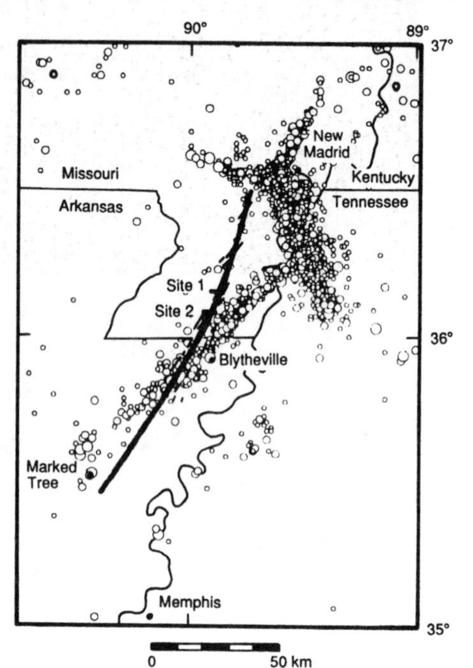


**FIGURE 3.** Bootheel Lineament shown in relation to NMSZ, earthquake epicenters plotted for 1974-1987. The heavy dark line from Marked Tree, Arkansas, to an area west of New Madrid marks location of Lineament approximated from various satellite images. The shorter black lines are the most prominent traces from aerial photography. Detailed Mapping is in progress for southern part of Lineament. Sites of two trenches by Memphis State University shown west of Steele, MO. The Lineament was discovered in 1989. It appears to be a strike-slip fault and may be the first known surface expression of a portion of the buried New Madrid Fault from which earthquakes originate. (From Schweig & Marple, 1991.)

In this book, we have adopted the engineering point of view. We have drawn the boundaries of the NMSZ to circumscribe the region that received the most intense ground shaking during the 1811-12 series of earthquakes. This is the area of most interest to people, in general, because the region most severely affected then will be the region most severely damaged in future. It is also within this region that one finds

**SLIDE #3** MAP

**Map of New Madrid Seismic Zone (NMSZ)**

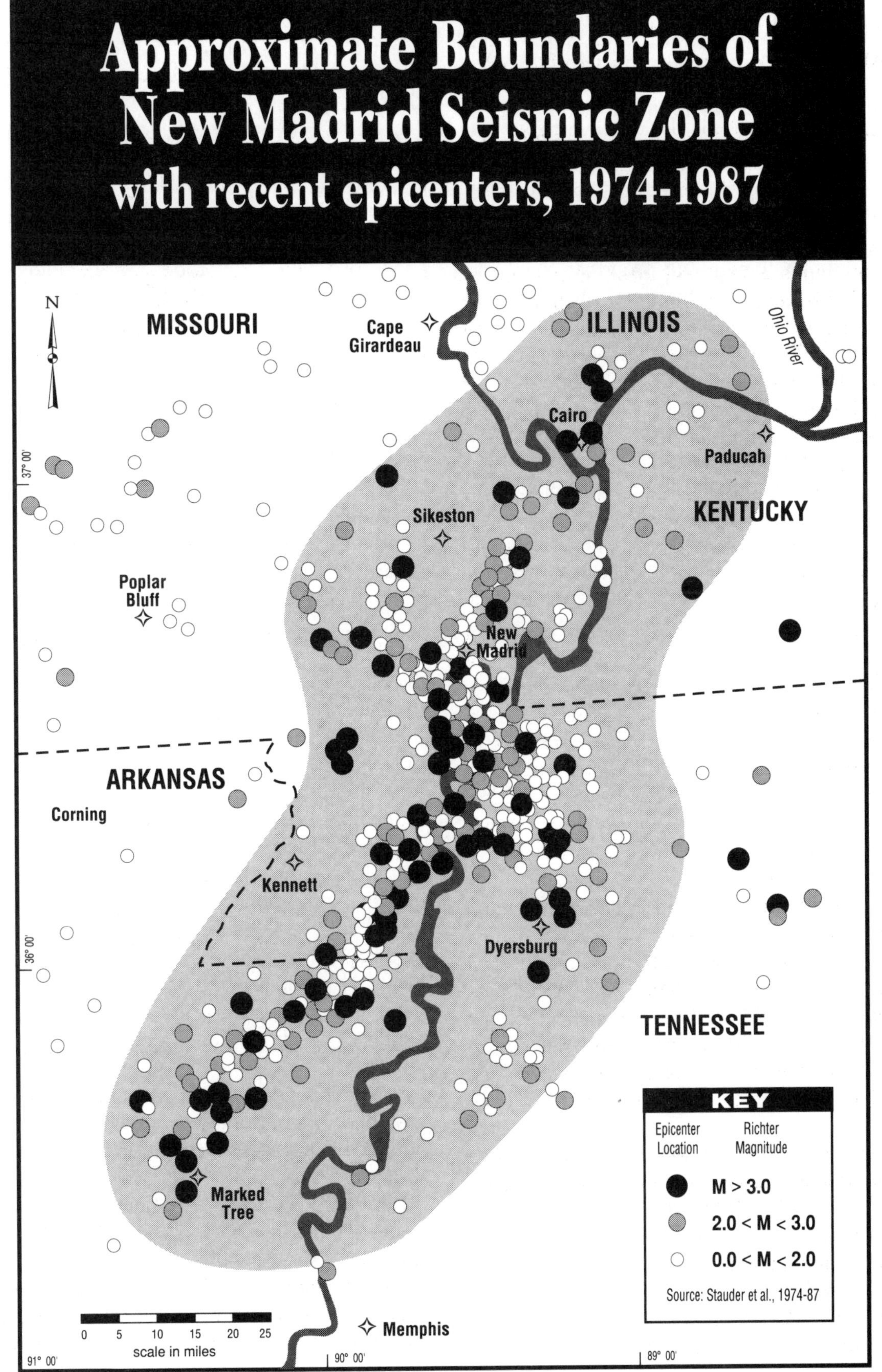

the most abundant evidence of the 1811-12 series in the form of permanent alterations in the landscape, the subject matter of the photographs of this book and slide set.

Therefore, in this book, we have taken the NMSZ to be a general region approximately 150 miles long (northeast to southwest) and about 50 miles wide—extending from south of Marked Tree, Arkansas, into southern Illinois, near Metropolis, above the famous bend of the Ohio called "Monkey's Eyebrow" in Kentucky. The NMSZ includes portions of five states as seen on Slide #3. Within this zone lies the most concentrated, currently active portions of the New Madrid Fault System, as seen in Figure 2c, as well as portions of the fault with less concentrated, more diffuse activity. The "Bootheel Lineament" is included in this zone. ( Slides #1, #102-#109, & #138.) It is an 85 mile long surface feature having the the appearance of a right-lateral strike slip fault. The lineament may mark a portion of the New Madrid Fault System that was active in former times but relatively inactive today. The most distinctive characteristic features of the NMSZ, as we are defining it, are the more than 5,000 square miles of disturbed landscape bearing permanent evidence of the cataclysms of 1811-12. It is these seismic landforms that comprise the central theme of this book and set of accompanying slides.

## What They Are And How They Happen

All of the features listed in the tables of Slides #4-#6 are described here in the same order as the tables. If you are giving a slide presentation, you will want to read through this section for your own background education. In your actual presentation, you may include or skip the information of this section depending on the nature of your audience and the time allotted. If you are mainly interested in a travelogue, then you may want to pass over Slides #4-#11 quickly, getting right into the photographs of actual features that start with Slide #12. If you are teaching a geophysics, geology, geography, earth science, or engineering class, slides #4 through #11 could be the basis for a full hour's presentation. In any case, if you are interested in the geologic details of these features, the forces that formed them, and how they appear today, this section is for you.

The table displayed in Slides #4, #5 and #6 classify the earthquake features of the New Madrid Seismic Zone into six major categories and twenty-four subcategories. In addition to photographs of these features, this book and the accompanying set of slides also contain pictures of seismically historic places such as sites where towns disappeared and where rivers ran backwards. Historical commentary will be reserved for the photo captions that follow in Slides #12-#149. In this section we shall define and describe the 24 types of morphoseismic features outlined and represented in the next eight Slides, #4-#11.

The primary energies released by earthquakes are vibrations released from a focal point at depth. These seismic shock waves expand from their subterranean source zone, or focus, until they reach the earth's surface and ripple across the upper crust shaking, cities and people. The point on the earth's surface directly above the focus is called the epicenter. Hence, earthquakes originate at a focus at depth, but are first perceived at ground zero, the epicenter from which the waves appear to expand radially to distant places. Sometimes seismic waves travel hundreds, or even thousands, of miles.

When the quake is over the shaking is over. But these movements, though transient, can permanently alter the landscape, causing visible rock and soil surfaces to uplift, downwarp, subside, move, break up, or fail in a variety of ways. All of the seismic features to be seen in the New Madrid Seismic Zone are related to various kinds of ground failure induced by earthquake shaking.

There are three principal types of seismically-induced ground failure: Liquefaction, Landsliding, and Secondary Faulting.

**LIQUEFACTION:** Earthquake liquefaction occurs when suitable soils temporarily become liquid or "quick" in response to seismic vibrations. Liquefaction is actually a hydrologic phenomena, being the response of groundwater to dynamic forces such as those generated by earthquake shock waves. A full understanding or liquefaction requires knowledge in three fields: Groundwater Hydrology, Soil Mechanics, and Seismology. The necessary conditions for liquefaction to occur are for the soils to be loose or unconsolidated, saturated with water, and sufficiently permeable for the groundwater to move through the pore spaces by the forces of the induced pressures.

For liquefaction phenomena to manifest at the surface water, tables must usually be less than 30 feet below. However, seismically induced liquefaction has been known to occur in layers of saturated sand buried 100 feet deep causing subsidence, landslides and ground failures above. There is reason to believe that liquefaction can be induced by earthquake forces near the focus of a quake at even greater depths, which can be reflected in surface subsidence over large areas as well as other permanent morphoseismic consequences. (See Knox & Stewart, 1993.)

Throughout most of the New Madrid Seismic Zone, as well as much of the surrounding region, water tables are typically less than 30 feet below the surface and often less than 15 feet down. This makes the area particularly prone to liquefaction phenomena during earthquakes, even in the case of moderate (magnitudes 5.0-5.4) tremors.

By contrast, California has many earthquakes but proportionately little liquefaction because the state is mostly arid. While there are plenty of valleys of loose sand in the West, the water tables are often hundreds of feet below surface so that the necessary conditions for liquefaction are not present. Seismically induced liquefaction in California occurs mostly along seashores, adjacent to other large bodies of water, or in valleys with streams that flow throughout the year. The Marina District of San Francisco which suffered severe liquefaction damage during the World Series Earthquake, October 17, 1989, is next to San Francisco Bay. A few blocks inland no liquefaction occurred.

The most common sites with high liquefaction potential in the Midwest are flood plains adjacent to perennial streams where water tables are near the surface and soils are loose and permeable. Most of the New Madrid Seismic Zone is underlaid by unconsolidated sediments of the Mississippi, Ohio, and St. Francis River flood plains which make the region highly prone to liquefaction during earthquakes.

Areas that have liquefied in previous earthquakes will liquefy in future ones. They can also exhibit liquefaction in response to mechanical vibrations and hydrologic pressures in the groundwater during high water conditions. Therefore, it is important for engineers, contractors, builders, developers, architects, regional planners, home owners, businessmen, and others to recognize earthquake liquefaction features from previous earthquakes and avoid building on those vulnerable sites, or make special provisions when building there is necessary. This book can serve as an excellent primer for such education, not only for the New Madrid Seismic Zone, but for the entire Midwest and other parts of the world, as well.

**SOIL TYPES THAT CAN LIQUEFY:** Normally, a potential for liquefaction requires layers of sand or silt, with little or no clay. However, under certain conditions, usually adjacent to bodies of salt water, some clays can also liquefy under earthquake loadings. Water-saturated gravels have also been known to temporarily liquefy during earthquakes.

A state of liquefaction or "earthflow" can also be stimulated in loess, a common soil type on the hilltops of the New Madrid Seismic Zone. Loess is a fine-grained, homogeneous soil, tan or light brown in color, which was deposited by the wind throughout the Midwest during ancient dust storms that blew 8,000 to 20,000 years ago during long periods of arid climatic conditions. Loess contains no rocks or gravel. Earth materials deposited by wind are referred to by geologists as "aeolian."

Liquefaction never happens in bedrock or in dry soils of any type. Except in rare instances, as mentioned above, liquefaction does not happen in clay, although water-saturated clay can amplify earthquake vibrations 20 times or more above the amplitudes experienced on nearby bedrock. As a rule of thumb, the least damaging ground motions from earthquakes are on sites underlaid by bedrock or by unsaturated soils where the water table is deep below the surface of the ground. The worst sites are where the saturated water zone is within 30 feet of ground surface in clay or sand. Clay amplifies. Sand liquefies. Both are destructive to any human constructions built upon such surfaces.

**HOW LIQUEFACTION OCCURS DURING QUAKES:** Liquefaction happens during an earthquake when vibrations over a period of time cause the pressures to build up in the ground water that occupies the pore spaces between the grains of sand, silt, or loess. The longer the duration of the earthquake the more likely that liquefaction will be induced. The only solid strength of such a deposit is provided by the friction between grains touching each other. When the pressure in the water that fills the pore space between the grains is sufficient to spread them apart, the solid nature of the sand, silt or loess deposit is changed into that of a viscous liquid: "quicksand" or "quickclay."

Because it takes time for the pressures to build up underground to produce liquefaction and because quicksand is a heavy, thick fluid that moves slowly, conditions of liquefaction, sand boiling, and associated phenomena may not be apparent during the shaking. In fact, it often does not manifest until after the shaking has already passed, sometimes not until 10-20 minutes later. The quick conditions or boiling of the sand can persist for hours or even days after the quake, sometimes as much as a week.

**HOW BIG DOES IT TAKE & HOW NEAR TO THE QUAKE?:** A natural question regarding seismically induced liquefaction is how big an earthquake is required to induce quick conditions and how close one has to be for such effects to be possible? With regards to size, several technical publications suggest that liquefaction does not occur for earthquakes less than body-wave magnitudes of 5.2. However, minor liquefaction effects in areas underlaid by particularly ideal predisposing conditions (loose sand deposits saturated with a near-surface water table) have been observed for earthquakes as small as 4.7 on the Richter scale in the New Madrid Seismic Zone. Minor damage to vulnerable structures has occurred in such areas.

With regards to distance, an earthquake in June of 1987 of magnitude 5.2 in southeastern Illinois caused liquefaction phenomena near Bell City, Missouri, 150 miles from the epicenter. A swimming pool, two large grain bins, a carport, and three houses were damaged (one severely). There was also fissuring and lateral spreading. At the same time, points nearer the epicenter of that quake did not experience such ground failures. Three years later (in 1990) this same area experienced no liquefaction phenomena when a 4.7 earthquake struck only 20 miles away.

Nearness to the epicenter implies greater amplitudes of ground motion, but distance implies a longer duration of shaking since the wave train consists of many waves traveling at a variety of speeds. The epicenter of the magnitude 8.1 earthquake that struck Mexico City in 1985 was 240 miles away and induced liquefaction that severely damaged some buildings. Although lasting less than a minute at its distant source, that quake lasted several minutes in Mexico City. However, ground shaking amplitudes within the city were never large. Yet, 400 buildings collapsed, resonating with the long lasting wave train amplified by underlying clays.

The great New Madrid earthquakes of 1811-12 induced extreme examples of liquefaction manifesting as sand boils and explosion cratering in the area of St. Louis, Missouri, and across the river in the flood plain of Illinois. Liquefaction also occurred from those quakes as far as Cincinnati, Ohio, more than 300 miles away.

It is evident that sometimes a low amplitude signal of longer duration remote from the epicenter can induce liquefaction when a high amplitude signal of shorter duration nearer the source will not. Seismically induced liquefaction remains a topic of current research. Scientists and engineers are still trying to understand it. One thing is certain, however. Areas liquefied in one earthquake can liquefy in subsequent quakes. They also remain liquefaction-prone between seismic events in response to periodic and seasonal mechanical or hydrologic forces.

Most of the time when earthquakes induce liquefaction, the ground simply becomes "mushy," stays that way for a while, and then firms up to its former hardness. No boiling occurs, and no permanent signs remain. It is only when the soil and ground water conditions are just right and the ground vibrations are extreme in amplitude and/or duration that the land surface is permanently defaced and deformed. There were probably very few locations in the New Madrid region that did not at least partially liquefy at some time during that long sequence of quakes. In most instances, no evidence remained. In others a "mottled" appearance can be seen in aerial photographs as evidence of former quick conditions. The boils, fissures, sand sloughs, explosion craters, and other features photographed and described here are at the extreme ends of the spectrum of liquefaction phenomena. So far as we know, the New Madrid Seismic Zone is the most extensive display of such features in the world.

**THREE WAYS TO INDUCE LIQUEFACTION:** Liquefaction in soils can be stimulated three ways: Seismically, Mechanically, and Hydrologically. Seismically-Induced Liquefaction (SIL) is caused by earthquake ground vibrations. Mechanically-Induced Liquefaction (MIL) is caused by vibrations that come from railroad trains, motor vehicles, tractors, and other mechanical sources of vibratory ground motion. Hydrologically-Induced Liquefaction (HIL) occurs when groundwater pressures increase due to rising stream levels during flooding conditions. HIL most commonly occurs on properties protected by levees where rivers can rise to levels above the land surface without actually flooding the land. Most of the New Madrid Seismic Zone falls into this category, being surrounded by levees that flank the rivers and drainage ditches throughout the area. Because of this, seismically induced-sand boils (SIL) become hydrologically active (HIL) during river flood stages, turn into quicksand, and boil again, just as they did during the earthquakes that formed them. Similarly, tractors, trains and trucks crossing over SIL sand fissures during times of high water table can mechanically induce liquefaction (MIL) causing highways to sag, railroad tracks to get out of parallel, and farm equipment to sink into the ground. The following slides are mostly about SIL, but examples of MIL and HIL are also shown.

**LANDSLIDING:** In addition to Liquefaction various kinds of landslides or lateral spreads can occur in response to seismic ground motion. These features occur when masses of earth actually move horizontally or down hill, sometimes hundreds of feet. Sometimes these moving blocks of earth, which can be a mile or more in size, are loosened during the earthquake by partial liquefaction.

While most earthquake induced landsliding occurs suddenly when the actual seismic shaking is taking place, it is important to know that sometimes there is a time delay. There have been cases where small cracks and fissures have formed in a hillside during the quake after which the slope appeared to be stable. Sometimes these weakened slopes have later began to creep slowly downwards after a few weeks or months. In some more dramatic cases, the fissured slope was not observed to move at all until as long as six months later when it failed catastrophically in seconds following a period of above average rainfall.

There is a saying among geotechnical engineers, "Once a landslide, always a landslide." It is important for builders and planners to be able to recognize sites of former earthquake landslides inasmuch as such slopes remain permanently unstable and ready to move again, not only from future quakes, but from heavy rains and the activities of people. Even 200 years after the earthquake, the risk of slope failure is still present, as you will see in Slides #141-#149.

Lateral spreading is a form of landsliding where slopes are almost zero. Lateral spreading almost always involves liquefaction of some layer below the surface which acts as a lubricated plane upon which the masses of more solid earth above can glide horizontally. Lateral spreads almost always move toward the nearest stream or body of water and can occur several miles back from the banks. Massive cave-ins of a river bank can be caused by lateral spreads miles inland pushing toward the stream. A number of towns and commercial constructions are built on the banks of the Mississippi. Some companies have eliminated the possibility of liquefaction directly under their industrial installations by numerous deep piles driven in the ground

**SLIDE #4**
**Extrusive and Intrusive Sand Features**

TABLE

## SEISMIC FEATURES FOUND IN THE NEW MADRID SEISMIC ZONE FROM THE 1811-12 SERIES OF GREAT EARTHQUAKES

**I. EXTRUSIVE SAND FEATURES**
- **A. Sand Blows**
  1. **Explosion Craters**
  2. **Filled Explosion Craters**
  3. **Earthquake Ponds**
- **B. Sand Boils**
  1. **Simple Sand Boils (Circular or Elliptic)**
  2. **Compound Sand Boils (Elongated or Irregular)**

**II. INTRUSIVE SAND FEATURES**
- **A. Sand Dikes (Discordant Intrusions)**
- **B. Sand Sills (Concordant Intrusions)**

**Continued . . .**

beneath their sites. But these plants are still in jeopardy of being shoved into the river during an earthquake by the forces of lateral spreading further inland.

**SECONDARY FAULTING:** A fault is a break in earth materials (rock or soil) with a relative displacement on both sides. The relative displacement can be horizontal or vertical (See Slide #10). There are two kinds of faults: Those that cause earthquakes and those that are caused by earthquakes. The first are called "Causative" or "Primary" faults. The second are called "Surface" or "Secondary" faults. The New Madrid Fault is a primary fault (or complex of faults) 2-20 miles below land surface. It is the source of the New Madrid earthquakes both past and present. It has never been seen. When it shakes the ground violently, the surface of the ground breaks into secondary faults. The only faults that have been visually identified in the New Madrid Seismic Zone are secondary. Simple fault features are not as common as lateral spread, landsliding, or liquefaction features, although surface faulting (relative ground displacement) is associated with all of these phenomena.

In any case, whether it be liquefaction, landsliding, lateral spreading, or surface faulting, the ground that was solid, strong, rigid and immobile before the earthquake becomes fluid, weak, broken and mobile during and after. The result at the ground surface is manifested in a variety of responses, all of which are potentially destructive during and following the earthquake. These are tabulated and described in the table and figures on Slides #4 through #11. We shall start with Slide #4 and briefly describe or define each of the terms given, from "Extrusive Features"

## SLIDE #5
## Lateral Spread/Differential Subsidence Features

TABLE

### SEISMIC FEATURES FOUND IN THE NEW MADRID SEISMIC ZONE FROM THE 1811-12 SERIES OF GREAT EARTHQUAKES

**III. LATERAL SPREAD FEATURES**
- **A. Sag Features**
- **B. Linear Crevasses**
- **C. Graben Fissures**
- **D. Sand Fissures**
- **E. Seismic Sand Ridges**
- **F. Sand Sloughs**

**IV. DIFFERENTIAL SUBSIDENCE FEATURES**
- **A. Sunk Lands**
- **B. Earthquake Lakes**
- **C. Discontinuous Channels**

**Continued . . .**

on Slide #4 to "Incoherent Landslides" on Slide #6, with reference to the figures depicting these features in Slides #7 - #11. The alphabetic, Roman and Arabic numerals preceding each of the named features correspond with those given in the Table presented on Slides #4-#6.

**I. EXTRUSIVE SAND FEATURES** are deposits of liquefied sand extruded upon the ground surface during or following an earthquake. Along with the extruded sand comes large quantities of water which can produce temporary flooding up to several feet deep. Included with the sand are other materials such as pea gravel, coarse gravel, coal, lignite (brown coal), carbonized wood, limonite nodules (little balls of iron oxide), and petroliferous nodules (they smell like petroleum and burn with a bright yellow flame). In the New Madrid Seismic Zone these features also commonly contain Indian artifacts. Since all seismically induced extrusive sand features have permanent direct connections with the water table and the sand layers below, once established they can respond to the vibrations of subsequent earthquakes of sufficient intensity, extruding their materials again and again, growing with each issue. Some of the extrusive features boiled repeatedly during the five-month sequence of more than 2,000 earthquakes comprising the Great New Madrid Earthquakes of 1811-12. Because of their permanent connections with the ground waters below, these features can also liquefy in response to mechanical or hydrologic forces between earthquakes. Extrusive sand features occur where a Liquefiable Saturated Sand (LSS) underlies either Dry Sand (DS) or a Non-Liquefiable Soil (NLS). A soil can be non-liquefiable (NLS) because it is either wrong

**SLIDE #6** TABLE

**Uplift, Surface Fault & Slope Failure Features**

**SEISMIC FEATURES FOUND IN THE NEW MADRID SEISMIC ZONE FROM THE 1811-12 SERIES OF GREAT EARTHQUAKES**

**V. UPLIFT & SECONDARY FAULT FEATURES**
- **A. Strike Slip Faults**
- **B. Normal Faults**
- **C. Domes or Horsts**
- **D. Altered Stream Gradients**

**VI. SLOPE FAILURE FEATURES**
- **A. Translational Block Slides**
- **B. Earth Flows**
- **C. Rotational Slumps**
- **D. Incoherent Landslides**

in composition (for example, too much clay) or unsaturated (for example, sand that would liquefy when saturated, but would not when dry).

A sagged, subsided, or depressed area can usually be found not far from an extrusive sand feature, indicating that a mass of earth material has moved from one area (the low spot) to the place where it was extruded (the higher ground). See diagrammatic Slide #7 and photo Slides #24, #54, #88, #89, and #99, which show sags or sunk lands adjacent to extrusive deposits. Nearby low spots are one of the things to look for when attempting to identify a sand deposit as an extrusive feature.

**I.A. SAND BLOWS** are extrusive sand features formed during earthquakes when the forces are such that liquefied sand explodes from the ground surface leaving a crater. These conical depressions can be up to 20 feet deep with rims several feet high at the time of their formation. They may remain a void or be filled by seismic sand boiling and other ways immediately following the quake. They can also be filled by non-seismic processes, such as wind, floods, erosion, and the activities of humans over longer spans of time. Unlike the gentle bubbling of a sand boil during its active phase, during the formation of sand blows extruded materials become airborne, sometimes reaching heights in excess of 25 feet above ground. Seismic sand blows occur where Dry Sand (DS) overlies Liquefiable Saturated Sand (LSS). Do not be confused by the use of the term "sand blow" or "blow sand" by longtime residents of the NMSZ who use these terms to refer to any sand deposit picked up by the wind and blown across the ground. It should also be noted that the term "sand blow" has been used in some geologic literature as a generic term for all earthquake sand features. We do not agree with this usage of the term. See Slide #7. Also see the discussion of "Sand Boils" discussed below.

**I.A.1. EXPLOSION CRATERS** are sand blow features that remain after the earthquake as cone or spoon-shaped depressions. The seismically-induced explosions that form these features consist of the rapid expulsion of both water and air. At the time of formation, they are more cone shaped with a sandy rim. However, as time passes, wind and water erosion bring sand back into the crater removing the rim and making them more spoon shaped. They are very permeable and have a direct connection with the water table below. Following their formation during an earthquake, they act as permanent surface water conduits into the groundwater. See Slides #80, #81, #84, & #85.

**I.A.2. FILLED EXPLOSION CRATERS** are explosion craters which filled and overflowed with ground water following the earthquake, carrying sediments to the surface of various sizes. These sediments range from coarse to fine, with the clays, silts and fine materials deposited on top and the gravels and coarser materials below. These remain as circular patches at ground surface where rain runoff can perch from time to time, supporting a variety of weeds, but not allowing farmers to plow and sow crops because of their tendency to liquefy (HIL or MIL) and remain "mushy" most of the year. See Slides #82 & #113.

**I.A.3. EARTHQUAKE PONDS** are explosion craters where the water table rises high enough to intersect and keep the bottoms full seasonally, if not the year round. They are not filled by surface runoff, like normal ponds, since they leak, have permeable bottoms, and act as direct conduits to the water table. When the water table falls below their bottoms, they are dry. When rivers rise high on the levees, they fill and overflow from the hydraulic pressures in the ground water below. Most have now been filled in and bulldozed over. Old-timers in New Madrid remember their childhood, when they swam in these ponds with sandy shores and clear spring waters that were cold even on the hottest of summer days. See Slides #22, #116 & #117. Also see "Earthquake Lakes" discussed later in this section.

**I.B. SAND BOILS** are extrusive sand features in which liquefied sand flows from below the ground to the land surface through a central vent or linear fissure, spreading a sand blanket from several inches to several feet thick. The extrusive orifice may be small, but the sand blanket can be very large, extending even hundreds of feet across the ground surface from the point of issue. Unlike sand blows, where the extruded materials become airborne during their formation, the formation of sand boils is not violent, but consists of a gentle boiling of sand and water, along with pea gravel, lignite, and other materials. Sand boils can continue to extrude their deposits for up to a week after an earthquake. In addition to the temporary quicksand conditions that accompany the seismic sand boiling phenomena, a considerable amount of water is discharged, causing ground water flooding that can be as destructive as the failed soils. Sand boils occur where a Non-Liquefiable Soil (NLS) overlies a Liquefiable Saturated Sand (LSS). See Slide #7 for a diagram. Numerous sand boils, still visible from the New Madrid earthquakes of 1811-12, can be seen in the slides that follow. However, these have been modified by the forces of time. When actively boiling they often form a volcano-shaped cone of sand with water and other materials flowing from a vent at the top. To see how a sand boil looks while it is boiling, including the appearance of a "sand volcano," see Slides #118-#121. Also see the discussion of "Sand Blow" above.

**I.B.1. SIMPLE SAND BOILS** are extruded from a single vent that extends from the ground surface to the water table and into source beds of sand. If the vent is like a pipe, the surface blanket of the sand boil will be circular. If the vent is elongated, as along a crack or fissure, the boil's surface appearance will be elliptic. Simple sand boils can be quite small, measured in inches or feet. Simple sand boils in the NMSZ also measure up to 500 feet in diameter. See Slides #24 & #25.

**I.B.2. COMPOUND SAND BOILS** are extruded from several vents and consist of more than one simple sand boil whose sand blankets

**SLIDE #7**
**Extrusive Sand Features**

FIGURE

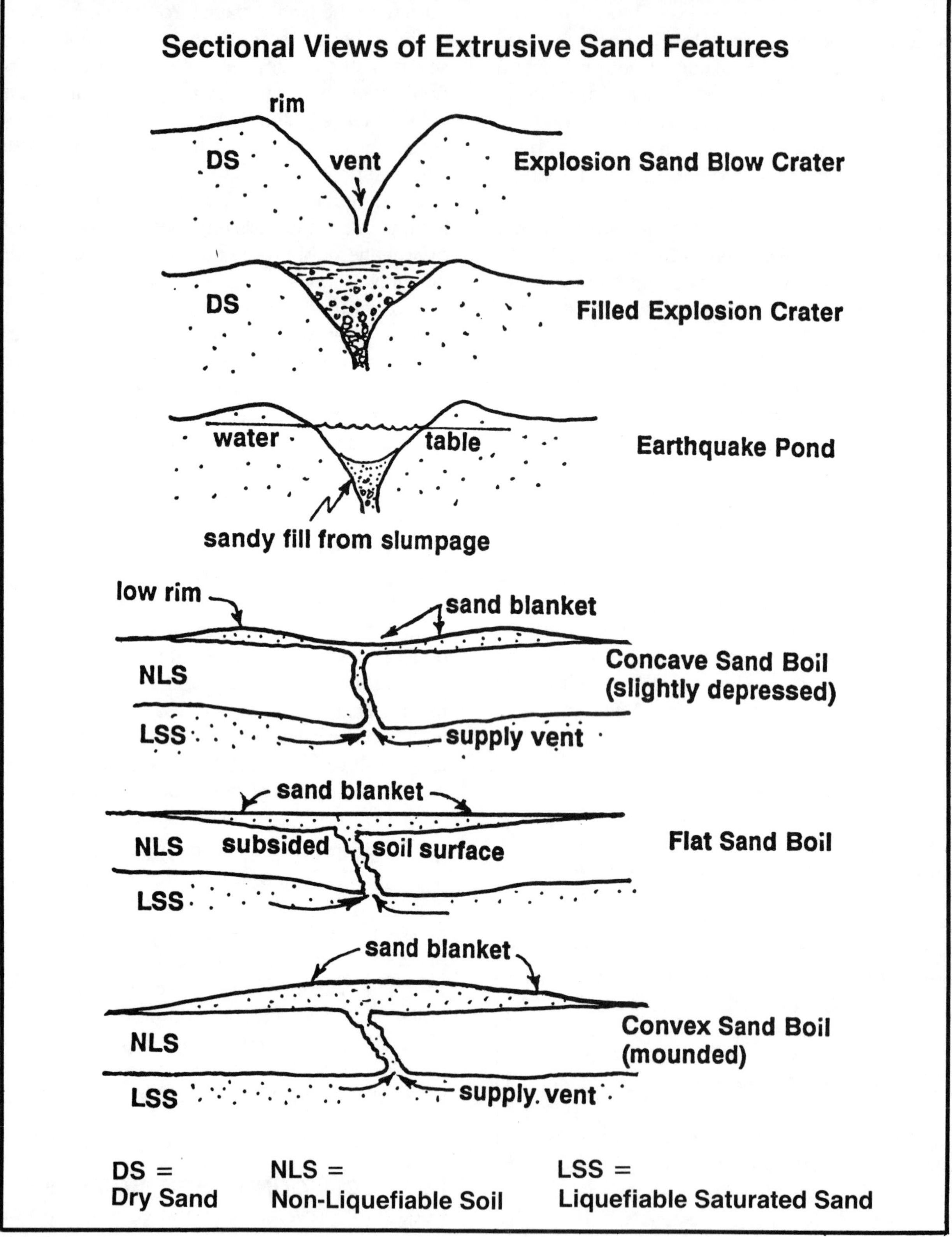

## SLIDE #8 Intrusive Sand Features

FIGURE

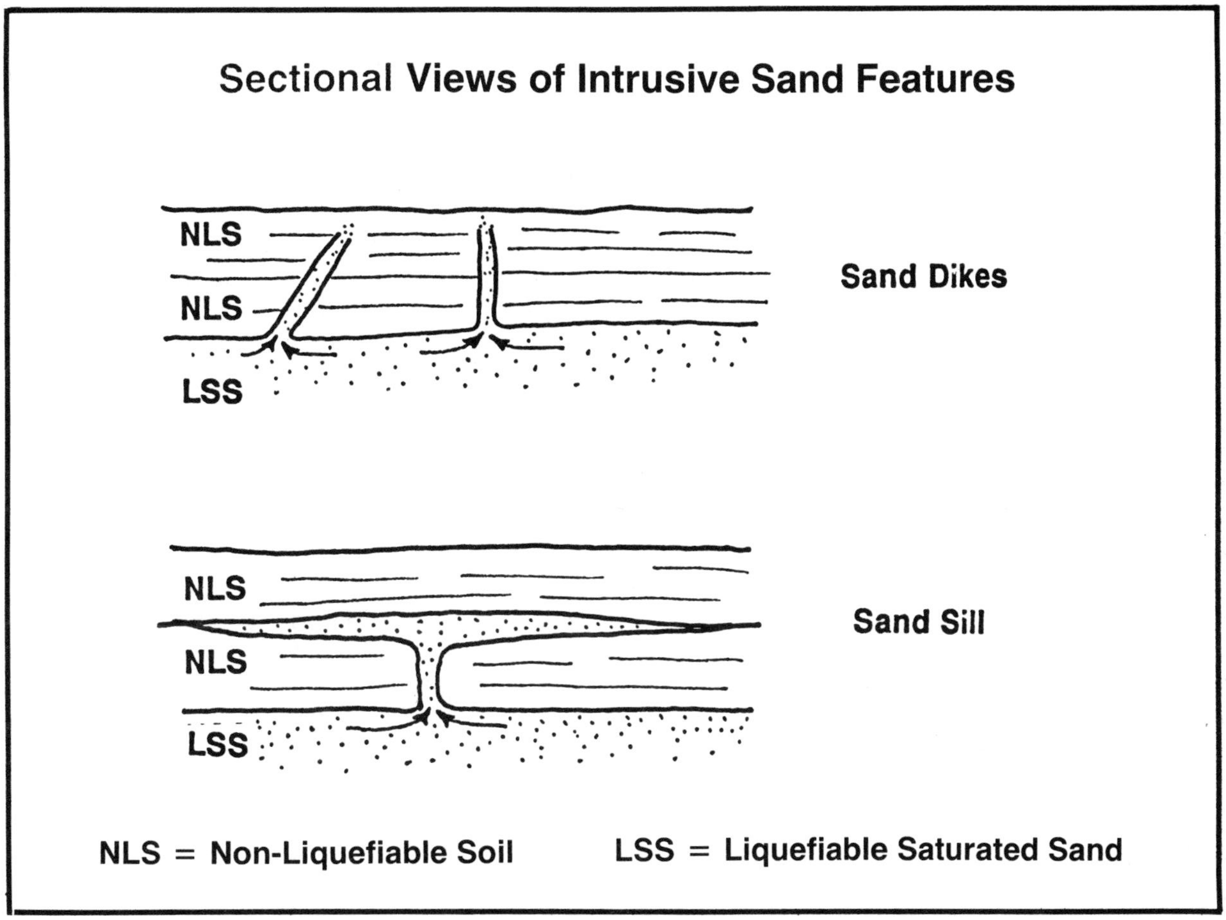

### Sectional Views of Intrusive Sand Features

NLS
NLS
LSS
**Sand Dikes**

NLS
NLS
LSS
**Sand Sill**

**NLS = Non-Liquefiable Soil** **LSS = Liquefiable Saturated Sand**

have merged into a single large deposit at the surface. These can be quite elongated where a string of circular and elliptic boils extruded along a crack have merged, or they can be quite irregular depending on the configuration of the several supply vents. Compound sand boils can be moderate in size, measured in feet, but can grow to enormous proportions measuring more than a mile. The largest compound sand boil in the world is shown in these slides, 1.4 miles in length and 136 acres in area. See Slides #102-109 at Location P.

**II. INTRUSIVE SAND FEATURES** are deposits of liquefied sand intruded into the layers of soil below the surface of the ground. Because they do not extend above ground, they cannot be seen unless intersected by digging or erosion that cuts down to give a sectional or sideways view of the bank of a ditch, stream, road cut, or eroded hillside. Seismically induced intrusive sand features occur where Liquefiable Saturated Sands (LSS) underlie Non-Liquefiable Soils (NLS). See Slides #8 & #74-#77.

**II.A. SAND DIKES** are intrusions of sand that liquefied during an earthquake. Dikes cut across the layers of non-liquefiable soil above. They may be at acute, oblique or perpendicular angles with the beds of soil across which they have intruded. Such deposits are called "Discordant." If the earthquake had lasted longer or had been of greater intensity, the dike may have continued to grow upwards breaking through to the ground surface and becoming a supply vent for an extrusive sand feature or sand boil. Existing sand dikes in the New Madrid Seismic Zone could become supply vents for sand boils in future earthquakes. See Slides #8 & #77.

**II.B. SAND SILLS** are intrusions of sand liquefied during an earthquake and squeezed between layers of non-liquefiable soils above. They are parallel or sub-parallel to the beds into which they have intruded. Such deposits are called "Concordant." When a sand boil is formed and extruded upon the surface, sediment deposited during subsequent centuries can bury and hide that boil. If exposed later in an excavation it may appear as a sand sill, intruded between layers, instead of appearing as buried sand boil. It is a challenge for geologists to figure out what they have discovered in such instances. See Slides #74-#76.

**III. LATERAL SPREAD FEATURES** are the result of liquefied, saturated sand moving horizontally beneath non-liquefiable soils. (See Slide #9.) As the viscous earth materials move laterally below, they stretch and pull on the soils above and are manifested by surface sags, crevasses, and fissures. When the overlying sediments are actually broken from the surface down to the liquefied sand beds, the quicksand is extruded leaving sand-filled fissures, sand ridges and sloughs. Lateral spreading usually takes place in a direction toward the nearest bodies of water and can occur several miles away from the water's edge. One of the dynamic manifestations of lateral spreading—bank failures in streams—can be photographed only during or shortly after an earthquake. The rivers of the New Madrid Seismic Zone suffered many cave-ins throughout the five-month series of quakes. Some bank failures were due to shaking during the tremors, themselves. Many, however, were due to lateral spreading further inland that literally shoved the banks into the channels. Along the Mississippi, sections of shoreline more than a mile in length were reported to have been thrown into the water, creating dangerous wakes that swamped boats and drowned boatmen. Some tributaries to the Mississippi were literally closed shut and rerouted by this process.

**III.A. SAG FEATURES** occur when liquefied sands that support a non-liquefiable surface deposit from below simply move out reducing the volume of supporting materials to hold up the surface, resulting in a low spot or "sag." Think of pushing down on the middle of an open tube of toothpaste lying on your sink. The viscous paste moves laterally toward the opening, reducing the volume of the contents and leaving a low spot where you pushed. Seismic sags can be thought of as small-scale versions of seismic sunk lands.

**III.B.LINEAR CREVASSES** occur when lateral underground movements of liquefied sand below stretch and tear at the surface, leaving cracks. These can vary in width from tiny cracks measured in inches to large gapping crevasses more than ten feet wide. Their lengths can measure from a few feet to more than a mile. People in the New Madrid area were terrified of being caught and swallowed up in such cracks. These features not only formed by the thousands, but some reported that the ground cracked open for a time and then slammed shut, violently ejecting sand and ground water "over the tops of tall trees." Sometimes they formed under large trees, splitting trunks with their spreading. Luckily, no human lives were lost, even though some people did actually fall into these crevasses, were injured, and had to be rescued by others. Some cattle fell into the crevasses and died. During the five-month siege of earth tremors the natives noted that in any given area the crevasses always seemed to orient the same way, often in a north-south direction. Cleverly, the residents felled large trees in a perpendicular direction. When a tremor would begin, they and their families rushed out to sit on a downed tree so that if a crevasse happened to open beneath them they would already have a bridge in place. Some reported that such enterprises actually saved them from being hurled into these horrifying holes.

**III.C. GRABEN FISSURES.** The word, "Graben," is German for "grave." It is also a technical geologic term referring to a pair of parallel normal faults with a downdropped keystone of rock or soil in between. (See Slide #10.)

**SLIDE #9** FIGURE

**Lateral Spread Features**

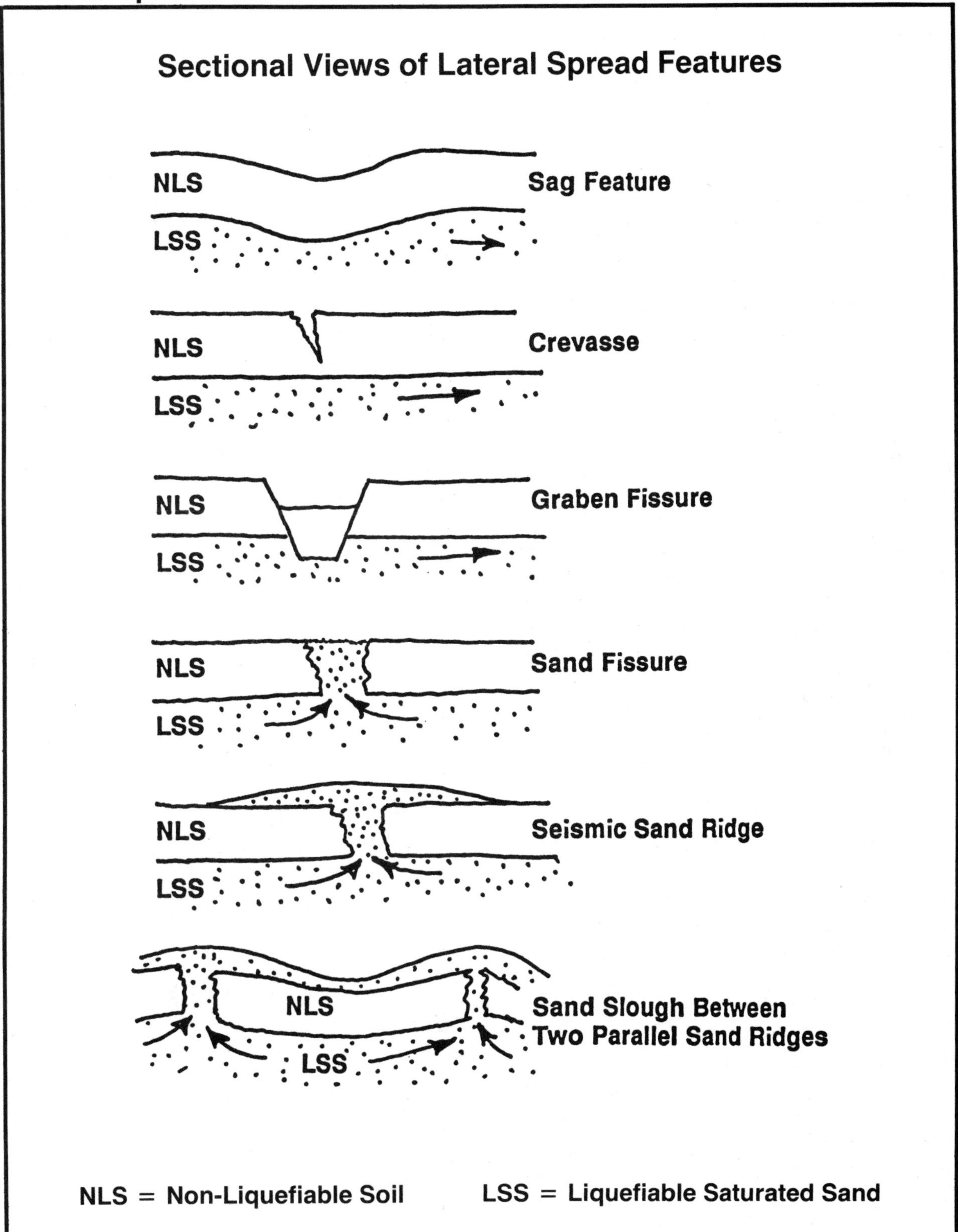

As a lateral spread feature, the paired faults of a graben are secondary and do not extend far below the surface soils. Grabens, whether in layers of soil or rock, are due to tensional forces. When liquefied sands move beneath non-liquefiable surface soils, tensions are produced that can pull the land apart, creating normal faults that form grabens. A graben fissure may have started as a sag feature when the liquefied sands first moved, but as more and more material moved away, the sag may have broken along its margins, creating faults and a separate keystone of soil that simply dropped down to fill the void left by the vacated sand. Graben fissures have sloping sides (the normal fault planes) and flat bottoms (the top of the downdropped block). They have been reported from a few hundred feet long to more than half a mile. Fuller (1912) describes them in detail. Graben fissures can be up to 20 feet deep and more than 100 feet wide. They can intermittently hold water, forming elongated ponds or lakes. The water they contain can be from surface runoff temporarily perched above the water table or they can be supplied from below during wet seasons by the rising of the water table. Graben fissures are long and narrow but pinch out on both ends giving them a "canoe" or "banana" shape in map view. See Slides #110-#112.

**III.D. SAND FISSURES** are crevasses that broke sufficiently deep and spread sufficiently wide that the liquefied sand below gushed up and filled the crack, leaving a streak of sand across the land surface. They are, therefore, a type of extrusive sand feature resulting from lateral spreading. Since their source was from below the water table and since sand is such a permeable medium, these surface features, like the other extrusive sand features, are points where rainfall and surface waters can disappear into the ground, recharging the ground waters that supply the water wells of the region. Because of their connection with the water table, sand fissures can also become unstable ground when river levels are high, sometimes making them impassible to agricultural equipment. Hydrologically- and/or mechanically-induced liquefaction can occur on these features during such times. There are thousands of linear sand fissures in the NMSZ measuring in width from a few feet to more than 200 feet. See Slides #92-#94 & #126-129.

**III.E. SEISMIC SAND RIDGES** are sand fissures that boiled enough sand through the crevasse to form a ridge. They are often more than 1000 feet long and can be hundreds of feet wide. When farmers scrape off a seismic sand ridge to level their land, they are surprised to discover that beneath the long, wide sand deposit they removed is a narrow strip of sand down the center axis of the ridge. What they removed was the extruded sand blanket. What they exposed was the sand fissure from which the ridge had been ejected. Sand ridges can be the locations of explosion craters. See Slides #84-#89.

**III.F. SAND SLOUGHS** are actually sags between two sand ridges where the volumes of extruded quicksands were so great that they flowed down into the sag and covered it with a layer of sand. Since the sagged area contains a non-permeable, non-liquefiable soil, it holds water thereby creating a long swampy deposit or slough. Fuller (1912) describes them in detail. Sand sloughs are also common locations of earthquake ponds or filled explosion craters. Hence, a seismic sand slough is one of the more extreme samples of seismic ground failures. They probably started out as sags that became flanked by crevasses that grew into sand fissures and became sand ridges that extruded so much material that a sand slough resulted. At the same time, explosion liquefaction during the shaking has left pocks and pits in their bottoms. See Slides #113-#115.

**IV. DIFFERENTIAL SUBSIDENCE FEATURES** are low spots on the land surface where the earthquake shaking caused compaction of the soil grains. It's like shaking a cup of sifted flour. You may have a full cup at first, but it will shake down to three-quarters of a cup. Liquefaction is usually a factor. When liquefaction occurs the grains of sand or silt are temporary separated. When they slowly settle back, then can sometimes pack more densely than before, thus reducing their volume and lowering the grade of the land surface. The adjective "differential" is applied in conjunction with the term "subsidence" to indicate the non-uniform fashion in which the land surface settles and compacts as a result of the earth shaking. Some areas will compact more than others. It is this "differential" that is so damaging to highways, airport runways, dams, levees, large buildings, and other constructions of people. If an entire structure subsided the same amount everywhere, it would suffer no damage at all. It is when one part sinks more than another that engineered structures can be seriously torn apart.

**IV.A. SUNK LANDS** are areas that have subsided but which do not hold water most of the time, either because they are too permeable or too high above the water table. Fuller (1912) describes them in detail. See Slides #83 & #101.

**IV.B. EARTHQUAKE LAKES** are sunk lands whose bottoms are below the perennial water table so that they contain water the year round. Earthquake ponds also contain water from the rise and fall of the water table, but they are formed by explosion craters which are round or elliptic in shape and small, their diameters being measurable in tens of feet. Earthquake lakes are formed by compaction of underlying sediments, although they can also be the result of regional downwarping from deep fault movements or a combination of both. In either case, earthquake lakes are irregular in shape and large, their dimensions being measured in miles. Earthquake Ponds seem to occur mostly in sand sloughs between seismic sand ridges while earthquake lakes occur in stream channels or flood plains. Perhaps as many as ten or more earthquake lakes were formed in 1811-12, two of which survive today: Reelfoot Lake, Tennessee, and Big Lake on the Missouri-Arkansas border. See Slides #49-#67.

**IV.C. DISCONTINUOUS CHANNELS** are stream-like, meandering features with water in portions of the channel (like a small linear lake or pond) and which can flow in two directions depending on prevailing surface and ground water levels. The distinctive features of a discontinuous channel are as follows: It has the appearance of a small or moderately-sized stream, but it has no surface outlet; It can flow both directions simultaneously in different reaches of the channel; And it can flow either direction or not at all at different times in any single reach. Their perennial water supply is ground water, but they also act as temporary diversion channels for surface runoff during heavy rains, directing most of their volume of water into the water table instead of flowing as a tributary into another stream. However, during times of flood or high water, they can act as tributaries, too. Discontinuous channels form from earthquakes in at least two ways. The first way is when existing streams have their gradients so disrupted by differential subsidence combined with sand boiling, bank caving, lateral spreading, land sliding, secondary faulting, tectonic uplift and downwarping, and other phenomena that they can no longer flow in a uniform direction toward their former mouths. Hence, they are broken up into "Discontinuous Channels" with all of the enigmatic characteristics described above. Another way discontinuous channels can form involves ancient stream channels. Long buried by more recent flood plain deposits, they are affected differentially by the seismic ground motion so that some parts of the old channel sink and subside while other stretches do not. This process leaves a meandering trace across the landscape, but with discontinuities that had no regular direction of flow, but which would be filled with ground waters and/or surface runoff according the seasons and changing rainfall conditions. While fascinating to study and visit, discontinuous channels are not as easy to portray in a photograph as many other seismic features. In addition to being complex, in and of themselves, the lands adjacent to discontinuous channels are often the locations of fissures, sand boils, explosion craters, and other seismic features. See Slides #20-#21 & #42 & 43.

**V. UPLIFT & SECONDARY FAULT FEATURES** deal with movements of blocks or regions of land, often as a reaction to tectonic movements at depth. The primary or causative faults that underlie the New Madrid Seismic Zone have never been seen and are not among the visible earthquake features of the region. Only secondary or surface faults, the consequences of the primary faults at depth, have been seen. (Refer to paragraphs on "Faulting" earlier in this section for more specific definitions.)

**V.A. STRIKE-SLIP FAULTS** are breaks in the earth with horizontal slippage. If you place yourself in line with the fault's trace, you'll see that one side of the fault moves toward you, the other away, regardless of which end of the fault you position yourself. If the right side is coming toward you, it is called a "right-lateral strike-slip fault." If the left side is coming toward you, it is called a "left-lateral strike-slip fault." The primary faults that comprise the NMSZ at depth and from which the earthquakes originate show a variety of relative motions. However, the major south leg (from Marked Tree, Arkansas, to near Reelfoot Lake, Tennessee) as well as the major north leg (from New Madrid, Missouri, to Metropolis, Illinois) has shown itself to have right-lateral strike-slip movement. This is determined by fault plane solutions to earthquake seismograms. Slide #3 shows how the epicenters line up to define these "legs". See Slide #10 for fault diagrams. The Bootheel Lineament, which bisects most of the NMSZ, is a recently discovered surface feature that may prove to be a surface expression of the New Madrid Fault deep in the earth below. It has the appearance of a right-lateral strike-slip fault and extends for more than 80 miles from Marked Tree, Arkansas, to a point 12 miles west of New Madrid. (See Schweig & Marple, 1991; Schweig, Marple & Li, 1992; Schweig, Shen, et al., 1992; & Sexton, et al., 1992) Also see Slides #1, #102-109 & #138.

**V.B. NORMAL FAULTS** have a predominantly vertical motion that appears as if one side is sliding down the fault plane. See Slide #10 for a diagram. Also see Graben Fissures discussed earlier. Also see Slides #45-#48 showing the Reelfoot Fault, which is a secondary normal fault.

**V.C. DOMES OR HORSTS** are uplift features. A dome is a large gentle mound formed when layers of the earth bend and warp due to vertical forces below. Domes can be many miles in diameter. Horsts form when the surface layers break from vertical forces below forming pairs of normal faults with a higher fault block between. The word "Horst" is used in German to designate a "high place." Note the "Tiptonville Horst" on Slide #1 bounded by the Reelfoot Fault on the east. There is also a "Tiptonville Dome," a much larger region including the "Tiptonville Horst" and consisting of a regional uplift that includes parts of Missouri, Tennessee, and Kentucky. A high point of the Tiptonville Dome is located at the Interstate 55 Rest Stop near Marston, Missouri, in the epicentral area of the February 7, 1812, 8.8 magnitude earthquake. See Slide #10 for a diagram of a horst. Also see Slides #36, #45-#48.

**V.D. ALTERED STREAM GRADIENTS** are simply the consequence of uplift (or downwarp) that causes streams to change their flow directions after an earthquake. Stream gradients can also be altered by differential subsidence. In the context referred to here, however, the altering forces have to do more with regional forces that create domes, horsts, and vertical faulting. See Slide #31 which shows where the Mississippi River temporarily reversed its gradient following the quake of February 7, 1812. Also See Slide #20.

**VI. SLOPE FAILURE FEATURES** refer to landslides of various types. More than 200 old landslides of possible 1811-12 origin have been mapped on the eastern side of the New Madrid Seismic Zone along the bluffs that line the Mississippi from Memphis, Tennessee, to Wickliffe, Kentucky. (See Jibson & Keefer, 1988.) Fuller (1912) remarked that as one traveled along the base of the Chickasaw Bluffs of Tennessee and Kentucky, one or more landslides were continually in sight along the way. Other landslides thought to have been caused by the New Madrid earthquakes have been noted along the western side of the New Madrid Seismic Zone along Crowley's Ridge in Arkansas and Missouri, as well as along the Benton Hills of Missouri. Slope failures were induced in the Benton Hills near the epicenter of a 4.7 magnitude quake in September, 1990, as well as in Piggott, Arkansas, 67 miles away on Crowley's Ridge. See Slide #11.

**SLIDE #10** FIGURE

**Types of Faults**

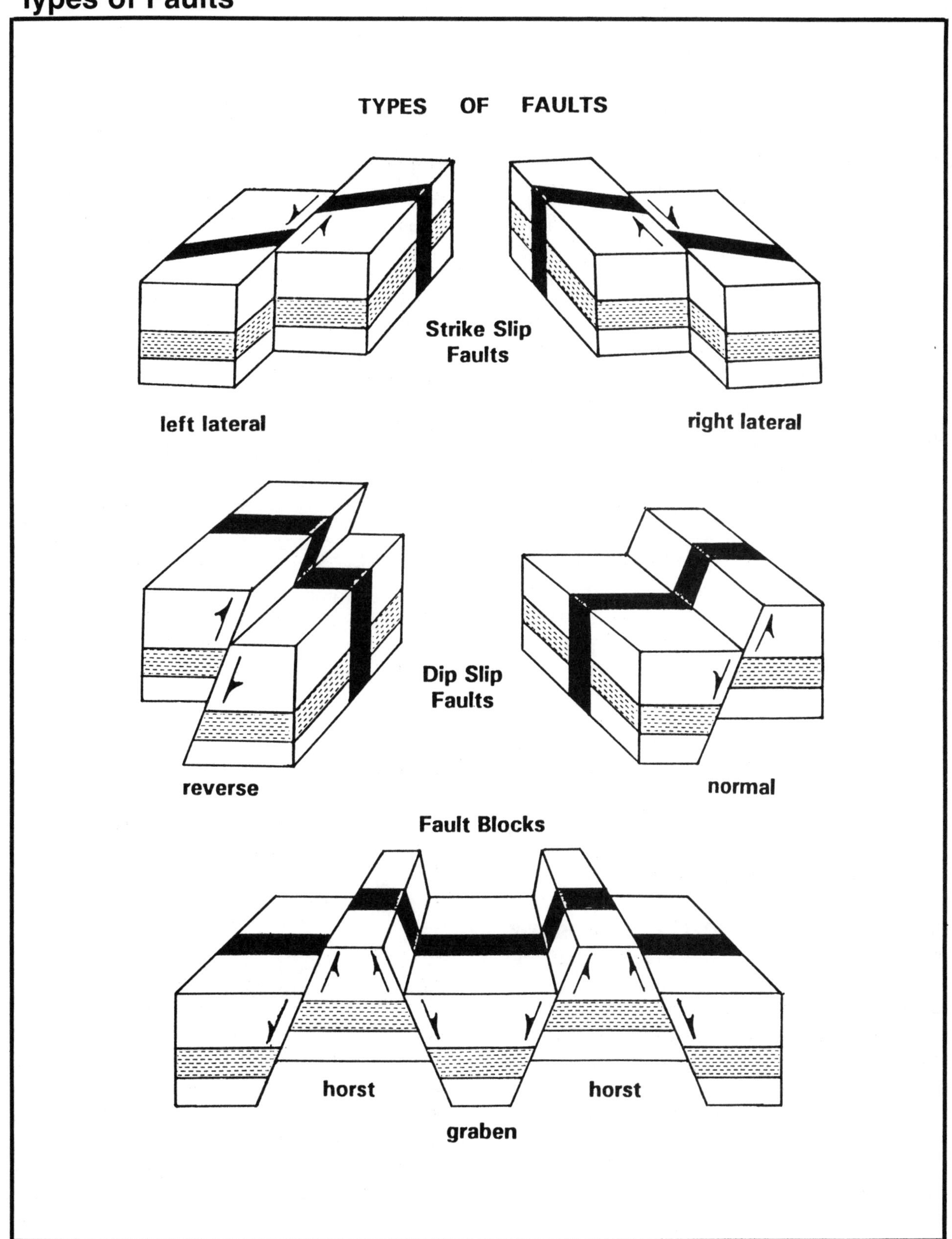

**VI.A. TRANSLATIONAL BLOCK SLIDES** occur when a bluff or hill breaks into large blocks that move horizontally. These blocks are actually bounded by normal faults, thus creating horsts and grabens. The blocks can move hundreds of feet. Their motion is facilitated by a slick glide plane at depth, usually a water-saturated clay or liquefied layer of sand. See Slide #10 for diagrams of horsts and grabens and see Slide #11 for a diagram of a translational block slide with a horst and graben. Translational block slides can be simple, as in the figure shown, or they can be compound, breaking into several fault blocks. See Slides #138-#140 for photos of an actual example of this kind of earthquake slide.

**VI.B. EARTH FLOWS** are examples of partial liquefaction of loess, a fine-grained wind deposit that covers the tops of the hills and bluffs of the New Madrid Seismic Zone to depths of more than 100 feet. See Slide #11 for a diagram. See Slides #134-#137 for an example.

**VI.C. ROTATIONAL SLUMPS** occur when a vertical crack forms parallel to the brink of a bluff or hill and when the loosened block then slumps and rotates downward. See Slide #11 for a diagram. See Slides 141-149 for examples.

**VI.D. INCOHERENT LANDSLIDES** are avalanches, rock falls, or other cases where the slope failed in a chaotic way. In a translational block slide or rotational slump, you can see quite clearly where the blocks used to be before they broke loose. In an incoherent slide you cannot.

**A COMPLEXITY OF FACTORS THAT FORM THESE FEATURES:** The 24 features listed and described above are all attributed to seismic causes. Unfortunately, it is not that simple.

First, there are non-seismic predisposing conditions that precede the earthquakes and make certain areas prone to liquefaction, landsliding, lateral spreading and/or secondary faulting. These conditions are neither seismic nor tectonic in origin. It was the activities of streams and rivers (fluvial factors) over geologic time that deposited the sands and silts that would later be vulnerable to seismically induced liquefaction. In some cases, it was the fine deposits of lakes or swamps (lacustrine factors) that influenced the appearances of these features. As for the fine uniform soils (loess) that top the bluffs and hills of the region that tend to slump, slide and flow during earthquake shaking, these were deposited by the work of wind (aeolian factors) over the past several tens of thousands of years. And as for the working and reworking of sand deposits between earthquakes that keeps them in a metastable state, ready to liquefy during the next quake when vibrations are large enough or long enough, that has been the work of ground water movement (hydrologic factors).

Furthermore, once an earthquake has occurred and altered the landscape via fissuring, faulting, etc., the resulting landforms are not static. They continue to be reshaped and sculptured by the ongoing and seasonal forces of streams (fluvial), wind (aeolian), ground water (hydrologic), and precipitation (meteotoric), freezing and thawing (climatologic) as well as the influences of vegetation (botanical), the workings of animals (zoological), and the activities of people (cultural). Therefore, the seismic features photographed today in the New Madrid Seismic Zone were all formed during and following the great earthquakes of 1811 and 1812, but their present-day appearance is the consequence many still active factors.

The abundance of seismic features in the New Madrid Seismic Zone has given birth to other landforms related to the wind. Over the centuries earthquakes have brought millions of tons of sand to the surface by the processes of sand boiling and sand fissuring. During periods of arid climatic conditions, the sand is picked up by the wind to form dunes which can migrate slowly across the landscape. During periods of higher precipitation the dunes support enough vegetation to become stable and immobile. Hundreds of these stabilized dunes can be observed in the NMSZ, sands that surfaced from seismic forces, now redistributed by the wind. Even today, farmers are plagued by the sands blown from the seismic sand ridges and other sand features. Abrasive sand crystals can move at high speed an inch or two above the ground during strong winds, cutting off crops at the base of the stem. Agricultural acreage with many

**SLIDE #11**
**Slope Failure Features**

FIGURE

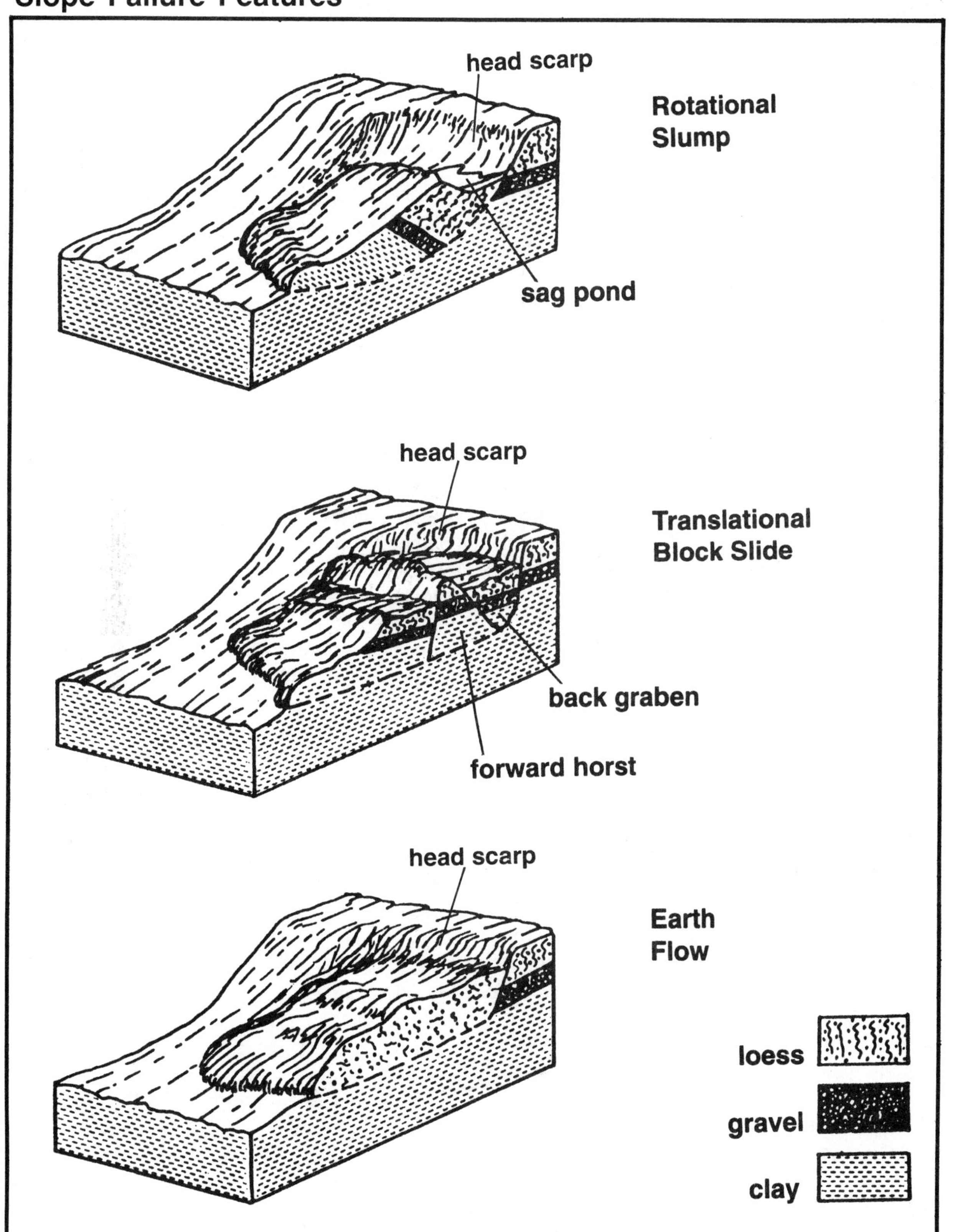

seismic sand features are referred to by local residents as "blow sand farms."

**CHAMELEONS AND CAMOUFLAGE:** Because of the incessant and continually changing forces of nature and because of the people that alter the appearances of these features almost daily, one cannot visit the New Madrid Seismic Zone once and see what has been captured in the photos of this book. These pictures were taken during many visits in all kinds of weather over a period of four years. These features are chameleons, looking one way today, another tomorrow. Furthermore, they occasionally adopt camouflage covers that can make them almost impossible to see. Many times the authors discovered a feature that was quite apparent upon first sight, but which became invisible or looked completely different on subsequent visits.

For example, the same sand boil or sand fissure will take on different appearances from day to day and month to month depending on recent moisture, temperature, and agricultural conditions. It is contrast between the color of the sand and the color of the surrounding clayey soil that makes extrusive sand features visible. When clay and sand are both wet, both are dark in appearance and a sand boil is difficult to discern. When clay and sand are both dry, both are light in appearance and a sand boil is, again, difficult, if not impossible to discern. But Sand dries more quickly than clay. Hence, the time when there is a maximum contrast between the appearance of the sand and surrounding clayey soils is after a rain when the sand has started to dry and the soil is still wet. In the summer, this period of maximum contrast may last only a few hours, or a day at the most, at which time the whole area becomes dry and light colored. In the winter, this contrast between the damp soil and drier sand can persist for three or four days after a shower, depending on wind conditions. Strong winds dry everything faster.

There are seasonal variations, too, related to crop cover and weeds. Just after a field has been planted and crops have sprouted, sand features are almost impossible to see. However, when the first dry spell comes with a hot sun and no rain for a couple of weeks, the crops on the sand features begin to wilt. Even if they survive, their growth is stunted. If dry weather persists, the crops on the sand features die out altogether, showing up dramatically as circles and streaks of yellow bordered by green. Hence, while the crops camouflage the features at first, they make them more visible as the summer wears on. See Slides #68 and #69.

After the harvest has cleared the land and temperatures cool in the fall, there are certain species of weeds that seem to thrive in the sand, but not on the more clayey soils. During these times, the sand features may be the only portions of the field with vegetation. Not only that, but the vegetation growing on these features is distinctive and different than the types of weeds growing elsewhere, making these seismic features stand out.

The filled explosion craters change their apparel seasonally as well. During cooler, wetter winter months, they appear as shallow circular patches of water. As spring comes to a close and temperatures rise, they change to circles of bright green, full of hydrophytic (water-loving) plants. As the summer heat takes toll, they dry up and turn into light gray circles of clay. Because they communicate with the water table through the vent below their fill, they remain mushy and soft most of the year. Farmers have learned to avoid them with their tractors and simply plant around them. Even when farmers try to fill and cover them, they remain as circles of liquefaction-prone, unfarmable land.

The old landslide slopes triggered by the 1811-12 earthquakes are also visible or invisible, depending on the vegetation. The best time to view them is in the late fall, winter, or early spring when the trees are without leaves. In summer months, they can become veritable jungles of tall weeds, leaved limbs, and climbing vines, not to mention the hawthorns, brambles and blackberry bushes.

And then there are the activities of farmers. Modern agricultural equipment, especially since 1980, has become so large and effective in molding the landscape to improve production that hundreds of seismic features are simply scraped off the landscape or filled in and covered over each year. Hence, a feature you saw last year may or may not be there the next time you visit.

All of this makes the New Madrid Seismic Zone a dynamic and exciting place to visit, even after you have been there many times. Once your eyes have been sensitized to see and recognize these features, you will never see the same thing twice on two visits, even when it is the same feature.

**THE WORLD'S GREATEST EARTHQUAKE LABORATORY:** To conclude this section, suffice it to say that the soils, slopes, and geology of the New Madrid Seismic Zone could hardly be more ideal in providing predisposing conditions for liquefaction, landsliding, lateral spreading, and secondary faulting. These unique passive conditions combine with the dynamics of ongoing processes of surface geology and the restless sleep of a subsurface seismic giant (who occasionally goes on a rampage). It is no wonder that in this sector of the earth's surface there exists the premier examples of morphoseismic phenomena to be seen and experienced anywhere on the planet.

Where else in the world can all 24 varieties of seismic land forms listed here all be found in one place? And in such abundance? And in such enormous dimensions? And remaining visible for so many decades? How many other seismic landforms remain there unrecognized and unidentified, awaiting yet another generation of scientists and non-scientists to discover and describe them?

Truly, the New Madrid Seismic Zone is one of the greatest outdoor earthquake laboratories in the world. Through this book we hope you will enjoy our sharing a sample of its innumerable secrets. And, hopefully, you will be able to go there some day, yourself, and make your own discoveries. And when you do visit, pick up a copy of *The New Madrid Fault Finders Guide*. (See back.) It will help you find your way around and see the features of this book, plus many more.

# Commentary

## A PHOTO ESSAY
## ON THE NEW MADRID FAULT ZONE

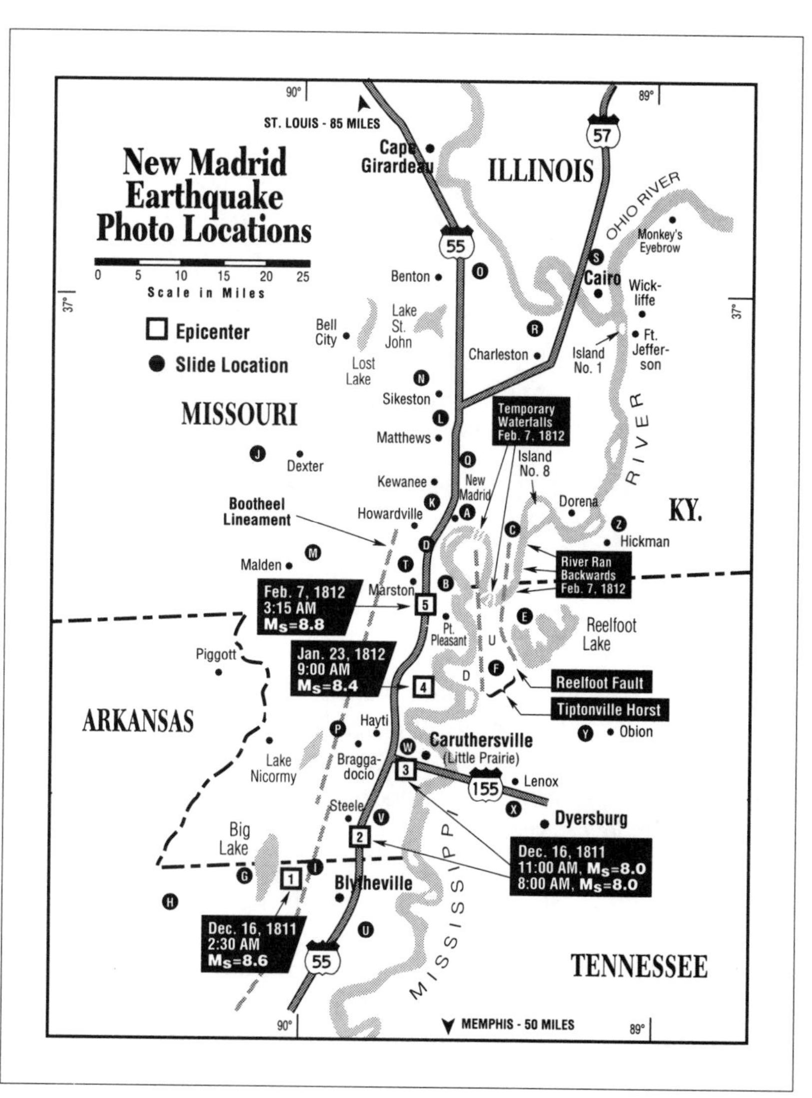

## SLIDE #12 LOCATION A

## Sand Boils in New Madrid, Aerial View Looking East

This airplane view of New Madrid was taken April, 1991. Look at all the light yellow patches scattered everywhere on the ground. They are sand boils from the great earthquakes of 1811-12. The city is covered with these features. They were quicksand then and they will become quicksand again. All it will take is another major earthquake. Even high water on the Mississippi has caused some of these to liquefy from time to time. Townspeople there know that when the river rises above street level on the outside of the levee, some places in town will become mushy and boil. The levee runs across the top of the slide (A1-A10), seen as a line of vegetation from left to right where a blue piece of the Mississippi River can be seen in the upper right corner (A10). The blue patches seen on the far side of the levee on the left are flood waters from St. John's Bayou. The mouth of St. John's, where it meets the Mississippi, is in the upper right (A10). The white objects clustered near the river (A9) are the Sinclair Oil Depot petroleum storage tanks. Remember these. In the slides that follow, they are a useful marker for identifying New Madrid from a distance. The New Madrid Museum is next to the river just to the right of the oil tanks. Highway 61 runs from left (D1) to right (D10). Highway U runs toward us off the bottom of the slide (G4). Near the center of the photo is the New Madrid Nursing Home, a building with five wings (E5). The adjacent housing development (F&G5 to F10) is surrounded by sand boils. There are boils under these buildings, too, but they have been covered over with grass and pavement. The quake is history. It was over in 1812. But plenty of evidence still remains. The landscape was permanently changed, as was the history of a whole region. In this sense, it really is "The Earthquake that Never Went Away." And the people who live here know it.

## SLIDE #13 — LOCATION A

## Five Flags Over Main Street, New Madrid, MO

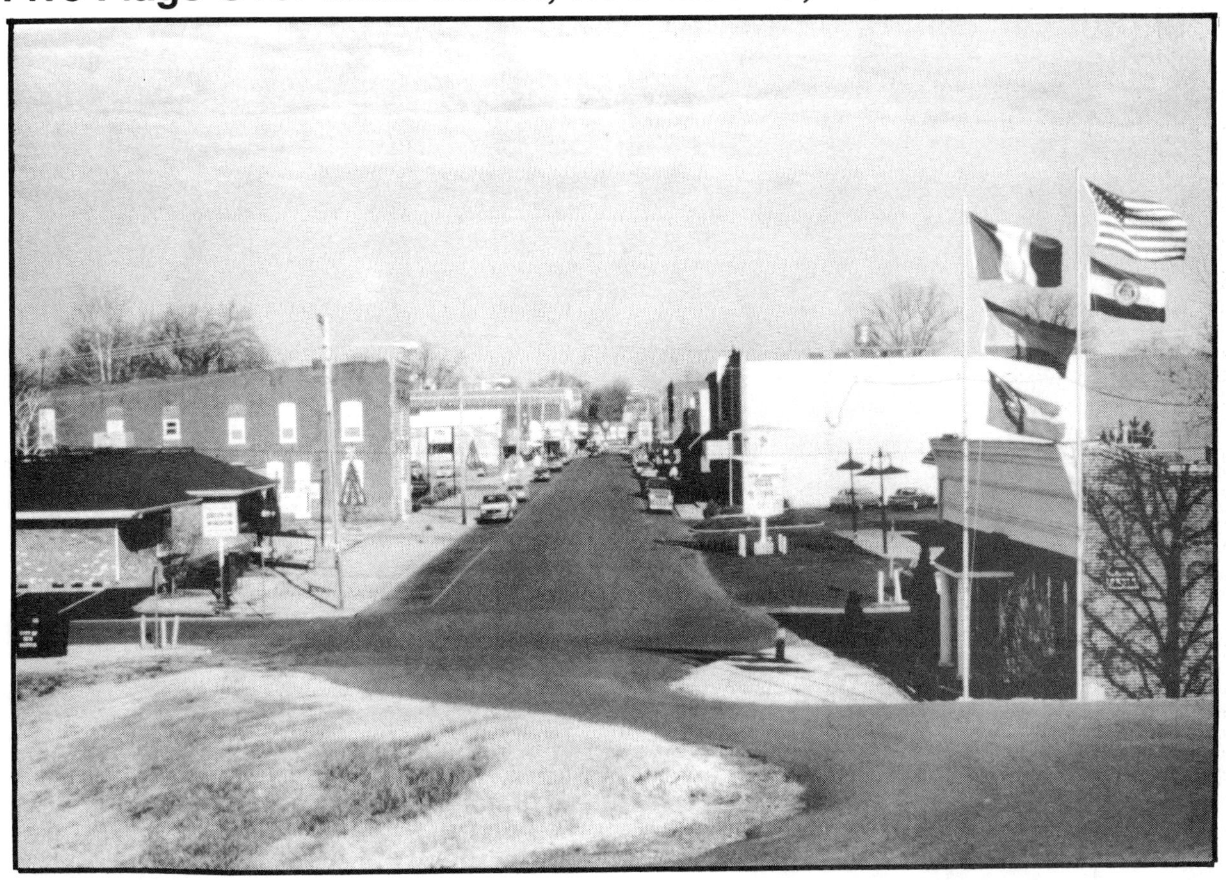

New Madrid not only has a unique seismic history, but a fascinating political history. American Indians had lived in the area for more than 10,000 years when the Spanish came in 1541 and claimed it. Later, in 1642, the French came from the north and claimed it. In 1760 control of the territory briefly fell to Great Britain, but in 1762 the Spanish regained it. In 1783, the same year the U.S. won the Revolution and obtained its freedom, the first permanent settlement was established at the site. At that time, the French outnumbered the Spanish, so it received a French name, "L'anse a la Graisse," or "Cove of Grease." Boatmen on the Mississippi stopped there to buy buffalo and bear meat. The name did not please the King of Spain, so in 1789 it was changed to "New Madrid," after Spain's capital. We Americans pronounce it MAD'-rid, instead of Ma-DREED' like the Spanish. It is probably good the original name was dropped or today's Americanized version would probably be "Greaseport." In 1800 France again obtained title to the land and in 1803 it became a U.S. territory via the Louisiana Purchase. In 1821 it became part of Missouri, the 19th State. Between 1861 and 1865 many in the New Madrid region pledged loyalty to the "CSA." (The Confederate States of America) The five flags waving over the New Madrid Historical Museum in the lower right-hand portion of the slide include America, Missouri, France, Spain, and the Confederacy. The Confederate flag you see is not the more commonly displayed battle flag. Rather it is the official flag of the CSA. Main Street is lined with unreinforced masonry buildings, some dating back more than 100 years. The white-sided building catching the morning sun is the old Dixie Theater built in the early 1930's. Across the street, on the left of the photo, is the old City Hall built in 1904. You can't buy buffalo and bear meat at New Madrid any more, but a few blocks down Main Street from where we are standing, you can buy an "Earthquake Burger." You'll have to go there and sample one to discover what it is.

## SLIDE #14 LOCATION A

## New Madrid Historical Museum Showing Seismically Designed Annex, Dedicated December 3, 1991

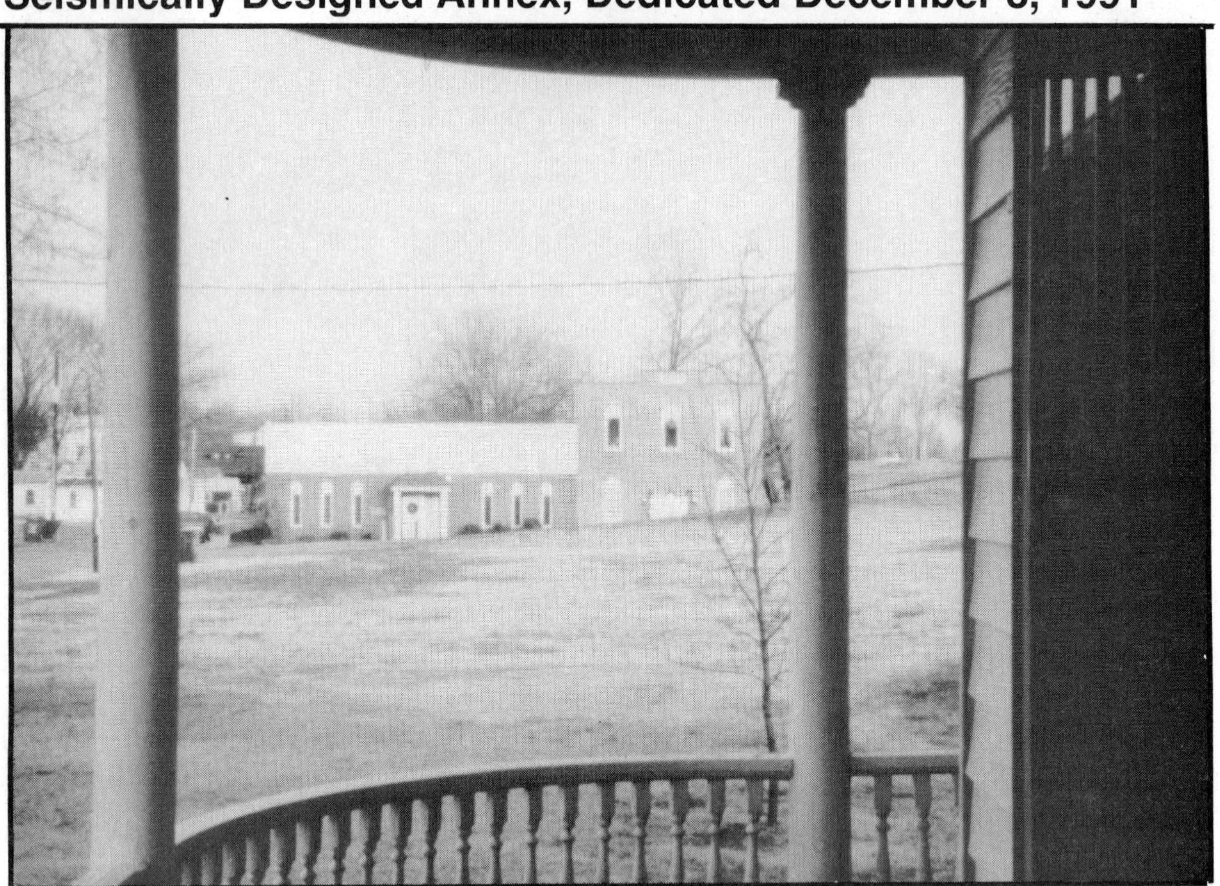

The porch from which this photo is taken is part of the home of Mrs. "Libba" Crisler.* The house was built between 1885 & 1889. The New Madrid Historical Museum is framed by the porch rail and columns. Organized in 1974, the Museum had more than 11,000 visitors from 15 countries in 1992. The building is in two parts The portion on the left has a new brick facade but is actually an old tavern built during the 1880's. It's close to the river. (The upward slope to the right is the levee; the Mississippi River Observation Deck is there just off the picture.) The tavern was a favorite place for boatmen to get their first drink when they landed and to enjoy their last drink before they left. That's why they called it "The First and Last Chance Saloon." The portion of the Museum on the right is a new annex dedicated on December 3, 1991. It is of steel frame construction with reinforced masonry walls, seismically designed to withstand earthquakes. The older saloon portion is unreinforced brick, not designed to resist earthquakes. The Museum contains many interesting displays about the Great New Madrid Earthquakes of 1811-12. There are also exhibits on their unique history prior to the Revolutionary War as well as during the Civil War. They also showcase the region's American Indian heritage. The Museum has many items for sale (including this book) that would make unique gifts. If you go visit, plan to spend several hours. It'll be well worth your time.

*Note: Mrs. Crisler's full name is Lilbourn Lewis Hunter Crisler, but her friends call her "Libba." Like many other residents of New Madrid, she is a descendant of the family of President Thomas Jefferson. Her grandfather, Lilbourn A. Lewis, is the man after whom the nearby town of Lilbourn is named. The intriguing saga of the "Jefferson Connection" to the New Madrid earthquakes is told in the book, *The Earthquake America Forgot.*

## SLIDE #15 LOCATION A

## Seismically Retrofitted Brick School, Outside View
## Immaculate Conception, New Madrid

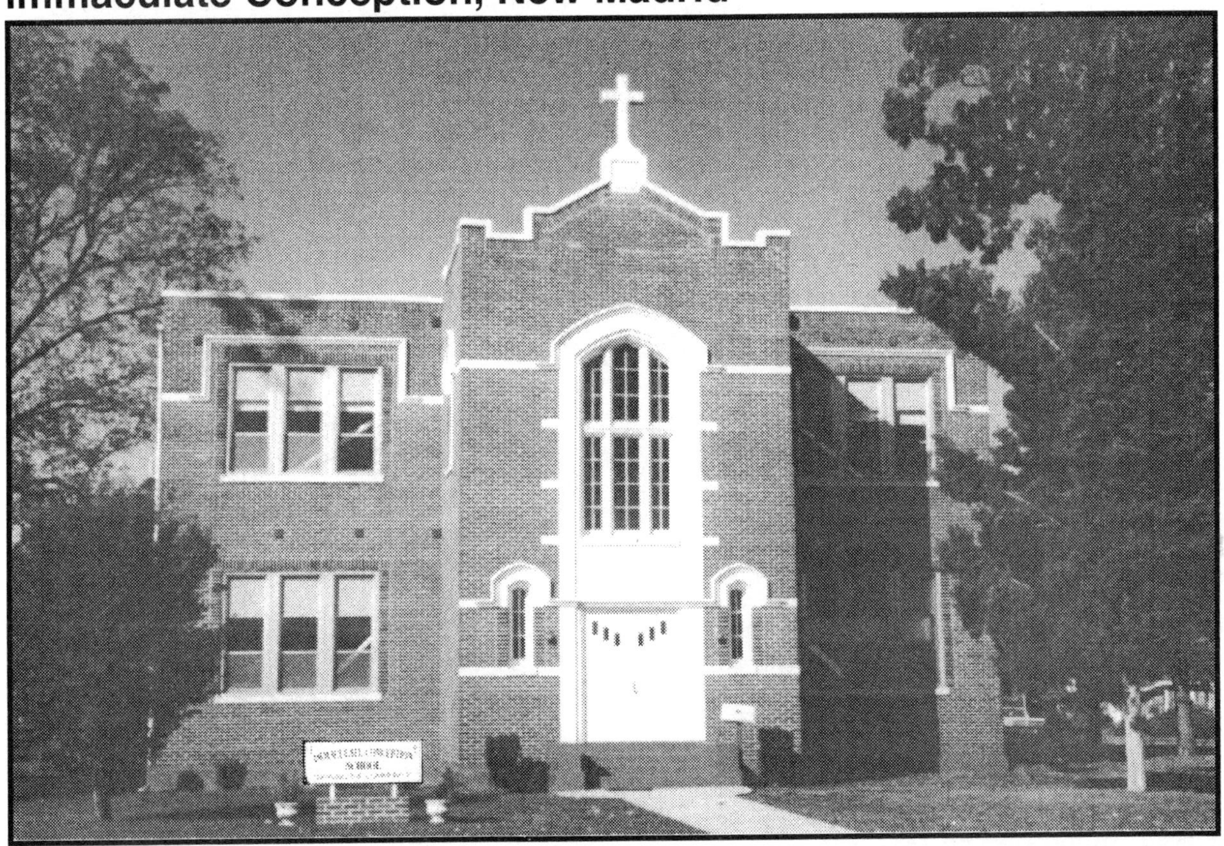

Here is an outside view of the Immaculate Conception School in New Madrid. It was built in 1921, a classic school design of unreinforced brick: Fireproof, but not earthquake-proof, a definite collapse hazard in the event of a big shake. The State of Missouri passed its first seismic building code requirement in May of 1990, effective January 1991. However, the law requires only new school buildings to be built to withstand earthquakes. The statute did not address existing buildings. The Immaculate Conception Parish decided to take a responsible stance voluntarily, even though the law did not require it. They decided to retrofit the building so that it would not collapse in an earthquake. This was accomplished before December, 1990. Look carefully. In the center panes of the two upper windows you will see diagonal braces inside the building. There is also a brace showing through one of the first floor windows on the left. Square metal plates are visible along the levels of the second floor and roof. These plates show where engineers have inserted heavy steel beams through the building. The beams are hidden in the ceilings but the diagonal braces are visible in each room. It gives you a feeling of security and safety to be inside this building and see the braces, knowing that during an earthquake the building cannot fall in and hurt its occupants. Now let us go inside and visit the kindergarten room behind the windows you see on the lower right.

## SLIDE #16 LOCATION A

## Seismically Retrofitted Brick School, Inside View
## Immaculate Conception, New Madrid

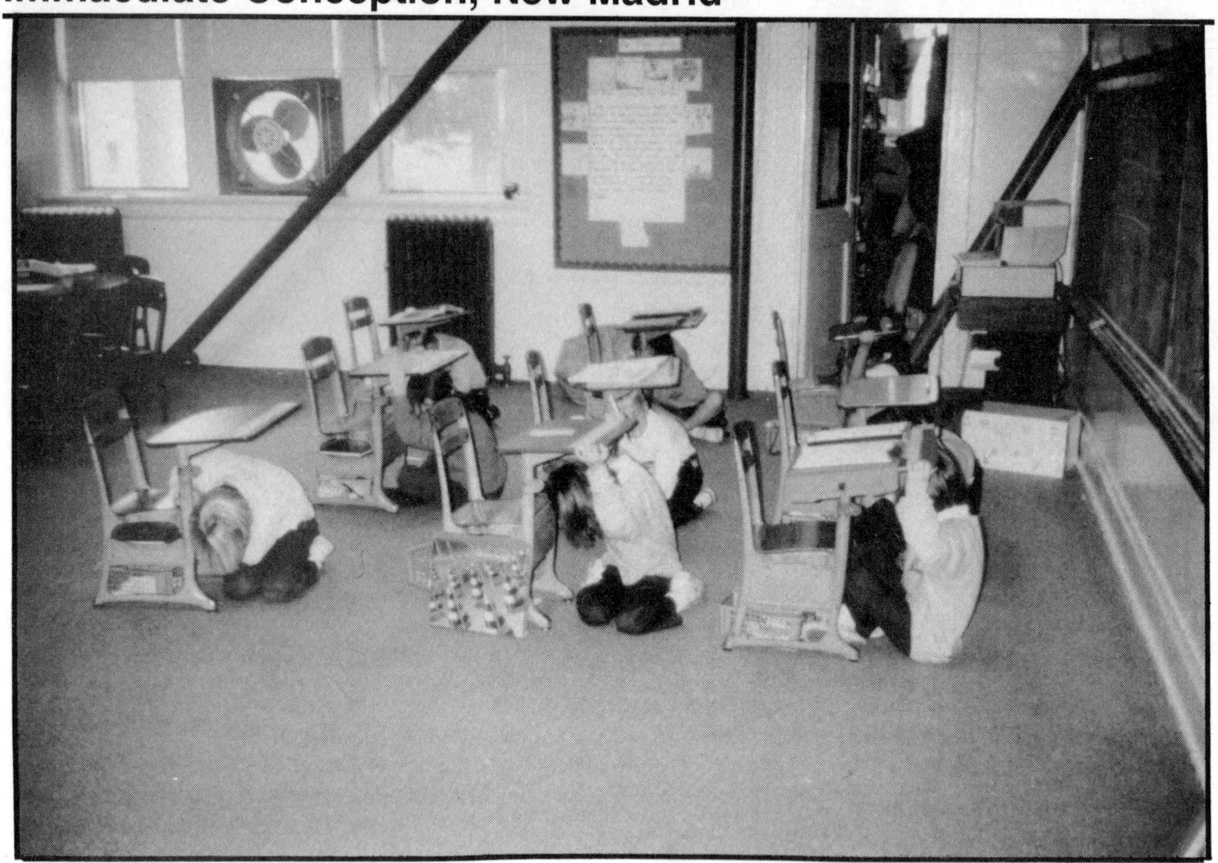

This is an inside view of the kindergarten classroom of Immaculate Conception School. Notice the braces and how they have been artfully painted to fit the colors of the room. Notice, also, that the children are engaged in a mock earthquake drill, ducking under their desks and covering their heads. They know what to do and they know their school has been made safe. The students, teachers, and supporters of the school are proud of what they have done. In fact, the kids sold T-shirts with a sketch of the school and the words, "I.C. School, Retrofitted to Rock n' Roll." What was the cost for this retrofit? About $500 per child—small insurance to protect so precious a treasure. If you want to know how they did it, write to them. The Parish has received inquiries from as far away as Italy! Better yet, take a trip to New Madrid and see it for yourself. The cost of retrofitting an existing school building is considerably more expensive than the additional cost of seismic design for a new building. But the I.C. School figured out a way to afford retrofit anyhow. Some day New Madrid will have another "Big One," but these students and teachers are ready.

LOCATION A

## SLIDE #17
## Original Site of New Madrid Beneath Mississippi and View of 8.8 Magnitude Quake Epicenter

Beneath these waters lies a city. Here we are standing on the Mississippi River Observation Deck just over the levee from the New Madrid Historical Museum (behind us). We are looking due south. The river is flowing from left to right in front of us, curving around the top of the largest bend of the entire Mississippi. On the left the river has flowed northward from a point 10 miles south while on the right it has turned 180 degrees and headed south where it will pass within a mile of itself at Bessie's Neck in Tennessee. Missourians call this "New Madrid Bend." Kentuckians call it "Kentucky Bend." Tennesseans call it "Bessie's Bend." The strip of land you see across the water is Kentucky. The river is a mile wide here. Look to a point about halfway across. From there to the Kentucky shoreline is the original site of New Madrid in 1811-12. From December 16, 1811, until February, 1812, the town had been repeatedly jolted by hundreds of earthquakes while the very ground itself was being fractured and torn apart by countless fissures and sand boils. Then on February 7, 1812, came the most violent shock of all, a record 8.8 magnitude on the Richter scale! What was left of the already devastated town shook loose from its foundations and slumped 15-20 feet downwards, almost to the level of the rushing Mississippi. The remaining town was washed away in the spring floods of 1812, never to be seen again. During the nearly 200 years since, the Mississippi has slowly cut the north bank and deposited sediments on the south bank causing the river to migrate northwards almost a mile from its course at the time of the great quakes. As you stand on the deck you can see two smoke stacks on the right. These are six miles downstream. The tallest is 812 feet high. On a clear day it can be seen up to 30 miles away. Scientists believe this marks the epicentral region of the largest of the New Madrid events, the great 8.8 magnitude quake of February 7, 1812.

## SLIDE #18 LOCATION A

## Location of Second Temporary Waterfall, Just Upstream from New Madrid, February 7, 1812

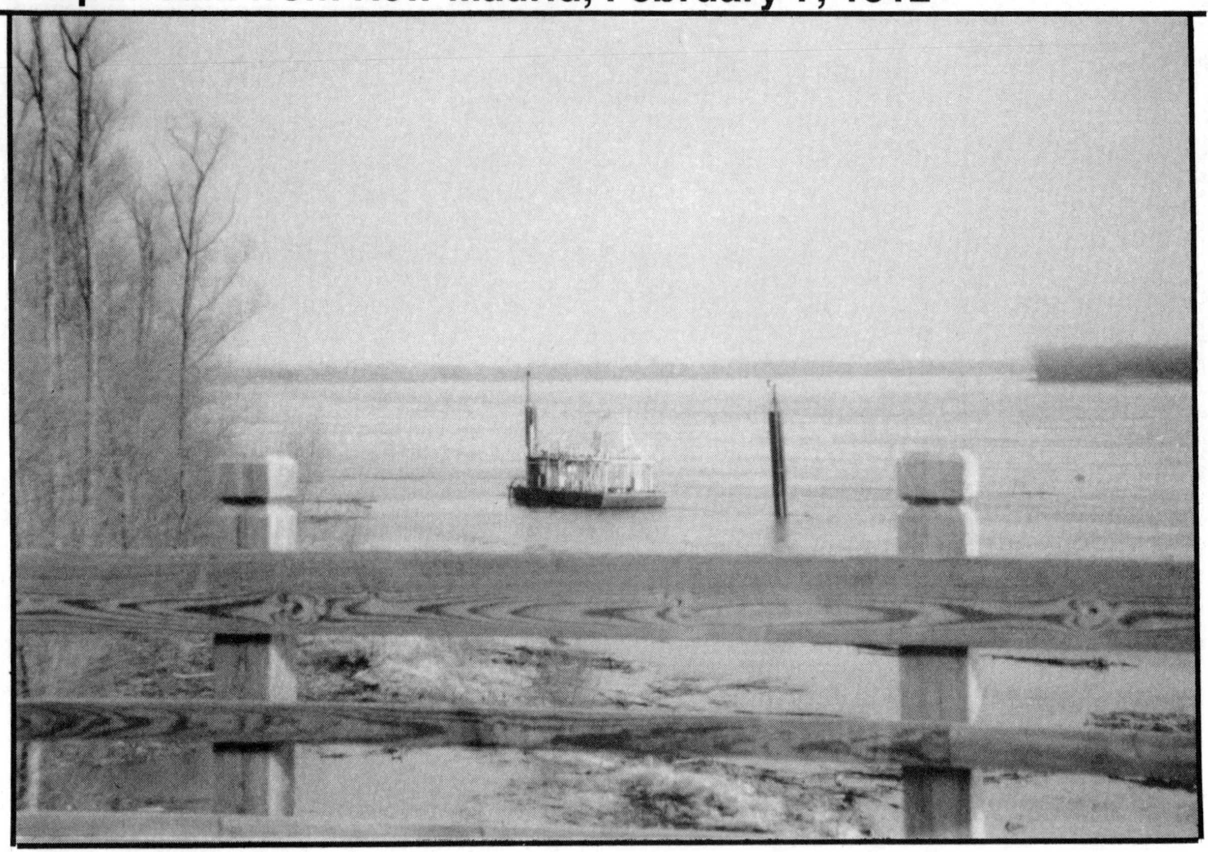

We are still standing on the Observation Deck at New Madrid, Missouri, but this time we are looking upstream and to the east. The small projection of land on the right is a piece of Kentucky at the upper part of "Kentucky Bend." The strip of land in the distance across the center of the picture is the west side of Donaldson Point in Missouri. Somewhere between the anchored boat and the Kentucky shore is where the second temporary waterfall appeared on the Mississippi River on February 7, 1812. It lasted several days. According to descriptions it was probably more of a shallow rapids than an abrupt waterfall, but it was very dangerous. The typical river boats of that time had no engines. They were either flat boats or keel boats powered by crewmen using poles and oars. In "white water" they were nearly helpless, at the mercy of the turbulence of the currents. During the waterfall's brief existence, 30 boats drifted around the bend towards our location and were swiftly drawn into the falls. 28 capsized and were swamped with almost total loss of lives. Witnesses watched helplessly from the banks at New Madrid where they could hear the frantic screams and cries of drowning boatmen. Behind the trees on the left is the mouth of St. John's Bayou. This was a natural harbor on the east side of New Madrid and one of the reasons the town was originally situated there in 1783. During the tectonic upheaval that formed the waterfall, boats in the New Madrid harbor were thrown up St. John's Bayou where they were left on dry land when the waters receded.

## SLIDE #19 LOCATION A

## St. John's Bayou Just East of New Madrid, Aerial View, Where Boats were Thrown up on Land, February 7, 1812

This aerial view can help you get your bearings on what we just saw in the previous slide. We are looking east and the east side of New Madrid can be seen across the photo in the foreground (G1-F10). The levee is marked by a gravel road on top that runs from the left corner (G1) to the right side of the picture (F10). In the lower right we see the Sinclair Oil Depot (F10), just inside the levee, and within sight of the Observation Deck just out of the picture on the right. From the airplane we have another view of where the second waterfall occurred on February 7, 1812, (C5-8) and where the boats were thrown up on land near the mouth of St. John's Bayou (D7). St. John's Bayou is that streak of water starting on the left center (D1) and moving horizontally across the picture to where it meets the Mississippi (D7) at the downstream point of that island. You can see a towboat with its long string of barges going upstream on the right (D8-10). The bend of the river wraps about the banks of Kentucky on the right (B7 to C10) with the shore of Donaldson's Point on the opposite side. The Mississippi is flowing northward into the photo from our right (B10) and then turns westward to flow off the picture also to our right (D10). All the way across the upper part of the photo (from 1 to 10 between A and B) is a faint light strip. This is actually the Mississippi River flowing south on the east side of Donaldson Point 6-10 miles away with more of Kentucky on the far side.

## SLIDE #20 LOCATION A

## Des Cyprie, Discontinuous Channel Beneath Highway I-55 Site of New Madrid Earthquake Refugee Camp, Winter, 1811-12

In the foreground you see the NW corner of New Madrid (EFG, 1-10). Interstate 55 extends left (E1) to right (D10), South to North. Notice the enormous sand boil in the lower right (FG, 8-10). The elevation of the boil is above the dark colored land to the left with Cypress trees and blue patches of standing water (EFG, 1-7). The main seismic feature is a discontinuous channel, called Des Cyprie (French for "of the cypress"). The SE end is a few blocks west of the New Madrid Museum. It meanders through the western edge of town (F1 to G4 to F5 to E5), passes under I-55 (E4), and winds to the west (E4 to D5 to C4) where it terminates as a body of water called "The Washout," a blue patch in the distance (B5), 2 miles north of Lilbourn. Its total length is 4.5 miles. 200 years ago it was a small stream called "St. Martens des Cyprie." It was seismically disrupted in 1811-12, so that it now flows both ways and has no normal surface outlets on either end. When it rains heavily NW of town, it flows toward New Madrid. But when the Mississippi is up, it can flow away from town toward The Washout (B5). In fact, The Washout was formed by the flood of 1912-13 when Mississippi overflow cut a deep, wide channel 1.5 miles long in the NW end of Des Cyprie. Today, it normally consists of ponds, dry patches and depressions where ground water flows into and out of the channel. North of Hwy U (just off the slide at lower left (G1)) ground water enters Des Cyprie east of I-55 (F1-E5) and flows into the Washout where it disappears into the ground (B5). South of Hwy U, it seeps intermittently toward the Mississippi, but the water seldom gets to the river above ground before it, too, disappears below surface near the City Golf Course. Des Cyprie is lined with seismic features. Look and you'll see yellow sand fissures (B7) and sand boils (C2, B2 and C4) in the distance. After the first great shock on December 16, 1811, almost everyone in New Madrid left town. Most camped at a site "about 3 miles to the northwest." The land on the left along I-55 (C,D and E, 1-4) is in the vicinity of the earthquake refugees encampment.

LOCATION A

## SLIDE #21
## East Terminus of Des Cyprie with Earthquake Pond and Land Fill by New Madrid Golf Course

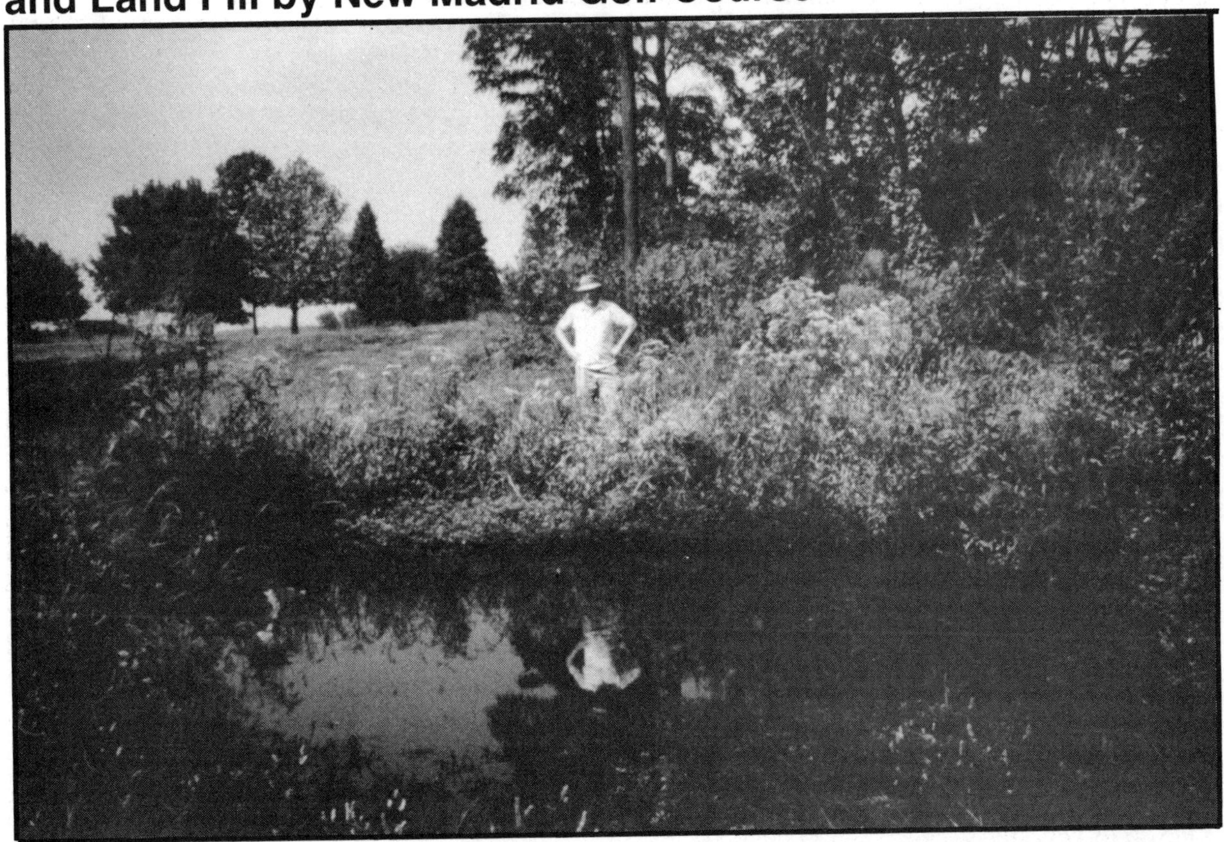

We are standing with the Mississippi River levee to our backs looking north at the southeastern end of Des Cyprie. This is an earthquake pond, a seismic explosion feature leaving a conical depression intersecting the water table. Earthquake ponds are not filled from above by surface runoff, like ordinary ponds. They are filled from below by the rise and fall of ground water. If the ground water level falls too far, they dry up and any surface water or precipitation that flows into them simply disappears through these orifices into the water table. On the other hand, when ground water pressures increase above land surface, these features fill and overflow. Earthquake ponds act as points of surface water recharge into the aquifer below as well as points of ground water discharge back to the surface. Unlike a regular pond, water flows both ways, in and out, through a permeable bottom. You will notice that the pond is almost perfectly round, about 45 feet in diameter. When it formed, it probably had a rim of sand and could have been more than 15 feet deep. At the time this photo was taken (Summer 1991) it was probably less than 6 feet deep. To the left, off of the photo, there used to be a grove of Cypress in Des Cyprie with a large seismic sunken area that held water most of the year. It was bulldozed, cleared off and filled in during the summer of 1990. We hope that the town does not forget that this is a covered earthquake feature. If a developer some day builds a housing subdivision over that filled portion of Des Cyprie, it would be extremely susceptible to liquefaction and ground failure during large earthquakes. This would not be good for paved streets or concrete foundations. Behind Dr. Knox (standing on the far side of the pond) is part of the New Madrid Golf Course. It is the only golf course we know of with natural seismic sand traps.

## SLIDE #22

LOCATION A

## Earthquake Pond & Seismic Dump at East Terminus of Des Cyprie in City Limits of New Madrid

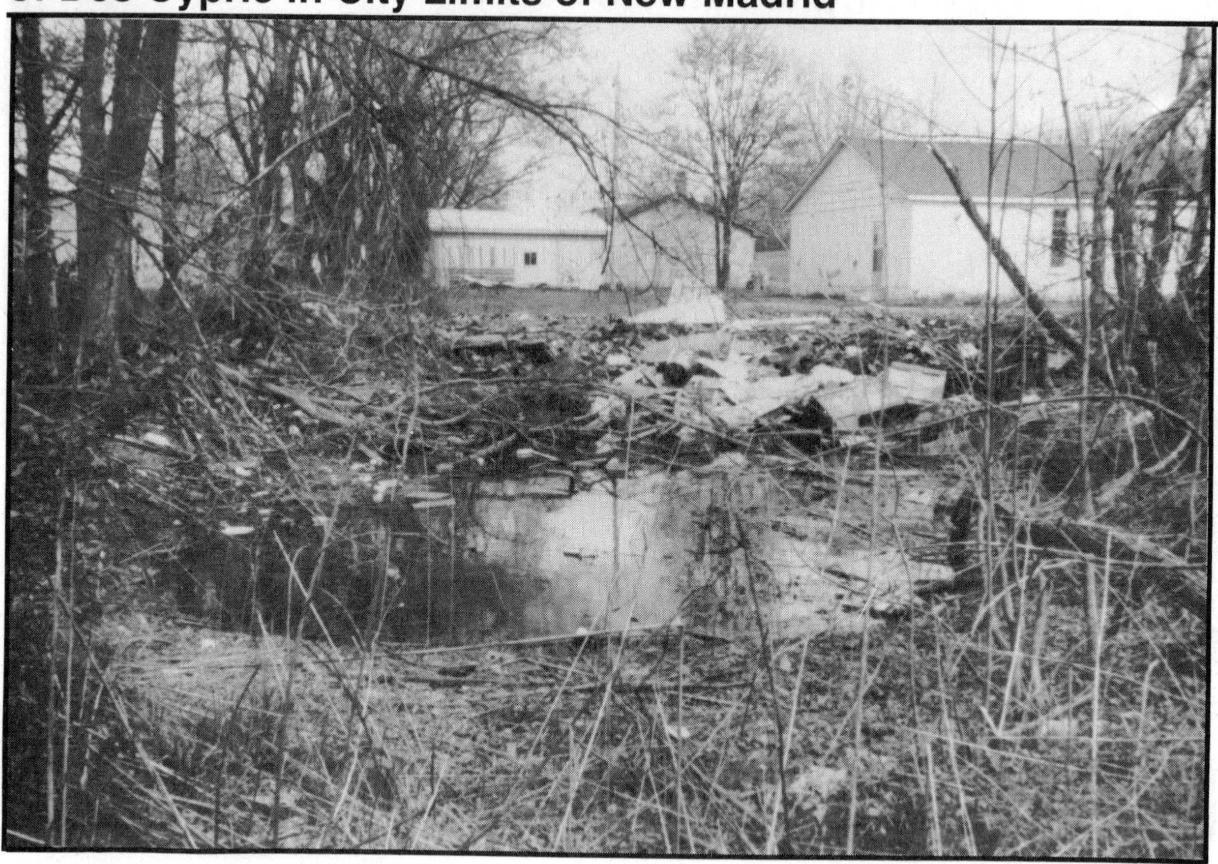

As we stand looking at this trash, the earthquake pond of the previous slide is behind us, the New Madrid Golf Course is beyond the trees to your left, and the white building in front of you in the upper right is the General Baptist Church of New Madrid. This earthquake pond has been used as a dump for years. It seems to work well. When the water table is rising, liquefaction in the bottom of the pond causes heavy items dumped in the pond to sink and disappear. You can keep putting trash into such holes for a long time and it seems like they never completely fill up. What the users of this site do not realize is that some day, during a major earthquake, that earthquake pond is going liquefy explosively and regurgitate all the debris it has been forced to swallow all these years. You are going to have old refrigerators, broken radio sets, dismantled television sets, used brick, concrete blocks, rusted buckets, crushed tin cans, bed springs, discarded bathtubs, worn furniture frames, and who knows what else belched back into view. There might even be some valuable antiques brought to light, hidden for generations in the sands beneath. This seismic dump is no longer visible, as such, today. It, and the earthquake pond of the previous slide, were filled and smoothed over in late 1991. This won't prevent them from exploding in a future earthquake and spitting up their contents, however. We can only hope no one inadvertently builds a house over one of these buried earthquake ponds.

## SLIDE #23 LOCATION A
## Mechanically Induced Liquefaction (MIL) by Trains on Tracks Over Seismic Sand Fissure

Once an area has liquefied in an earthquake, it can liquefy again and again, not only from subsequent earthquakes, but by any force that increases groundwater pressure. Here is a railroad track crossing a seismic sand fissure. It is next to Hwy 61 in the SW city limits of New Madrid. The New Madrid substation is in the center of the photo. You can see Interstate-55 passing beyond this 161,000 volt electrical facility. A large white trailer truck can be seen on I-55 to the left of the substation. Every time a train passes, the mechanical vibrations can cause partial liquefaction in the fissure. This causes subsidence. In turn, this causes the tracks to settle out-of-level and out-of-parallel. As a result, trains are periodically derailed here. The latest was in 1993. Tons of soil and gravel have been dumped here, but it just keeps sinking in. Not far below surface is a vast reservoir of liquefiable sand. When pushed down with the weight of a rock load the mushy sand below just spreads underneath. You could probably push stone into this fissure for 100 years and still have the problem. Normally, you would not see water standing on a sand fissure. They are like sponges. Rain and runoff soak in as fast as they hit the permeable sand. This patch of standing water represents a part of the fissure where impermeable soil has been added to firm up the foundation beneath the tracks. Mechanically induced liquefaction (MIL) from train vibrations is a problem worldwide—even where no quakes occur. Europe and Japan have ultra-high-speed trains whose tracks must be in perfect alignment to prevent disastrous derailments. Engineers there have some solutions that might fix tracks in New Madrid. In Tennessee, west of Reelfoot Lake along Hwy 78, between Ridgely and the KY-TN State Line, the railroad tracks have a problem with MIL for more than 50 miles. When driving through there, notice the unevenness of the rails. Several derailments have occurred along that stretch. The New Madrid quakes stopped shaking in 1812, but they created problems for railroads that will never go away. Imagine! Trains being derailed today by an earthquake that happened two-hundred years ago!

## SLIDE #24 — LOCATION A

## Seismic Sag & Largest Sand Boil in New Madrid, By Sinclair Station, Aerial View

This is the largest sand boil in the City Limits of New Madrid (D3-6). It forms an almost perfect circle about 500 feet in diameter. It is so big that from an airplane it can be spotted more than two miles away as a distinctive yellow-orange spot. In this photo, we are only a few thousand feet away. It is located on the west side of town, about a mile NW of the original site of New Madrid. Hwy 61 (D1 to E10) cuts across the south edge of the sand blanket (D3-5). A black man was reported to have drowned in a sand boil, December 16, 1811, "about a mile NW of town." This could have been the site of that tragedy. When large amounts of sand like this boil are extruded, somewhere nearby there is usually a low place from which the sandy material came. The grey road seen diagonally across the left lower corner (G7 to E1) is on the levee. The dark corner outside the levee is part of a large seismic sag, a natural dry depression without a surface outlet. Just off the picture in the upper right corner (A10) is the site of the historic, pre-Civil War Bloomfield House, lost in a fire a few years back. In front of this house was a large earthquake pond next to Des Cyprie. It has now been completely filled in and smoothed over. Old-timers remember its cool clear spring waters issuing from the ground. Removal of all the fill would not only restore the earthquake pond to its natural appearance after 1812 but would also bring up artifacts dating back more than a century, including items from before and during the Civil War. The light green patch across the lower right corner is the airplane wing. Now let's land the plane and take a look at the Sinclair Sand Boil from the ground.

## SLIDE #25

LOCATION A

## Sinclair Sand Boil, View from Ground Standing on the Sand Blanket Facing Sinclair Station

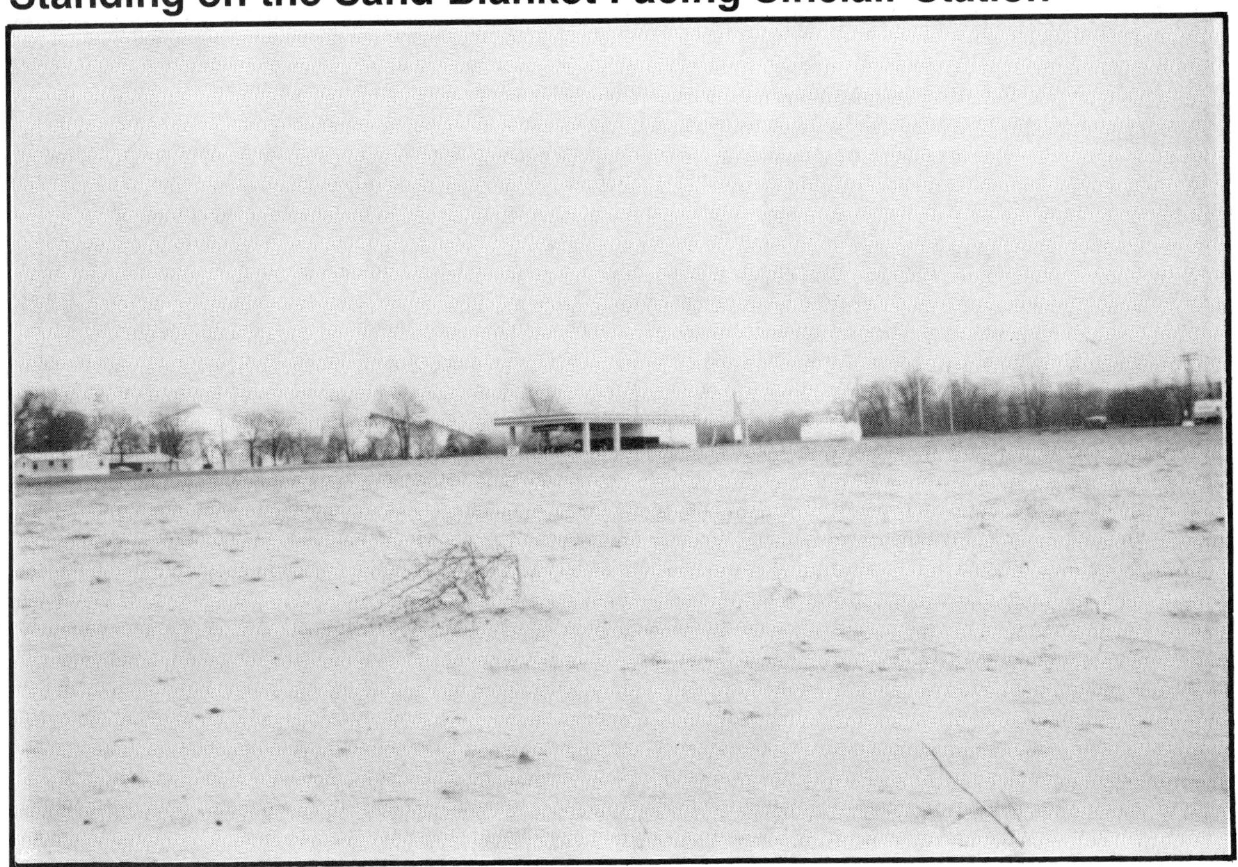

Here we are, standing in the middle of the largest sand boil in New Madrid. It looks like a desert. Crops don't grow well in sand. For one thing, sand contains very few nutrients. Even so, weeds and sown crops will at least sprout when weather is wet and cool. A couple of weeks of hot dry weather will wilt them all. Sand does not retain water very well. (It takes some clay in the soil to do that.) In the center of the picture you see the Sinclair Station that gives this boil its name. The treetops that appear to be sticking out of a low place in the distant right are in the large seismic sag mentioned in the previous slide. The white objects behind the trees to the left of the Sinclair station are the storage bins of the Cargill Seed Company. Mr. Robert Riley, owner of the boil, has kindly given permission for visitors to explore this mammoth sand deposit. When you stop, you will find cold drinks and tasty food at the Sinclair Snack Bar across the road. You will also find a variety of interesting things in the boil, itself. For instance, there are lots of Indian flint chips and shards of broken Indian pottery. Native Americans used to make grass baskets and press clay against the insides to mold a pot. Then they would fire the pot, burning off the grass. This would leave an impression of the grass form on the outside. You can find pottery pieces in this sand boil with the weave of the basket showing on one side. The smooth side of the shard was the inside of the pot. You won't always find the Sinclair sand boil as desolate and barren as it appears here. It depends on the time of the year. Sometimes vegetation covers the ground, and sometimes it does not. But the sand is always there.

## SLIDE #26 LOCATION A

## Sand Boils in West New Madrid, Aerial View Looking South Down West Leg of New Madrid Bend

We are now looking south from the north side of New Madrid. Many features mentioned in the previous slides can be identified in this view. Starting on the left we see Highway 61 entering town from the north (G1-D3). Evergreen Cemetery is near the lower left corner (F1). Many historic New Madrid names can be found there, including several Lilbourn Lewis's whose dramatic story is told in the book *The Earthquake America Forgot.* Next to the Cemetery is the New Madrid Elementary School (E1). See that white cluster of objects next to the river on the upper right (between B1 and C1). That's the Sinclair Oil Depot and Tank Farm seen in Slides #12 and #19. St. John's Bayou is to the left and the New Madrid Museum to the immediate right of the Sinclair Depot. Highway U runs across the center from its intersection with Highway 61 (D3) to the right edge of the photo (D10). Highway U was seen in Slide #12 and was mentioned in relationship to Slide #20. The New Madrid Nursing Home (between D5 & C6), also seen in Slide #12, is visible here to the right of the intersection (D3) of Highways U & 61. The Cargill Seed silos and storage bins (seen in the last slide) are visible here on the river's edge in the upper right (C8). To the right of Cargill (C9) you can see a faint light (yellow-orange) spot. That's the Sinclair Sand Boil seen from more than two miles away. Des Cyprie runs from the right (D10) to a point just east of Cargill. The Mississippi runs from left to right (B1-B10) where it turns southward around New Madrid Bend (B8 to A6). In the far distance, between A4 and A6, you can actually make out Bessie's Neck, 10 miles south of New Madrid. You'll see more of Bessie's Neck in Slides #27, #29, #30, #44 & #46. The prominent island you see (B6-B10) is relatively new, deposited by river sediments during the 1927 flood. It is called "New Madrid Island." Between A8 and B8 you can see the white plume of the Associated Electric smoke stack, marker for the epicentral region of the magnitude 8.8 earthquake of February 7, 1812. Note the numerous sand boils and liquefaction features on the ground, including those surrounding the Elementary School. Now let's fly down the river to the power plant.

## SLIDE #27 LOCATION B
## Associated Electric Plant & Smoke Stack, Marker for Epicentral Region of 8.8 Quake of 1812

Epicentral ground zero for the biggest earthquake in American history outside of Alaska. That's what you are looking at here. The temblor struck at 3:15 a.m. on February 7, 1812, with a surface wave magnitude of 8.8 on the Richter scale. The Good Friday Earthquake in Alaska, March 27, 1964, with a magnitude of 9.3, was bigger. But in the lower 48 states, nothing yet has topped this New Madrid event. By comparison, California's biggest event so far was the Great San Francisco Quake of April 18, 1906, measuring 8.3 on the Richter scale. Three of the New Madrid events were bigger than that. You see three smoke stacks here. The two tallest ones in the center (D6 & D7) are the Associated Electric Company. The smallest one on the right (D9) is the Noranda Aluminum Company. Evidence of liquefaction can be seen by the mottled appearance of the soils in the foreground. Why would anyone build here? From a commercial point of view, it is ideal. Water supply is abundant, railway connections are good, and the river provides easy shipping for coal, aluminum ore, and other goods. Actually, when these facilities were built, scientists had not figured out the location of the epicentral area of the largest New Madrid quake. It's exact location is still not known but is thought to be within a 10 mile circle marked by these smoke stacks. The tallest one, 812 feet high, is certainly a most convenient marker as a field guide in the NMSZ. It can be seen from as far as Hickman, Kentucky, Reelfoot Lake, Malden, Missouri, and Lenox, Tennessee, 30 miles away. So when you are exploring the NMSZ for seismic landforms, you can often use this smoke stack to orient yourself on where the "really big one" was centered relative to where you are. The river is flowing south from left to right (CDE-1 to C10) with Kentucky on the opposite bank. Bessie's Neck can be seen behind the smoke plume (B9) with the southern tip of Donaldson Point to the east (A8). Scarcely visible near the horizon on the extreme right is Reelfoot Lake, Tennessee, 15 miles away (A10).

## SLIDE #28 String of Circular Sand Boils South of Associated Electric Plant

LOCATION B

Here we are looking back up the river toward New Madrid from south of the Associated Electric Plant. The cluster of white objects in the distance (C5) is the Sinclair Tank Farm six miles north of where we are. Remember Slide #17 where we stood on the Mississippi Observation Deck outside the New Madrid Museum and looked six miles south to see this same smoke stack. The river flows around New Madrid Bend from right (C10) to left (D1) and back to the right (D10). The piece of land circled by the river (CD6 to CD10) is part of Kentucky. Notice the string of sand boils in the foreground curving up toward the Aluminum and Electric Plants (G5 to E4). Another large boil is visible on the right (E9). The location of this plant on the banks of the Mississippi River (in the center of the most active portion of the New Madrid Fault Zone surrounded and underlain by by liquefiable soils) places it at very high risk of being shut down by an earthquake some day. However, not to worry. As with all electric power plants, the New Madrid Plant is part of a grid so that if one plant goes down another takes over to keep the supply of power continuous. The back-up plant for this one is the Sikeston Power Plant discussed on pages 134-136, Slides #91-#93.

## SLIDE #29 — LOCATION B

## Bessie's Neck & Donaldson Point,
## Site of First Waterfall on Mississippi, February 7, 1812

Bessie's Neck is at the center of this photo. This peculiar isthmus with the Mississippi on both sides is only three-quarters of a mile wide while the distance the river travels from one side to the other is slightly over 20 miles. The view from our plane is toward the east. At the center on the left (C1) you see a blue thread of the Mississippi 7 miles away flowing southward on the far side of Donaldson Point. The river makes a 180 degree turn about the tip of Donaldson Point (between C5 and D5) heading in the opposite direction (D5 to D1). From there it flows northward 10 miles until it makes another 180 degree turn around the top of New Madrid Bend. A piece of Kentucky is found on the inside of the loop, which is why Kentuckians call it "Kentucky Bend." This bend is seen in map view in Slide #1 and in photo view in Slides #17, #18, #19, #26 and #28. From there, the river descends 10 miles southward back to the west side of Bessie's Neck where a towboat and barge train can be seen headed downstream in the photo (E7). We are looking at three states here. Across the entire horizon in the distance (C1 – C10) are the Chickasaw Bluffs in Tennessee, which contain more than 200 earthquake landslides from the 1811-12 temblors. The thin strip of blue on the right (C9) is Reelfoot Lake, about 9 miles away. The tongue of Donaldson Point on the left (CD1 – CD5) and the land in the right foreground is Missouri. Along the isthmus on the left edge of the picture and north of Bessie's Neck is the Kentucky-Tennessee State Line (D1-E1). Bessie's Neck, itself, is actually in Tennessee, and that's why Tennesseans call this "Bessie's Bend." In the late 1800's when the town of Bessie was there, boats coming down the river would stop opposite Donaldson Point for the boat-weary passengers to disembark and relax on land while their boat continued on. They would spend the night in the Bessie Hotel and then be taken across the isthmus the next day to catch their boat, now 20 miles further downstream.

## SLIDE #30 LOCATION B

## Ten Mile View of New Madrid Bend from 5000 Feet Altitude Looking North from Tennessee

Here you can see the entire New Madrid Bend. A blue ribbon of river enters the picture on the right (E10), flows around Donaldson Point (D8-9), turns north at Bessie's Neck (D6), flows northward away from us until it turns west (C7-9) around the top of the bend (C4-7), turns southward (D2-3), flows towards us past the west side of Bessie's Neck (D4), and exits from the picture on the left (E1). Across Bessie's Neck by land is but a short walk, but by river it is more than 20 miles. (See Slide #1.) This is the biggest bend on the entire Mississippi. Why? Because it is an earthquake feature. The most active portion of the New Madrid Fault lies pulsating 2-8 miles beneath this area. (See Slide #3.) This stretch of the NMSZ is underlaid by a thrust fault (a low angle reverse fault). (See Slide #10.) Beneath this location the two sides of the New Madrid fault are being pushed towards each other. Take a sheet of paper, lay it on a flat surface, and push the two ends toward each other. The middle will hump up. Similarly, the New Madrid Fault below, pushing toward itself in an east-west direction, causes the land to hump upward here. The resultant regional upwarp is called the "Lake County Uplift." (Lake County is the part of Tennessee seen in the foreground.) Now you can understand why the bend in the river. The Mississippi flowing southward encounters this region of uplifted ground, reverses itself at Donaldson's point and cuts a channel at New Madrid, ten miles north, to get around the high ground. Erosion has slowly narrowed Bessie's Neck since 1811-12. At that time it was more than 2 miles wide. Now it is less than a mile. Straight below the tip of the airplane wing, at the top of the bend, you can barely make out a cluster of white objects. This is the Sinclair Tank Farm in New Madrid, more than 10 miles away (between C4 and D4). The Associated Electric Plant on the left (D1) marks the epicenter of the 8.8 magnitude quake. Reelfoot Lake is behind us, to the right. Note the sand features in the foreground, several of which are boils and fissures.

LOCATION B

## SLIDE #31
## View of Where Mississippi River Ran Backwards From Site of First Waterfall Looking Northward to Island #8

Here we can see all of Donaldson Point (D2-7). On the right, the river flows toward us from Island #8, 12 miles north in the distance (C8-9). On the left the river flows away from us toward New Madrid, 12 miles away (C1). On February 7, 1812, following the largest of the New Madrid Series (magnitude 8.8) the river flowed backwards for several hours and two waterfalls formed. The retrograde portion of the river stretched from the tip of Donaldson Point (D4) to Island #8 (C8). The site of the first waterfall was just around the tip of Donaldson Point (E3-4) while the second fall was a mile upstream from New Madrid (C1). The waterfalls lasted 2-3 days before they eroded away. One boat captain, Mathias Speed, was tied up on Island #8 for the night. After the quake, which hit at 3:15 a.m., he cut loose his moorings and drifted in the river. He was one who testified to the retrograde motion. Later in the day, when the river again flowed south, he rounded Donaldson Point to encounter the first waterfall near Island #10. Unable to steer his boat to shore or reverse his collision course with the falls, he and his crew plummeted over the rapids and survived without capsizing. Behind them in the distance, they saw another boat floating downstream. That crew, seeing the disappearance of the raft ahead, abandoned ship, took a lifeboat to shore, and walked from the tip of Donaldson Point to New Madrid, letting their vessel crash over the falls without them. Prior to 1890 the position of Donaldson Point was actually a mile east (to the right) of where it is now. Island #10 has become incorporated into the point (D3), existing no more as an island. Island #9 has become incorporated into the mainland of Tennessee on the right (D10). The small town in the left foreground is Cates, Tennessee (F1-4). At the upper end of the retrograde river stretch (CD-7) the river was so violently thrown over its banks that the waves destroyed several thousand acres of forestland. Some of those broken stumps are still visible today. Let's look at them.

## SLIDE #32 — LOCATION C

## Stump Hole With Quake Shattered Cypress Stumps

We are looking at the "Stump Hole." The Mississippi is across the pond on the other side of the field. This is a "borrow pit," a place where soil was excavated (borrowed) to build up the levee behind us. These cypress stumps were buried in soil deposited by the river since 1812. You can easily drive to the Stump Hole from New Madrid, which is located about 8 miles due west. It used to be a favorite fishing hole for area residents. The field beyond is also underlaid by stumps, a whole forest of them. The great earthquake reduced this mature virgin forest into splintered rubble and jagged stumps. Subsequent floods gradually deposited silt and sand over the remains, thus creating a vast arboreal graveyard. These stumps were exposed because of excavation for the levee. Others have been made visible by erosion in the Mississippi River bank on the other side of the field. You can walk across the field and look at them when the river is low. But the best view of these shattered casualties of the earthquake is from a boat in the river. Let's get in a boat and take a look.

## SLIDE #33 LOCATION C

## Broken Cypress Stumps on West Bank of Mississippi Opposite Island #8

Now we are out in a boat on the Mississippi looking westward toward the Missouri bank at the north end of Donaldson Point. Island #8 and the Kentucky shore are behind us. Dr. Knox is on land. He is 6 feet, 2 inches tall, so you can get an idea of how large these cypress stumps have to be. The level of the land is about 15-20 feet above the water. These stumps were buried in flood deposits after 1812, which is why they have been preserved so long. Cypress is also a wood that does not rapidly decay, since standing trees of this species can live 500 years or more. The skeletons of these stumps are being exposed because the river bank is eroding here. Imagine the utter chaos and violence of the river on that dark morning of February 7, 1812, when 30-foot waves rushed recklessly over the banks, snapping oak, cottonwood, tulip and cypress into splinters and stumps. When the great waves receded back into the river, they carried thousands of trunks and logs, clogging the channel and creating hazards to boats for miles downstream. For decades after the quakes, boatmen passing by noted the vast wasteland of stumps, thousands of acres of them, mown down with such regularity it appeared as if some giant lumberjack had topped them all 10-12 feet above ground with a single swing of a monster axe. Year after year, as the Mississippi flooded the dead forest, the stumps retarded the flow, trapping sediments until they were buried where they fell, like soldiers on a battlefield. This is a thousand-acre cemetery for earthquake victims. This scene helps us to realize that people are not the only casualties of earthquakes. Trees and animals are victims, too. When a million trees were destroyed in a few seconds, like these, a million creatures living there were also destroyed. The number of men in boats and Native Americans on land, also swept away by that tempestuous flood, will never be known. Few traces of former life remain to be counted after such a gargantuan cataclysm. One doesn't even want to imagine what would have happened had a city been on that site.

## SLIDE #34 LOCATION C

## Close Up of Broken Stumps on West River Bank With Author, Ray Knox

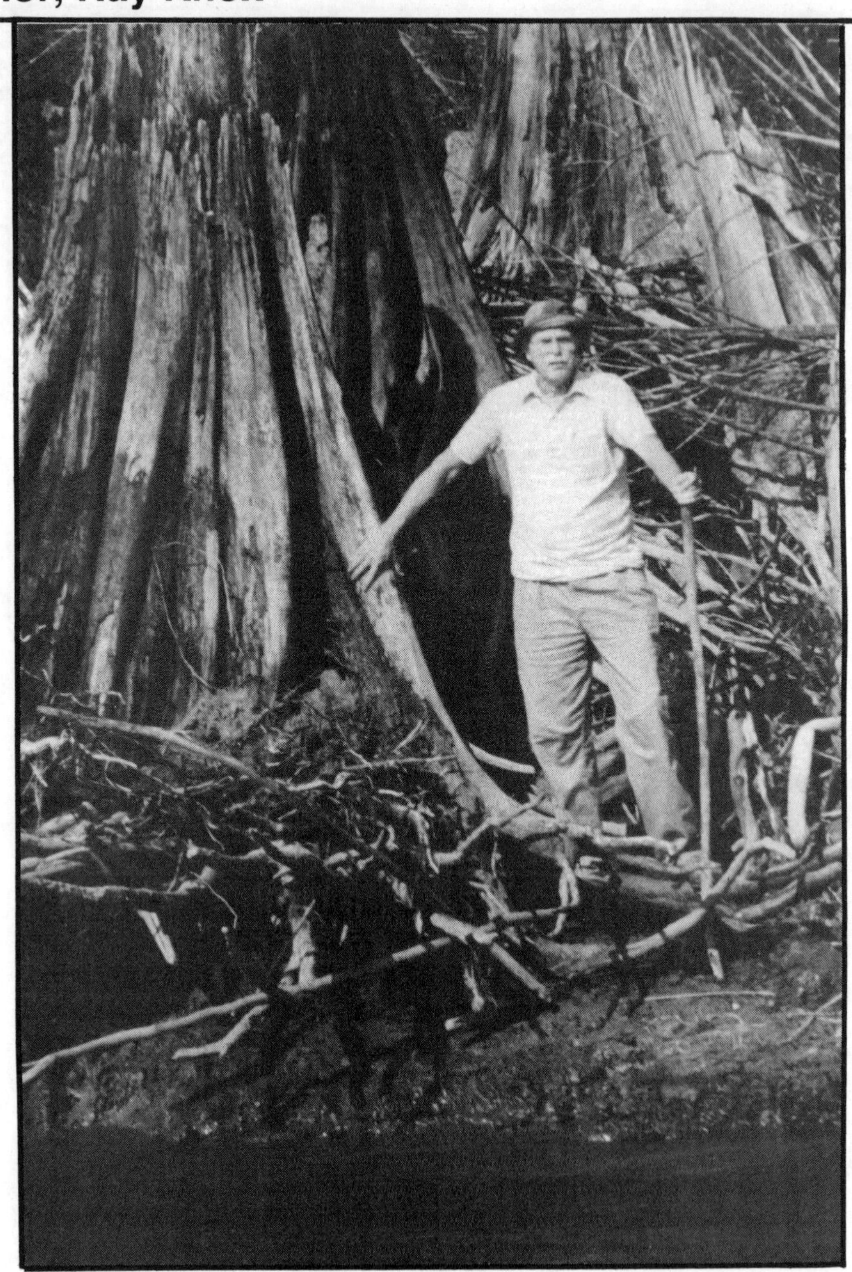

A close-up view of these stumps better portrays the maturity of their size when their lives were so abruptly ended on February 7, 1812. Already centuries old at the time of their untimely deaths, they could still be alive today had it not been for the events of 1811-12. Note the shattered tops.

## SLIDE #35 — LOCATION C

## Buried Broken Cypress Stump in River Bank Emerging into View by Erosion

Here we see a cypress stump half buried (or half exposed) in the bank of the Mississippi. As the river erodes this bank, the seismically shattered stumps preserved there emerge into daylight. Whether these stumps will remain visible for long is a question. The U.S. Army Corps of Engineers is engaged in a project upstream from here to halt the erosion. Tons of rock boulders are being placed against the shore, lining the banks and covering everything visible. This and the last two photos were taken on a sunny morning in 1991. If the Corps follows its schedule, 1991 may have been the last year these photos were possible. However, thousands of these earthquake stumps remain buried and preserved beneath the corn, cotton and bean fields above. Future generations will still be able to dig and find them, as the Stump Hole has demonstrated. And nature always has the last word. The work of the Corps won't last forever, but the forces of the river will.

## SLIDE #36 LOCATION D

## New Madrid-Marston Rest Area on Interstate-55

This is the New Madrid Rest Stop and Visitors' Center on Interstate 55 (D4 – D7). It is actually located a few miles south of town between New Madrid and Marston, Missouri. The view from our plane is toward the northwest. Note the numerous sand boils and signs of liquefaction in the mottled soils that surround the rest stop. A particularly large sand boil is clearly seen two miles in the distance (A4 – A6). This area is a topographic high, a tectonic dome, part of the "Lake County Uplift" associated with the active thrusting of the New Madrid Fault in the bedrock 2-8 miles below ground. There should be a large billboard on the Interstate here that says something like, "YOU ARE NOW PASSING THROUGH EPICENTRAL GROUND ZERO OF THE LARGEST EARTHQUAKE IN AMERICAN HISTORY, 8.8 RICHTER, FEBRUARY 7, 1812." The 15-mile stretch of I-55 centered on the New Madrid Rest Stop passes over one of the most active portions of the New Madrid Fault today (See the maps of Slides #1 and #3). There is a 33% chance of a measurable earthquake on the New Madrid Fault any day you drive through. You probably won't feel it. It would most likely be too small for that, something less than 2.5 on the Richter scale. But it will be detected by one or more of the dozens of seismic stations scattered throughout the NMSZ. This is one of the world's most dynamic portions of the earth's crust. Today it is just restless, popping off small reminders every week. But some day, it will rise up and explode again like a dozing giant jarred suddenly into full wakefulness, raging in anger over his disrupted sleep.

## SLIDE #37 — LOCATION D

### Large Sand Fissure at Mile Post 44
### Under Interstate-55, Railroad & Levee, Aerial View from North

Part of a huge sand fissure can be seen in the center of this photo (D4-E6. Actually, the fissure is more than twice as long as what you see, extending almost the entire width of the picture (D1-E9). It is 200 feet wide and extends, from right to left, under Interstate Highway 55 (E6-E8), under the railroad track (D4), and under the levee (D2-3) along the edge of a borrow pit containing some water (D1-2). The west end of the fissure terminates in a huge sand boil under the Interstate, sticking out on both sides of the highway (F6 and E8-9). Don't count on being able to use this portion of I-55 when the next major New Madrid earthquake happens. Liquefaction will break it up, making it impassable. The railroad track won't be passable, either. And as for the levee, just hope the Mississippi isn't at flood stage when it hits. The fissure is at Interstate Mile Marker #44, so we call it it the "Mile Post #44 Fissure." The New Madrid City Limit sign stands east of the highway just south of this fissure, putting this seismic feature within the boundaries of the town. When you are driving by, a clump of willow trees marks the west side of the feature (F8). The triangular light colored area in the center just east of the Interstate (C4-C6) is a borrow pit being filled with rice hulls. Looking down the Interstate toward the top of the picture you can see the New Madrid Rest Stop and Visitors Center 1.5 miles to the south (A7). This fissure and sand boil are within the region of Epicentral Ground Zero for the "Big One " the 8.8 event in 1812. Now let's land our airplane at the New Madrid-Marston Airport nearby, and drive up to take a look at this morphoseismic feature from Interstate 55.

## SLIDE #38

## Mile Post 44 Sand Fissure As Seen From I-55

Here is how the "Mile Post #44 Fissure" looks from the highway. You can see the levee extending across the picture behind the trees along the fence line on the far side of the field. The grade of the railroad track can be seen running along the base of the levee. Sometimes the sand fissure shows up better. At other times it is hardly visible. It depends on the moisture conditions and whether it is temporarily covered with weeds or crops at the time. Today, as we view it from our car in January of 1990, it is a relatively bare strip of yellow sand with the dark brown remnants of wilted vegetation clinging to the soils on either side. In direct alignment with this fissure is the Associated Electric smokestack 3.5 miles away, our handy marker for the 8.8 epicentral region. Actually, the epicentral area is not known precisely. It is thought to be within a ten mile circle containing the smoke stack and containing the location of this fissure, too. So far as damage and the intensity of the shaking is concerned, it wouldn't make much difference if you were exactly on the true epicenter of an 8.8 magnitude quake, or ten miles away. For that matter, even 50 miles away would probably mean total destruction to any human-built constructions. This sand fissure and connecting sand boil were active bogs of quicksand during the great quakes. They become mushy from hydrologic pressures (HIL) even now when river levels rise on the outside of the levee. Tractors tilling the adjacent fields north and south of this fissure cannot cross it when water tables rise high or they will induce liquefaction by their vibrations (MIL) and sink in. Can you imagine what will happen to this highway, railway, and levee when the next major New Madrid earthquake hits? Hopefully, that won't be soon.

## SLIDE #39 LOCATION D

## Aerial View of MP-44 Fissure, Howardville Sand Boil, Lake St. Anne, New Madrid Central High School

We are back in our airplane now. In this view we can see some features already seen before and some new ones not previously shown. In the lower left we see part of the large borrow pit being filled with rice hulls (FG1-2). The levee and railroad track run diagonally from the bottom (G3 to D10) while Interstate 55 angles across the photo left to right (F1-C10). The Mile Post 44 Fissure can be seen in the center (E6-F6) where it passes under the levee and railroad track to emerge on the other side near the bottom center of the photo (G7). We are looking northwest. A mile away, in the distance, you can see New Madrid Central High School—a cluster of circular buildings in the upper right corner (A9). On the upper left we see the town of Howardville (A1-B5). A long wide yellow streak cuts left to right across the corner of Howardville (B3-B6). This is the 25-acre "Howardville Sand Boil"—one of the largest in the NMSZ. In front of New Madrid High School (C8-B8) is a clump of willow trees. They mark the location of old Lake Ste. Anne—an earthquake lake formed by the events of 1811-12. It is dry most of the year now, but temporarily fills with water after a heavy rain. It has no surface outlets. The intermittent waters of the lake soak in and move underground toward the Mississippi under I-55 and under the levee and through the Mile Post 44 Fissure. Lake Ste. Anne is a discontinuous channel like Des Cyprie. Before the earthquakes this was a navigable stream shown as "Gut Ste. Anne" on 18th century maps. "Gut" is a truncated version of an old French word, "Gutiere" meaning "ditch, channel or gutter." The Mile Post 44 Fissure is actually an extension of the old stream channel of Gut Ste. Anne filled by quicksand in 1811-12. The vibrations of heavy traffic on I-55 over this feature causes enough liquefaction (MIL) to pose an ongoing problem with the shoulders and highway here. Imagine a modern highway being damaged today by an earthquake that happened two centuries ago. This is another example of why we say "The earthquake never went away." More on this is found in the book, *The New Madrid Fault Finders Guide,* mentioned on page 216.

## SLIDE #40 LOCATION D

## Howardville Sand Boil (25 Acres) and Lake St. Anne, Aerial View from East

Seismic sand boils are not uncommon to large earthquakes anywhere in the world if soils are sandy and saturated with ground water. But to see one this big is truly rare. Most seismic sand boils are less than 10 feet in diameter. The Howardville Sand Boil seen here (C2-C8) is a world-class champion. The clump of willow trees from right to left (E10-E5) occupy the bed of Lake Ste. Anne—a former stream channel prior to the earthquakes of 1811-12. Gut Ste. Anne was a commercial artery of a complex stream system that connected the Mississippi, the Little, and the St. Francis rivers. Prior to the quakes Spanish keelboats, French pirogues, and Indian canoes traveled along this navigable waterway carrying furs and other items of trade back and forth across the Missouri Bootheel. Just beyond the northwest end of Lake Ste. Anne at D9-D10 in the photo where it passes just west of the Lilbourn Indian Mound (seen in the next photo, Slide #41) there was a ferry. Prior to 1811 people actually paid a ferry toll to cross the spot where Hwy 61 now passes over. There is no trace of a stream there now. It was destroyed by the earthquakes. More on Gut Ste. Anne, its significance to Native Americans, and its destruction in 1811-12 can be read in the other two books of this trilogy—*The Earthquake America Forgot & The New Madrid Fault Finders Guide*—discussed on pages 214 & 216. The New Madrid Central High School is just out of the picture on the right. Let's get back on the ground again, walk across the Howardville Sand Boil, and get a view of the Indian Mound.

## SLIDE #41 — LOCATION D

## Howardville Sand Boil, Large Indian Mound, New Madrid Central High, Lake St. Anne, Ground View

It looks like a desert. Pure sand. No vegetation. And this is just the NE end of the Howardville Sand Boil—about 7 acres of it. The willow trees (D6-D10) mark the location of Lake Ste. Anne situated on the end of the boil. Here, again, we find a high place (the sand boil) next to a low place (the Lake), as is so often the case with extrusive seismic sand features. In the center, behind the willows, is a group of buildings. This is New Madrid Central High School. On the left, where some trees stand, is the "Mound Cemetery" (D1-D4). White folks are buried there. The name of the cemetery comes from a large Indian Mound visible behind the trees (D2-D4). It is known to archeologists as the "Lilbourn Mound." Indians are buried there. Hernando Desoto is thought to have erected a cross on the Lilbourn Mound around 1540. There are also some grave stones on top of the mound where white settlers were buried around the turn of the century. New Madrid Central High School is on the site of an ancient Indian city, abandoned some time before the settlers came from Europe. Many wooden buildings were there, long decayed into dust. For centuries the Mississipian Indians lived, worshiped, farmed, fished, and raised families there. Gut Ste. Anne flowed by the Mound giving them access to the navigable streams of the region which were destroyed in 1811-12. It was a center for Indian commerce for hundreds of miles up and down the Mississippi River—one of the more important Native American settlements of its day. When the site was selected for the new school, historians protested. It was to no avail. Archeologists were allowed to find what they could before construction began. The New Madrid Historical Museum contains many of these artifacts. More than a hundred skeletons were unearthed—bodily remains of previous dwellers in the fault zone. Archeologists were still working when bulldozers moved in to raze the site in preparation for the new buildings. They followed in the tracks of the dozers picking up what final artifacts they could salvage before everything was paved or grassed over. The school was finished in the 1970's.

## SLIDE #42 LOCATION D

## Lake St. Anne, New Madrid Central High, Large Sand Boil Northwest of School, Aerial View

Here's a better view of the New Madrid Central High School property (D5-9)) and the features that surround it. Highway 61 cuts up from the bottom of the picture (G4-5) straight into Howardville (AB-2,3,4,5) and curves out of town behind the strut of our airplane (A1). See the Howardville Sand Boil where it cuts across the corner of town from the strut to Lake St. Anne (D1-4). Mound cemetery lies between the circular school buildings and Howardville (C5). The large Indian Mound is on the east side of the cemetery, adjacent to the school property near the silver water tower (C6). About half a mile to the northwest of the school buildings is a large sand boil (B8). A thin line of trees from the boil southward past the cemetery marks another discontinuous channel, having the appearance of a small stream or ditch, but not going anywhere, having no surface outlets on either end. It is a fragment of old "Gut St. Anne" before the earthquakes stopped its normal flow. When the school was planned in the early 1970's, the people of New Madrid were aware that great earthquakes had struck the region in 1811 and 1812, but that was history. This is the present. No one at that time had effectively translated these historic facts into the realization that "if it happened once, it will happen again." History can and does repeat itself. The school was built at a cost of $5 million. It is a beautiful structure, inside and out. The school cafeteria even has chandeliers, donated by a school benefactor. It could have been seismically designed for the same amount, but it wasn't. New Madrid officials now realize that was a mistake. But at the time these decisions were made, in the early 1970's, earthquake awareness in the Midwest was almost nil. Now we know better, thanks to the tremendous amount of new research and earthquake education since 1985. We can only hope that when the next "Big One" happens, it won't be during school hours.

## SLIDE #43 — LOCATION D

## View of New Madrid Central High From Large Sand Boil Northwest of School, Ground View

This photo looks strangely similar to Slide #41. In both we see a barren sand boil in the foreground, a patch of willows to the right, and the New Madrid High School in the background. Only this time, we are 1/2 mile NW of the school (instead of SW). The boil is soft. You can see our footsteps crossing the sand to where we stand. The water tower with its bulbous silver top can be seen over the trees. The Indian Mound is located through the trees to the right of the tower. The willows actually mark a discontinuous channel, a seismic feature, a former small stream that flowed uninhibited toward the River before 1811. It had a name, "Gut St. Anne." The earthquakes so disturbed its gradients and clogged its channel that it became permanently broken up and unable to flow. If you go to the trees and walk to the right it looks like a normal shallow stream channel, dry most of the year. But if you continue walking, you find that near the Mound cemetery it simply ends, going nowhere. Any water that finds its way into the depression simply soaks into the ground, having no surface outlet. This sand boil is about 5 acres in size. It has an interesting story. In September of 1990 a TV station from St. Louis wanted to fly over the NMSZ and photograph some seismic features. Dr. Stewart was their guide. As they flew around with cameras rolling, the TV Newsman asked if they could land the helicopter and take some ground shots. Dr. Stewart suggested this boil. When the copter touched down, it kept its blades whirling in idle. The vibrations started to induce liquefaction in the ground (MIL). The metal runners upon which the aircraft was resting began to disappear into the sand. No one had gotten out yet. Realizing that the helicopter was sinking, the pilot shouted, "Fasten your seat belts! We're going up!" Again we were reminded, "if a spot was quicksand once, it can become quicksand again, and it doesn't take an earthquake to do it." We never named this feature. Maybe it should be called the "Helicopter Sand Boil."

## SLIDE #44 LOCATION E

## Reelfoot Fault, Site of First Waterfall, and Retrograde River Stretch, Feb. 7, 1812, View Looking North

Now let's leave New Madrid and head for Reelfoot Lake, Tennessee, for a look at the world's most famous earthquake lake. On our way we pass by Bessie's Neck (D1) and Donaldson Point (C2-8). Once again we can look straight up the River toward Island #8 where the water ran backwards in 1812 (D5-9 to C9). We can also take another grand view of the east half of New Madrid Bend (D1 to C4 back to C1). The tiny white spot on the left (C1) at the top of the bend is, you guessed it, the Sinclair Oil Tank Farm at New Madrid, about 12 miles from where we are flying. In the immediate foreground below we see a prison compound (G-4,5,6), a Tennessee Correctional Facility. (We wonder if this penal complex was seismically designed. Who needs a major earthquake that turns into a major jailbreak?) From a point east of the prison farm (G8) the Reelfoot Fault strikes northward straight across the zigzags of the roads and farm boundaries (G8 to D9), straight up the river bank along the east side of Donaldson Point. There are actually a pair of surface faults here. The other one runs along the east edge of Bessie's Neck (D1), slicing northward toward St. John's Bayou on the east side of New Madrid (C2). (See Slide #1.) Together, these two surface faults form a pair with a block of uplifted ground between them bounded by normal faults. This is called a "horst." (See Slide #10.) This horst has a name. (Every horst should have a name, don't you think?) It is called the "Tiptonville Horst," a secondary fault feature associated with the "Lake County Uplift." It is identified on the map on Slide #1. If you imagine the effect of uplifting the Tiptonville Horst (between D1 and D8), noting where the pair of faults cross the Mississippi (at C2 & D8), you can begin to see why the river ran backwards, why two waterfalls were formed, and why waves were thrown over the banks along Donaldson Point (C9) destroying the forestland. And considering that the land sank on the east side of the fault (FG-8,9,10), you can also see part of the reason why Reelfoot Lake (just off the right of the picture) formed.

## SLIDE #45 LOCATION E

## Closer Aerial View of Reelfoot Fault and Stretch Where Mississippi River Ran Backwards

Here we have an excellent aerial view of the Reelfoot Fault. Starting with that odd shaped piece of land at the bottom center (G5) the fault strikes northward to the right of the farm house and barn (D7), across the river and up the east side of Donaldson Point (B8 to A9). Reelfoot Lake and swampland are off the photo to the right. There are two kinds of faults: Primary faults that cause earthquakes and secondary faults that are caused by earthquakes. The Reelfoot Fault is a secondary fault, a surface break in the land caused by the movement of the primary New Madrid Fault deep below. The Reelfoot Fault is a normal fault, moving up on the west and down on the east, with 15 feet difference in elevation (See Slide #10.) The causative fault branch of the New Madrid system (where the quakes originate) lies 2-8 miles below land surface and is a reverse or thrust fault. Here is an example where the motion of the causative fault below does not directly correspond to the relative displacement of the surface fault above. So far, scientists have not yet discovered any surface fault in the NMSZ that has been proven to be a direct upward extension of the any part of the seismically active New Madrid Fault System below. The Bootheel Lineament, discovered by satellite imagery in 1989, may turn out to be the first, but we'll say more about the Bootheel Lineament when we get to Slides #102-#109 and Slide #129.

## SLIDE #46 — LOCATION E

## Ten Mile View of Relationship Between Reelfoot Fault, Town of New Madrid & 8.8 Magnitude Epicenter

Reelfoot Fault strikes straight across this photo (E1 to E10). The fault displacement is down in the foreground and up on the far side. The buildings on the right (D9) are on the high side. Reelfoot Lake is directly behind us. Here is another view of where the River ran backwards (B5-B10), as well as the site of the first waterfall (B2-3). (See Slide #1.) You can see Bessie's Neck on the left (between A1 and B1) with both branches of the Mississippi, one flowing north (B1-4), the other flowing south (A1-5). The Associated Electric Company and smokestack earthquake marker, 10 miles away, can be seen at the top left (A1). The white gleam of the Sinclair Oil Tank Farm at New Madrid, 13 miles away, can be seen at the top right (B9). This photo helps to establish how close New Madrid is to Reelfoot Lake, which is not at all obvious from the ground. They are less than 15 miles apart "as the crow flies." However, the driving distance, via the nearest bridge over the Mississippi, through Caruthersville, Missouri, and Dyersburg, Tennessee, is more than 75 miles. (See Slide #1.) There used to be a ferry between Dorena, Missouri, and Hickman, Kentucky, that shortened the driving distance between New Madrid and Reelfoot. But even by that route, it was over 50 miles. And even though the ferry was a pleasant cruise over the river, and we would highly recommend your taking it if it were still in operation, the ferry route was probably longer time-wise than the 75-mile route through Caruthersville. It is difficult to study a fault zone that passes through parts of five states and crosses one of the world's largest rivers in three places.

## SLIDE #47 LOCATION E

## Ground View of Reelfoot Fault from Downthrown Side Looking West

Now we are on the ground walking toward the Reelfoot Fault. Reelfoot Lake is to our backs, 2-3 miles away. You can see a ridge ahead. This is the top of the fault scarp, 15 feet higher than the field where we are walking. The roof and gable of one of the farm houses noted in the two previous slides can be seen located at the top of the horst. The group shown walking toward the slope of the fault's incline, is an international party on a NMSZ field trip sponsored by the Geological Society of America (GSA) in November, 1989. The trip was led by Dr. Buddy Schweig of Memphis State and Dr. Randy Jipson of the U.S. Geological Survey. We had gotten up pretty early in the morning to get here. The man on crutches was from California, which goes to prove that nothing will stop a dedicated geologist from going to the field to see things for him or herself, even an injured foot.

## SLIDE #48

LOCATION E

## Ground View of Reelfoot Fault from Upthrown Side Looking East, Reelfoot Lake in Distance

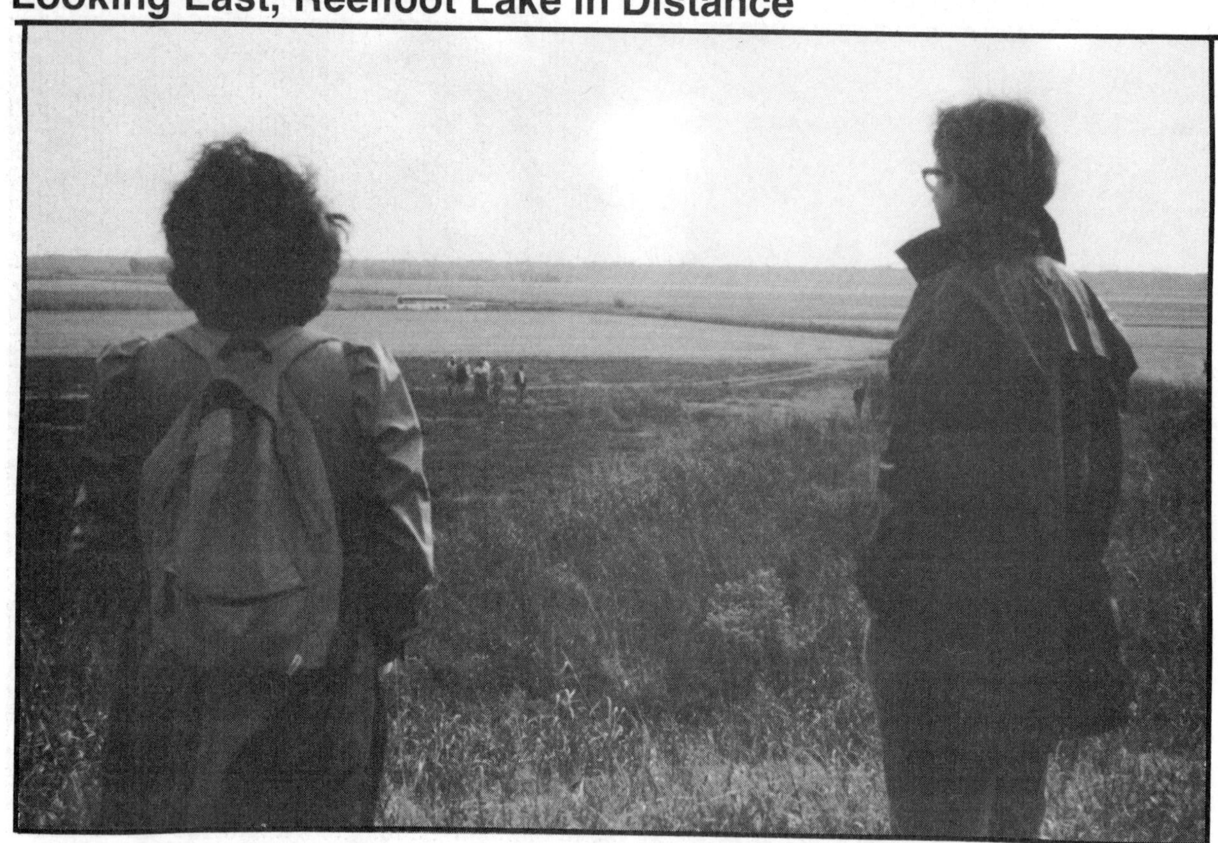

From this vantage point we are standing at the top of the Reelfoot Fault looking east into the Reelfoot Basin. The other side of the fault, where the small group of scientists are standing, is 15 feet lower than we are. Along the horizon, about 6 miles away, we see the line of the Chickasaw Bluffs containing many earthquake landslides, some of which we shall see later in Slides #134-#149. Between us and the bluffs, dimly visible just below the horizon, are the tops of thousands of cypress trees. This marks the location of Reelfoot Lake whose length of more than 16 miles completely spans width of this photo. An old map of Western Tennessee published in 1795 does not show any lake here at that time—only a hardwood forest sprinkled with groves of cypress and a few cypress-lined streams meandering through. So what happened? How did such a huge body of water come to be? Let's board a plane, fly over the lake and take a look.

## SLIDE #49 LOCATION F
## Aerial View of Reelfoot Lake Visitor's Center

Reelfoot Lake covers the top of the photo. The Visitors' Center and Museum can be seen below (D7). Highway 21-22 curves along the lakeside from left to right (B1 – E10). The streets and houses below make up the little town of Blue Bank, Tennessee. Reelfoot is a popular resort area, great for camping, boating, fishing, and exploring. The black-roofed building diagonally across from the Visitors' Center is Boyette's Restaurant (E7). We recommend the catfish, but they serve a great breakfast, too. Notice the numerous green cypress trees along the lake's edge (B1 – D10).Look at the ones projecting into the lake, getting shorter and shorter until they seem to disappear into the water (C10 – A4) It looks like the earth sank and submerged these trees. And that is exactly right. It happened in 1812 with the Great New Madrid Earthquakes. A Tennessee National Guard Armory is located near the lakeshore on the left (between C3 and C4). The Reelfoot Fault is located less than a quarter of a mile in front of the Armory Building which is partially constructed of unreinforced brick. We will need the equipment and manpower of the National Guard in the event of a major earthquake here. The location of this facility is convenient and strategic in a way. But will it still exist after the "Big One" hits? Behind the Reelfoot Lake Visitors' Center is a system of boardwalks over the waters of the lake's edge (CD – 7,8,9). Let's go down and take a walk on the boardwalk.

## SLIDE #50 LOCATION F

## 200-300 Year Old Cypress Trees, Submerged Near Shore in Reelfoot Lake

These cypress trees were here when the great quakes hit in 1811-12. The ground beneath them subsided some, but not much. They have survived well in these shallow waters. As you walk along the boardwalk, take your time and enjoy the peace, the bird songs, the wind whispers, the frogs talking, and look for turtles sunning themselves on fallen limbs. There is a fascinating Indian legend at least partially true about the formation of Reelfoot Lake and how it drowned the wedding party of Chief Reelfoot (a Chickasaw) who had broken tradition by marrying "Laughing Eyes," a beautiful maiden of a rival tribe (Choctaw). Native Americans had long known that this area was an active seismic zone. Some tribes had preserved a verbal account of a previous sequence of great quakes in this area that must have equaled the magnitudes of those of 1811-12 that occurred about a hundred years before Columbus discovered America. The Shawnee name for the region of the New Madrid Fault is "Wabukeegu," which translates as "ground that shakes." The New Madrid earthquakes of 1811-12 drove out the Native Americans, but their numbers had already been reduced before the settlers came. When the first Spanish explorer, Hernando Desoto, passed through the fault zone about 1540 A.D. he brought European diseases which had already decimated the Indian population long before the migrations of the settlers had become significant. Ironically, Desoto, himself, never got back to Spain—dying on the banks of the Mississippi of a sickness he and his men has brought with them from abroad. These stories are told in great detail in the book, *The Earthquake America Forgot*, mentioned on page 214.

## SLIDE #51 LOCATION F

## Old Cypress Trees in Deeper Water, Submerged During Formation of Reelfoot Lake in 1811-12

Look at that solitary cypress in deep water. It is a stunted survivor of the great cataclysms of 1811-12. Focus in the distance where the Chickasaw bluffs make a thin blue strand across the horizon. Sit awhile, feel the breeze brush against your face, and study the calm waters. Maybe you'll see a fish jump. As you can see in the previous photo and those that follow, the trunks of the trees are enlarged at the base in a unique way characteristic of the baldcypress (Taxodium distichum). Under normal circumstances, the enlarged base or "buttress" is at ground level. But these cypress trees are not situated in normal circumstances. Cypress cannot germinate under water and even though they like wet, swampy conditions, their sprouting requires dry or semi-dry land at least part of the year. Hence, every baldcypress tree seen here in deep perennial waters predates the earthquakes of 1811-12, even though some are rather small—stunted by their submergence. What is interesting is that enlarged trunks are now seen at the water level of the lake on these submerged trees. These are called "flying buttresses." In the decades following the earthquake the trees, which already had a buttress at the soil line, grew another buttress at the water line. Hence, these "earthquake trees" in deep water all have double buttresses. If you go out to one of them in a boat you can reach under the flying buttress with your paddle—good places for fish to hide and for you to catch them!

## SLIDE #52 LOCATION F

## Old Cypress Trees in Even Deeper Water, Submerged During Formation of Reelfoot, 1811-12

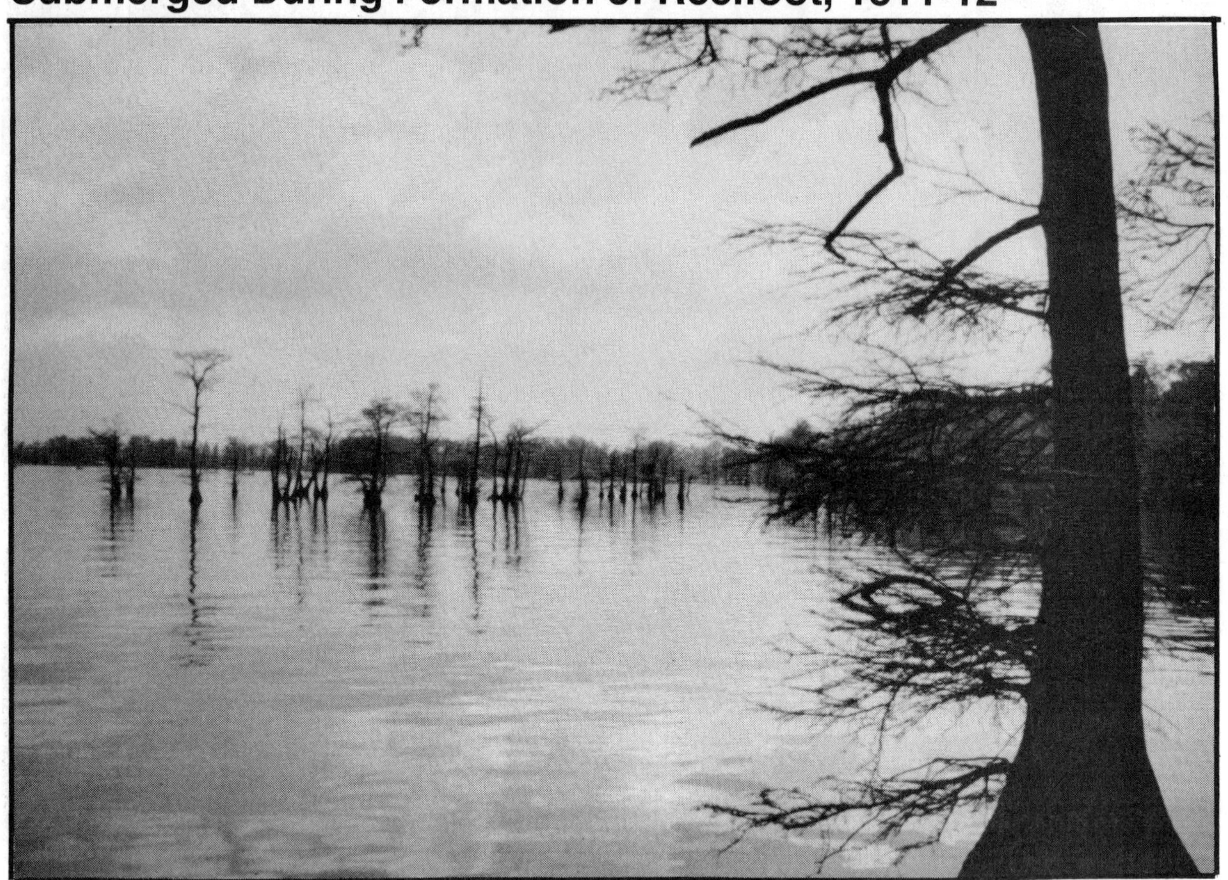

Here you can see some more partially submerged survivors of the earthquakes. These cypress trees have been stunted, but still live. Their neighbors, however, have long since drowned. Victims of the earthquakes. From a boat you can see the dead remains of their stumps lying just below the surface of the lake, peering through the waters in murky silence, full of stories to tell, but mute, unable to speak. Reelfoot Lake is a graveyard of these stumps, tens of thousands of them. Only shallow-draft boats can navigate these waters. Boats with moters must keep their propellers high, just below the lake's surface. Enjoy the delicate pinks and blues reflected in the rippled waters from the sky above in this tranquill scene and meditate for a while. Consider the awesome life-and-death forces of nature that gave birth to this enchanting lake and created the haunting scenery that surrounds it. Major earthquakes can bring death, but also life. There was destruction with the Great New Madrid Earthquakes, but also rebirth. Reelfoot Lake exemplifies both: The death of a cypress wilderness. The birth of a living lake.

## SLIDE #53 LOCATION F
## Fishermen in Boat, Reelfoot Lake, Fall 1990

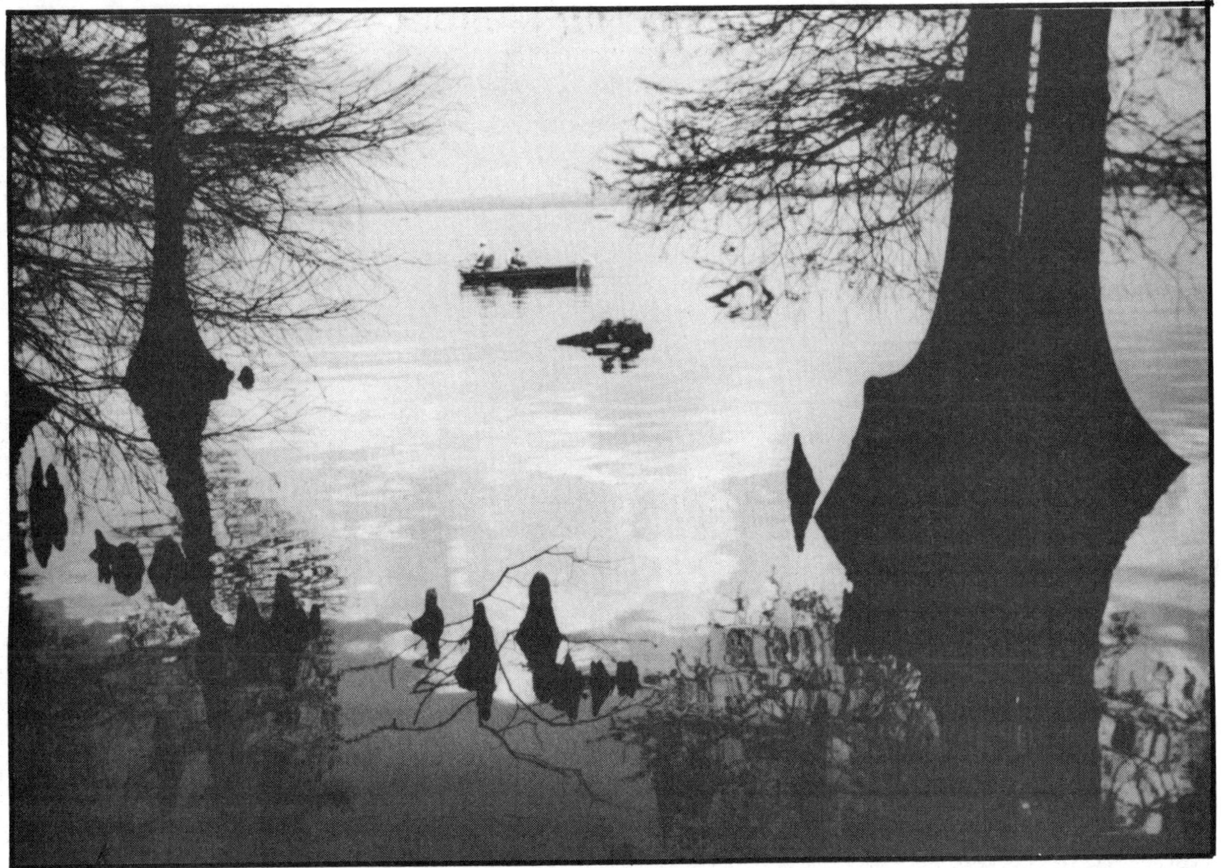

Fishermen love Reelfoot Lake. Several world champion fish have been caught here. This man and his wife are enjoying an early morning of calm on the lake. Reelfoot is not a place to rush. If you come here, set aside ample time for a relaxed visit. You can easily spend several hours in the Visitors' Center and Museum, alone. And on the lake, itself, you could spend a whole vacation. Many people have bought summer cabins or have retired here to live the year round. The shaking of the Great New Madrid Earthquakes stopped long ago, but the impact goes on. Some of that impact is good. Earthquakes are not all bad. They create beautiful scenery, natural harbors, majestic mountains, picturesque islands, flowing springs, fertile soils, high ground and panoramic river views on great rivers like New Madrid Bend, and wonderful recreational lakes like Reelfoot. This book (and slide set) are about the consequences of the Great New Madrid Earthquakes that "never went away." Of course, most of the consequences of these great quakes have already disappeared, and much that remains today will be gone tomorrow. But Reelfoot Lake, we hope, will last a long, long time for many future generations to enjoy.

## SLIDE #54 LOCATION F
## Large Sand Boils at South End of Reelfoot Lake

According to one theory, Reelfoot Lake began to form during the great 8.4 magnitude earthquake of January 23, 1812, when some huge sand boils dammed Reelfoot Creek. This started an impondment that eventually became a permanent lake when on February 7, 1812, the whole area subsided and sank, blocked by the Reelfoot Fault on one side. The original water surface of the lake was almost 20 miles long and 5 miles wide, almost 100 square miles or 64,000 acres. It's a shallow lake, maximum depth about 20 feet. Today it has silted in to an area about 16 miles long and 4 miles wide, or 41,000 acres, less than two thirds its original size. About one-third of the former lake is now swampy forestland, but it is still a huge and impressive body of water. And to think it formed precipitously by an earthquake! In this photo we are standing on the edge of two huge sand boils on the south end of the lake along Highway 21-22. Could it be that these are the culprits that started it all on January 23, 1812?

## SLIDE #55 Aerial View of Submerged Cypress Forest, Central Portion of Reelfoot Lake

LOCATION F

Now we are back in the air at an altitude of about 1,000 feet above the center portion of Reelfoot Lake. You can see from here that the water is shallow and that the cypress forest stands in water a few feet deep.

## SLIDE #56 — LOCATION F
## High Altitude View of Flooded Cypress Forest, Reelfoot Lake, Tennessee

Here we have climbed to an altitude of 5,000 feet. We are one mile above Reelfoot Lake. From this vantage point the scene looks like an area under current flooding conditions. As a matter of fact, that is exactly what we are looking at except that the flood started almost 200 years ago and never subsided.

## SLIDE #57 LOCATION G

## High Altitude View of Flooded Cypress Forest, Big Lake, Arkansas

Here we are flying high over flooded cypress again. It may look similar to Reelfoot Lake, but it is not. We are in Arkansas looking northward toward the Missouri state line along the sole of the Bootheel. This is Big Lake, another earthquake lake formed on December 16, 1811, the first day of the Great New Madrid Earthquake series. It's not as famous as Reelfoot, but it was just as big. When it formed it was around 20 miles long and 5 miles wide, about 100 square miles or 64,000 acres in water surface, the same as the original size of Reelfoot. Now it has shrunk to less than half its original size, partly because of natural silting in, but largely due to engineered drainage systems. The white line wandering from the bottom center off to the left is a siltation control levee. As in Reelfoot, this view looks like we are flying over a flooded area with trees temporarily standing in the water. It is a flood, all right, but one that happened back in 1811 and never went away.

## SLIDE #58 LOCATION G
## Aerial View of Big Lake Visitor's Center

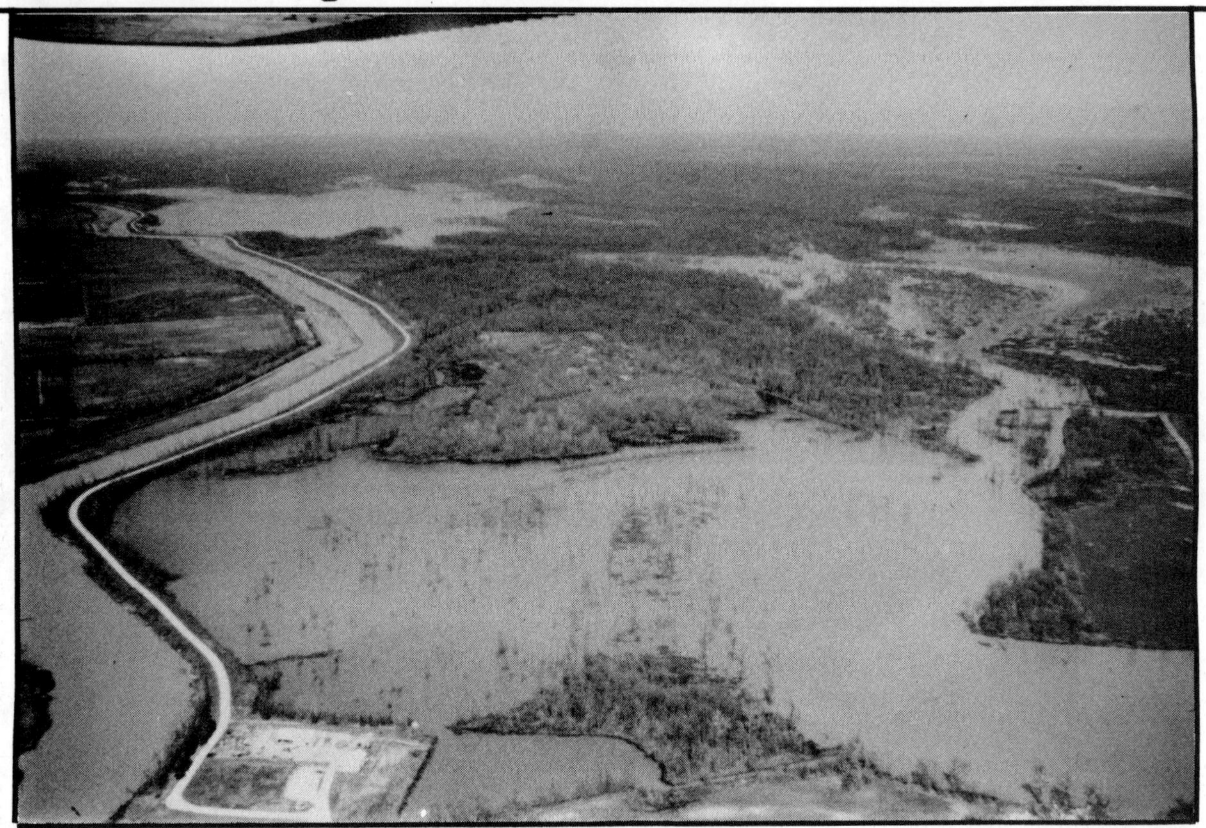

This is another view of the south end of Big Lake, Arkansas, looking north. The land along the horizon is in Missouri, about 12 miles away. The cluster of buildings in the lower left is the Big Lake Visitor's Center, a facility of the State of Arkansas. Winding along the left you see a major drainage canal and levee with a gravel road along the top. This is called the "Main Ditch," the principal channel by which the Bootheel of Missouri is drained into Arkansas and, eventually, into the Mississippi River. As you can see, most of the water that would naturally flow into Big Lake now bypasses on the west side.

## SLIDE #59 LOCATION G

## Old Cypress Submerged During Formation of Big Lake, The First Great New Madrid Earthquake, December 16, 1811

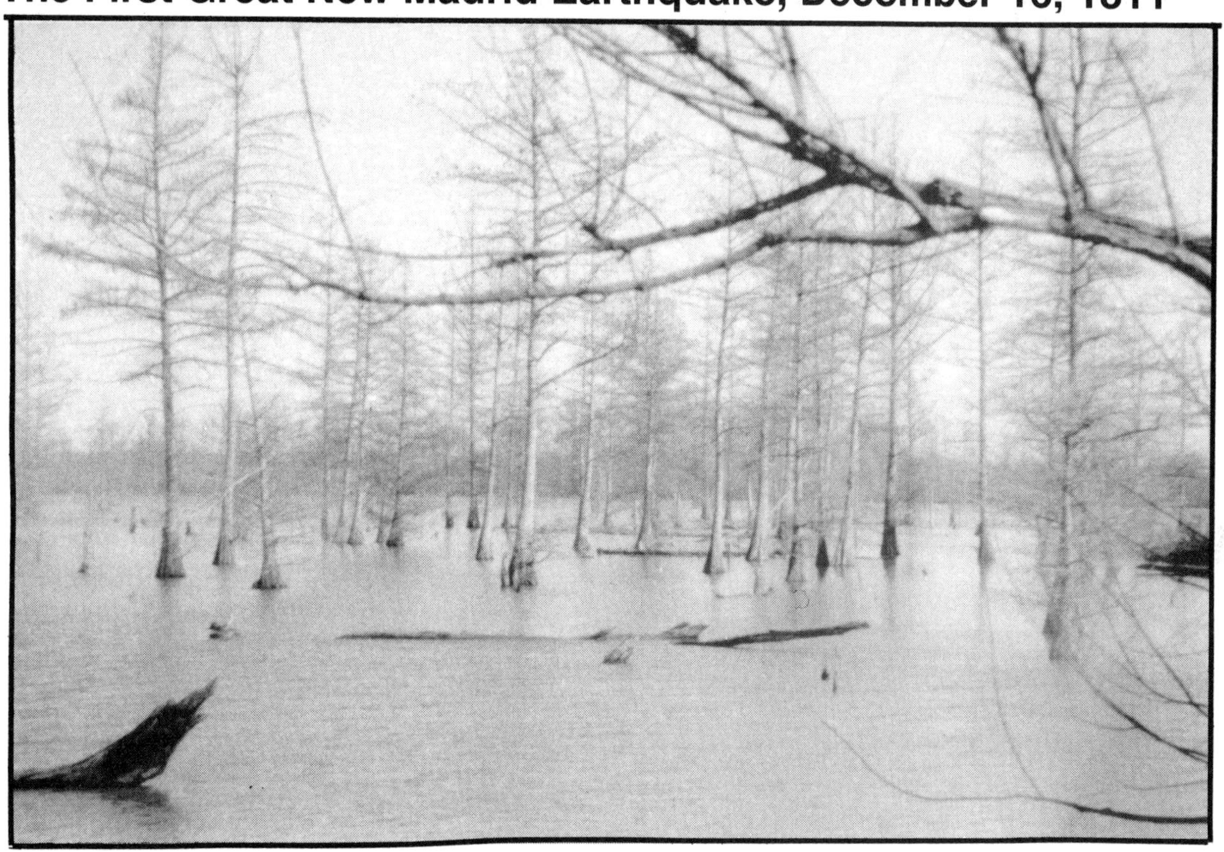

This scene could be mistaken for some of the scenes along the shore of Reelfoot Lake, but, again, we are in Arkansas on the shore of Big Lake. We are standing just north of the Big Lake Visitors' Center in this photo. The water is less than 10 feet deep here. Big Lake and Reelfoot Lake were not the only lakes created by the New Madrid Earthquakes, but they are the only ones that still remain as perennial lakes. The others have all been drained for farmland, as has been the upper portion of Big Lake that lies on the Missouri side of the state line. There were at least six other earthquake lakes. Most lasted for more than 100 years, having been drained only since 1918. The next largest of these lakes was Lake Nicormy, between Kennett and Hayti, Missouri. Lake Nicormy was about 3 miles wide and almost 10 miles long. (See Slide #1.) The southernmost of the earthquake lakes was Lake Tyronza, east of Marked Tree, Arkansas. The northernmost lake was Lake St. John, between Sikeston and Benton, Missouri. (See Slide #1.) It was drained around 1920 via St. John's Ditch which runs south along the east side of Sikeston Ridge and into the Mississippi River at St. John's Bayou near New Madrid.

## SLIDE #60 LOCATION G

## Isolated Cypress Submerged in Deep Water During Formation of Big Lake, December 16, 1811

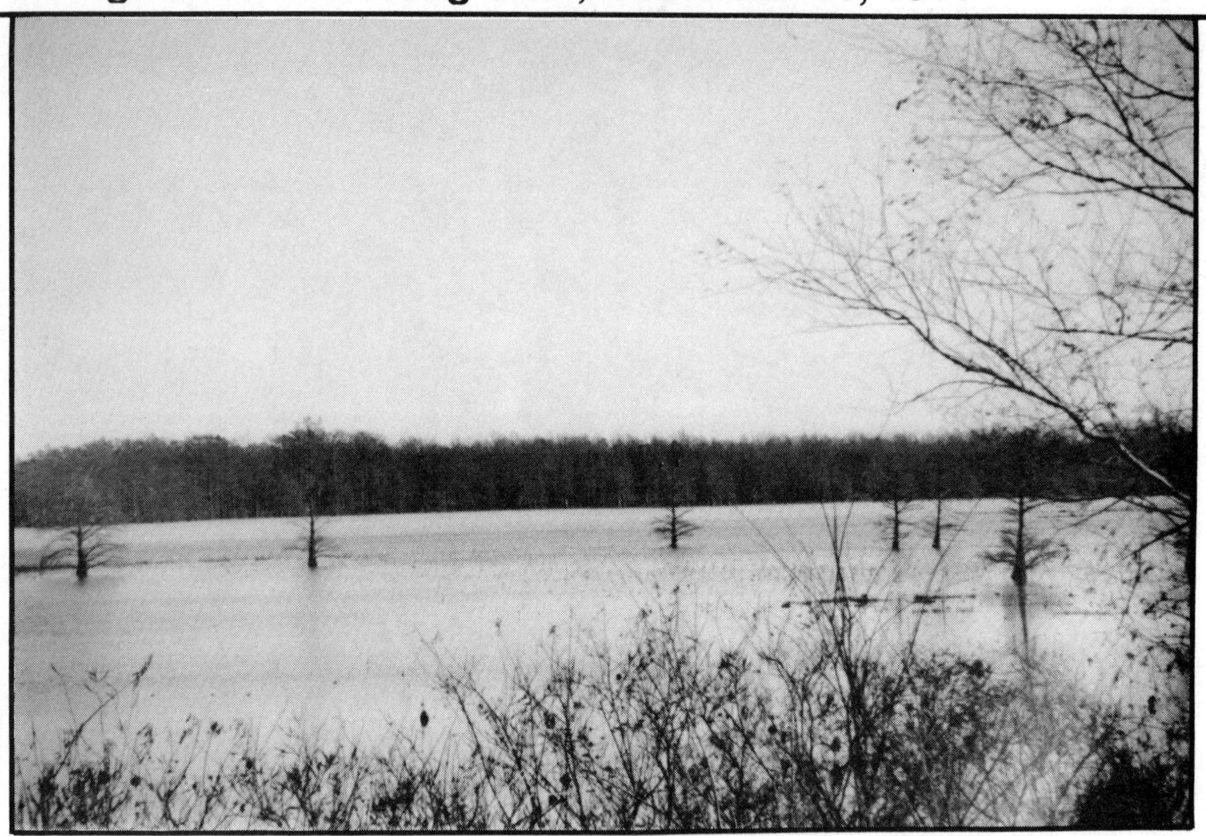

Most of the cypress were drowned in this area of Big Lake. However, just like in Reelfoot, a few survived the deep water, as you can see here. These trees don't look big enough to be several centuries old, but they have been stunted in their growth by the seismic inundation of 1811. They are lucky to still be alive. Today eagles build nests in the tops of some of these trees. In fact, there are two bald eagles barely visible sitting in the top of the tree just right of center in this photo. Look closely and you will see two white dots (their heads) with black forms below (their bodies). Big Lake is a wildlife refuge, like Reelfoot, where eagles and other endangered species can live in security and multiply. If you visit either Big Lake or Reelfoot Lake, perhaps you will be fortunate enough to see some of these majestic, winged monarchs in their natural habitat, a refuge provided today because of an earthquake of yesterday.

## SLIDE #61 LOCATION G

## Man and Boy Fishing, South End of Big Lake, Arkansas, Numerous Stumps of Dead Cypress

Fishing is good at Big Lake. Here we see a man and his young boy fishing together on the south end of Big Lake, just off of Highway 18, between Blytheville and Manila. In the distance you can see hundreds of cypress stumps sticking out of the water, the remains of trees killed in 1811. But yesterday's loss of a forest is today's legacy of a lake, another gift of the Great New Madrid Earthquakes.

## SLIDE #62 LOCATION G

## Sand Boils in Manila, Arkansas, Big Lake in Background And Blytheville, Arkansas, in Distance, Aerial View

Manila, Arkansas, is spread out before you in this photo. Notice the numerous sand boil features still visible in the undeveloped portions of town. These seismic features actually underlie the whole town. You just don't see them because they have been covered by turf, pavement and buildings. A part of Big Lake can be seen in the background. The white spot in the upper right corner is the city of Blytheville, Arkansas, 15 miles to the east.

## SLIDE #63 LOCATION G

## Unusual Sand Fissure/Sand Boil Patterns Around Farm West of Big Lake, Arkansas

Look at the interesting sand fissure patterns around this farmhouse and old brick building. Can you imagine the boiling and surging of the ground here during the earthquakes? We are now located about 7 miles north of Manila and 7 miles east of Leachville, Arkansas. The "Main Ditch" that drains the Missouri Bootheel and bypasses Big Lake runs across the top of the photo from left to right. Big Lake is located just to the other side, seen as forested swampland and a few patches of blue water. The white spot in the upper left corner is the city of Blytheville, again, still about 15 miles away to the east.

## SLIDE #64 LOCATION G

## Closer View of Unusual Sand Fissure/Sand Boil Patterns Around Farm West of Big Lake, Arkansas

Now we have zoomed in on the same farm and brick building seen in the previous photo. The turmoil of those great cataclysms of 1811-12 is even more evident in this closer view. Notice that these features have a prevailing SW to NE direction. This could have been due to seismic standing wave patterns during the earthquakes, harmonics caused by reflections from special configurations of geologic and tectonic structures in the earth beneath. A set of standing waves lasting 2-3 minutes could set up fissure patterns like these through which sand ejections could occur. These are speculations. There are a number of hypotheses that might explain what you see here, all awaiting adequate research.

## SLIDE #65 LOCATION G

## Complex Sand Fissure Patterns West of Big Lake

Continuing northward, along the west side of Big Lake, Arkansas, we spot some more interesting seismic sand features below. Notice that they seem to be oriented in two "preferred" directions. "Criss-cross" pairs of "preferred" fissure directions can be found in many places within the NMSZ. Does this mean more than one earthquake caused them?

## SLIDE #66 LOCATION G

## Sand Boils on Arkansas-Missouri State Line Between Manila, Arkansas & Hornersville, Missouri

We are now crossing the Arkansas-Missouri state line (G4-A6) south of Arbyrd and Hornersville, Missouri. We are a mile or two west of Big Lake. Notice how the State Line Road is smeared by a sand boil in the upper center of the picture (A6). As you drive down the country road that runs from left to right, from Missouri into Arkansas, you will notice that the Missouri and Arkansas sides do not quite line up. There is a slight bend to bring the two state roads together. On the ground, as you drive by the big tree on your right (going south) and enter Arkansas on this road, you will be struck by the sight of an enormous sand boil on the west side of the road more than 500 feet long (E6-E10). Maybe the reason the Arkansas end of the road jogs to the east here is to avoid the sand boil.

## SLIDE #67 LOCATION G

## Large Sand Boils North of Hornersville, Missouri, With Big Lake Swamp in Background, Aerial View

Big Lake is seen across the top of this photo. The "Main Ditch" crosses from left to right along the edge of the Big Lake Swamp. We are now a few miles north of Hornersville, Missouri, looking east. Look at the huge linear sand boil extending from the center of the picture to the right. And notice the spiral sand feature on the left.

## SLIDE #68 LOCATION H

## Sand Boil by Roadside in Bean Field Near Monette, Arkansas, Showing Distressed Crop Growth

Sand boils do not support crops very well. There are few nutrients and sand doesn't hold water. Here we are in a soybean field in northeastern Arkansas near Monette. The beans sprouted in the spring, but here in late June, after a couple of dry spells, the beans that were planted in sand have wilted and all but disappeared. Spots with stunted or missing crops can be seen on seismic sand features in fields throughout the New Madrid Seismic Zone.

## SLIDE #69 LOCATION H

## Sand Boils by Fence & Tree Row in Bean Field Near Monette, Arkansas, Showing Distressed Crop Growth

Here we have another bean field in late June, only a few miles from the one we just saw. Here we see a sand boil in the foreground with stunted bean plants, starved for both water and nutrition. In the distance, along the fence row, you can see another area where the bean plants are distressed and short. This is another sand boil. At certain times of the year, you can spot sand boils by growth patterns of the crops. In the wet spring when crops are first planted, the seeds sprout in the good soil and sand alike, making it impossible to spot seismic sand features. But when the summer heat comes and precipitation becomes less, whatever is rooted in sand stops growing or wilts. Farmers do not like these features because of their unproductivity. But they always seed and plant them to reduce the problem of wind erosion. High winds pick up the dry sand, blow it across the ground about an inch high, and cut off young, tender newly-sprouted crops at base of their stems. Wind blown sand is highly abrasive, sawing like a serrated knife. In some areas of the NMSZ where seismic sand features are abundant, power companies have to wrap wooden telephone poles with metal to keep the sand from wearing them away at their bases.

## SLIDE #70 LOCATION I

## Sand Boil Acres, More than 1,000 Boils Per Square Mile Epicentral Area of First Great NM Quake, December 16, 1811

More than 1,000 sand boils per square mile! That's what you are looking at now. We are flying on the east side of Big Lake, just south of the Arkansas-Missouri state line, a few miles west of Blytheville. This is thought to be the epicentral region of the first Great New Madrid Earthquake, at 2:30 a.m. on December 16, 1811. There are no towns in this region, only a few widely scattered farm houses. The distance between the roads on either side of the center fields is one quarter of a mile. You can count about 70 boils in the quarter-mile, 40-acre section you see below. There are sixteen such areas in a square mile, which adds up to more than 1,000 boils per square mile. The boils you can still see today in this area range in size from 15 to 80 feet in diameter. At the time of the temblor dozens of smaller ones were also there, boiling away, long since obscured by the disc and plow. Notice the left-to-right zone just above the center of the photo. It is conspicuous because it has no visible boils. Ground motion during the earthquake was probably as severe in this "boil-free" zone as it was all around it. The reason for the lack of boils may be because little or no boil-making sand exists near the surface here. Who knows? Field research in the NMSZ always seems to pose more questions than answers. From the mottled appearance of this land, you can imagine how the earth must have tossed, tumbled, seethed and churned during that cataclysm, like waves on a turbulent sea. And along with the boiling sand imagine copious discharges of ground water gushing and spewing forth, temporarily flooding the land before the waters could run off into the newly formed Big Lake. Add to that chaos the sounds of gurgling, hissing, exploding fluids and gases rushing from the ground accompanied by the screams of desperate wildlife, the roar of the earth like a growling drumhead, and the smells and fumes of rotted organic matter released from their ancient burial cells. Some day, it will happen again.

## SLIDE #71 LOCATION I

## Sand Boils in Wheat Field Near Gosnell, Arkansas, Between Big Lake & Blytheville, Arkansas

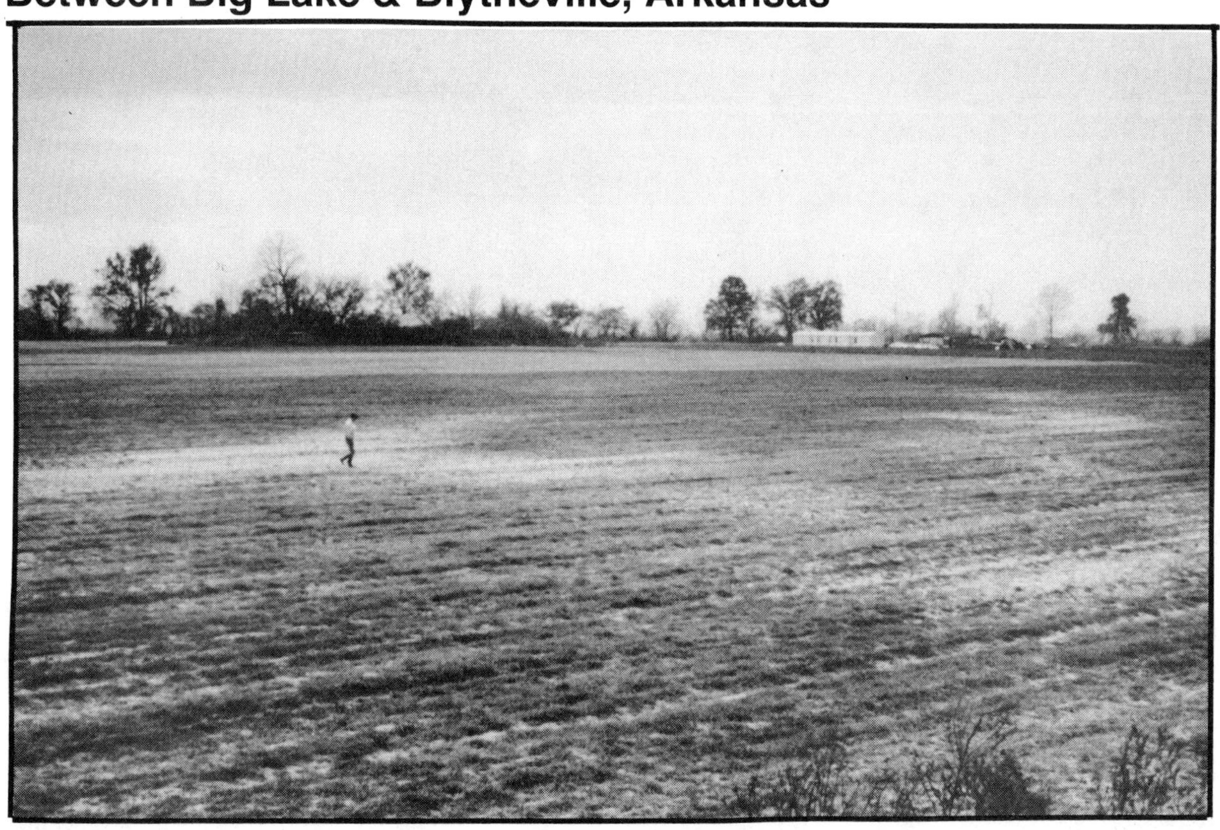

Standing on the edge of the State Line Ditch looking south into Arkansas, we are looking across a field of newly-sprouted winter wheat. We are still in the same area as the last slide, the epicentral region of the first great quake, the 8.6 magnitude event of December 16, 1811. The sand boils we saw from the air in the last slide look like this from the ground. Now let's climb down into the drainage ditch and look at a sand boil from the side in sectional view.

## SLIDE #72 LOCATION I

## Sectional View of Sand Boil in Side of Drainage Ditch Showing a Small Secondary Fault

Now we are standing in the bottom of the State Line Drainage Ditch looking at the Arkansas side. In the grass and weeds you see along the top (A3 – B10) is where we were standing when we took the previous photograph of the field of winter wheat. The top layer of light-colored soil is the plow zone, the surface of agricultural tillage for almost a hundred years (B1 – C10). There may also be some Mississippi River flood sediments deposited since 1812 in this top layer (B1 – C10). On the extreme left, the next layer is a light grey sand (BCDE1-5) with a layer of dark clay below (EFG1). Follow the top of the dark clay layer from left to right to the center of the photo (E1 – E6). Notice that at this point the dark layer has a discontinuity, jumping up about 5 feet (E6 – C6) and then continues to the end of the excavation (C6 – C7). This is a little secondary fault. The dark clay layer used to be continuous at the higher level. During earthquakes of 1811-12 the clay layer broke, and the left end sank down five feet while sand boiled through the breach (E6 – C6) in the clay layer creating a sand boil on top (BCDE1-5). We are looking at a side view of a sand boil (sand over clay) with a plow zone and recent flood deposits on top. The secondary "fault zone" in the clay is the vent by which this sand boil was supplied from beneath. In fact, before the quake the sand was under the clay. After the quake the clay on the left was under the sand. The clay is denser and heavier than the sand so that when the earthquake broke the clay layer and liquefied the sand below, a combination of gravity and seismic ground motion caused the clay to sink into the liquefied sand, displacing the sand and forcing it up through the vent as a sand boil on the surface. The clay and sand literally traded places during the earthquakes. What was on top (the denser clay) went to the bottom. What was underneath (the less dense sand) flowed out on top. Let's take a closer look at the little fault zone and supply vent.

## SLIDE #73 LOCATION I

## Sectional View of Sand Boil Supply Vent Showing Flow Lines & a Secondary Fault Displacement

We are standing a few feet back from the vertical wall of the State Line Ditch looking at where the clay layer observed in the previous slide broke. Here, in the lower left, you can clearly see where the dark clay layer sank down five feet below its former elevation, as evidenced by the undisturbed dark horizon on the right. The squares of white string mark square meters of area. In the "faulted zone" between the offset clay layers you can see the flow features of the liquefied sand that gushed through the break. Little pieces of wood, limonite, clay bits, lignite, pea gravel, and other materials are also carried into the sand boil by the force of the flowing sand. See how it curves upward and deflects to the left. Most of the sand boil is to the left, but some lapped over the top of the high side of the fault on the right, too. This seismic feature shows up clearly in the side of this drainage ditch. There are hundreds of miles of drainage ditches in southeast Missouri and northeast Arkansas. They are probably all lined with numerous faults, fissures, vents, dikes, sills, and sand boils. But don't expect to climb down into just any ditch and see features as clearly as this one. Weeds and the smearing effect of runoff flowing down the sides of the ditch almost completely hide these features unless you dig with a bulldozer and shovel, as has been done here. Even then, the clarity of visibility lasts only until the next heavy rain. The arduous work of excavating this site was carried out in 1989 by S.G. Wesnousky and other researchers from Memphis State University, Center for Earthquake Research & Information. This exposure was viewed by an international group of geologists, seismologists, and engineers on a field trip sponsored by the Geological Society of America in November, 1989.

## SLIDE #74 LOCATION J

## Sectional View of Seismic Sand Sill and Supply Vent In Side of Drainage Ditch Near Dudley, Missouri

Here is another sectional view of a seismic feature exposed in a drainage ditch. Only this time we are more than 50 miles north of the State Line Ditch shown in the last photo. We are west of Dexter, Missouri, near Dudley. (See Location Map in Slide #1.) Across the ditch (in the center of the photo) we see a seismic sand sill and its supply vent, an intrusive seismic feature (See Slide #8 for a diagram of a sill.) Let's wade across and take a closer look, but walk carefully. At certain times of the year the banks and bottoms of these ditches become easily liquefiable. You don't want to sink up to your knees in quicksand. In fact, when the water table is high in the vicinity of a ditch, you can jump up and down in certain places in these canals and induce liquefaction and sand boiling. Jump up and down several times and the soil can get mushy, rippling like a water bed. Pretty soon, a few seconds after you stop jumping, you will see water starting to seep through in a few places followed with flowing grains of sand and pieces of floating lignite or carbonized wood. You can then actually see a miniature sand boil in action. The boiling can continue for 10-15 minutes after you have stopped jumping. The vibrations of an earthquake causes liquefaction in much the same way as vibrations caused by a person jumping, except on a much larger scale.

## SLIDE #75 LOCATION J

## Closer Look at Sectional View of Seismic Sand Sill In Side of Drainage Ditch Near Dudley, Missouri

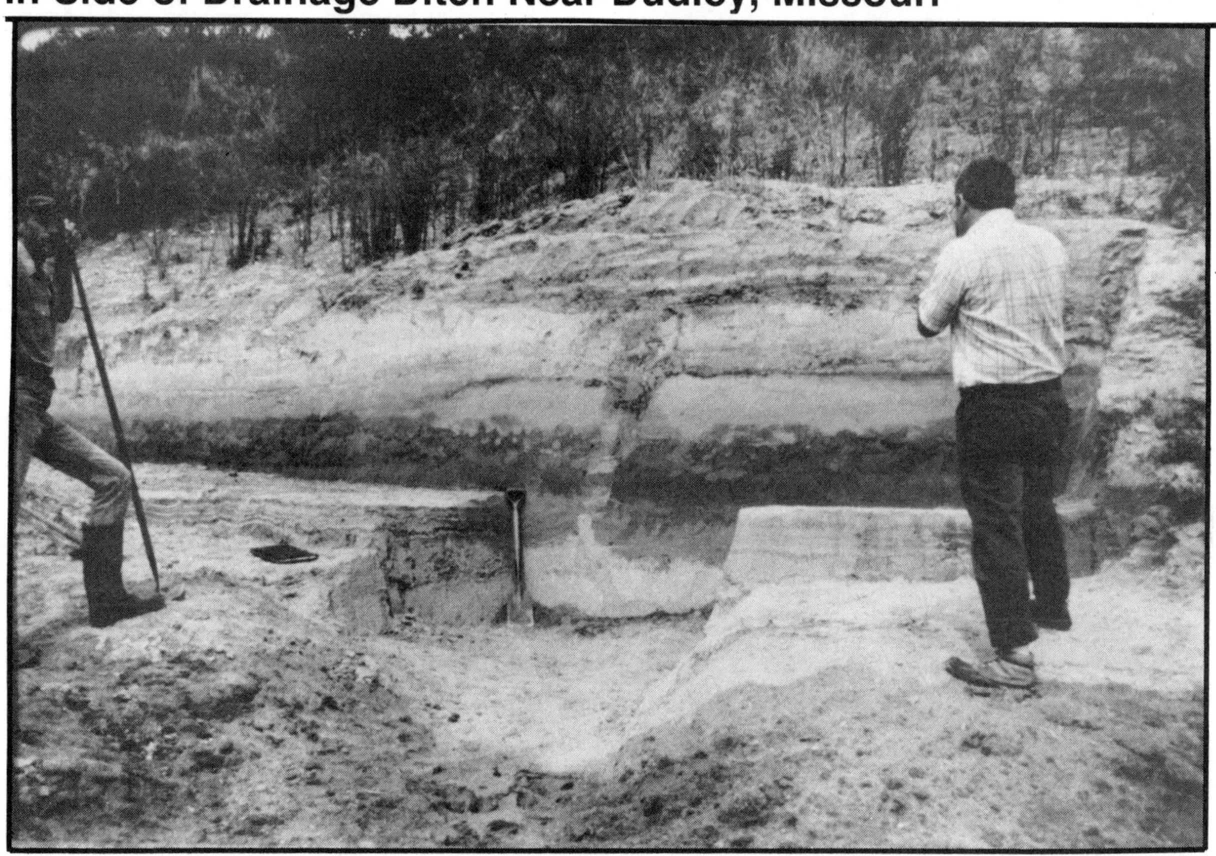

The sand sill and its supply vent are clearly visible here. You can get an idea of the scale of this feature by comparing it with the men standing by. Sectional views of sand boils and sand sills are similar. (See Slides #7 & #8.) The difference is that the boil was extruded out onto the top of the ground surface while the sill was intruded in between two horizontal layers below land surface. Sills are buried features. They cannot be seen from above. They can only be seen in side view, like this one. The age of this seismic feature has not yet been definitely determined. The evidence suggests that it is much older than 1811-12. In fact, it may be centuries older or, perhaps, even more than a thousand years older. This means that great earthquakes like the sequence of 1811-12 have happened in the New Madrid Seismic Zone before. Other lines of research have suggested a repeat interval or 500-700 years. Furthermore, the size of this sill and the numerous other seismic features around the Dudley, Missouri, area suggest that the epicentral region of former great earthquakes in the NMSZ may be different than the one for 1811-12. In 1811-12, the active part of the fault zone seemed to be along the river, 25 miles east of here. The feature in this slide, and others nearby, could mean that when they were created, a western branch of the New Madrid Fault Zone was the cause, a branch relatively inactive and unknown today. Now let's climb up the bank and take an even closer look at this ancient record of a great earthquake.

## SLIDE #76 LOCATION J

## Close Up View of Supply Vent to Seismic Sand Sill With Jim Vaughn, Geologist

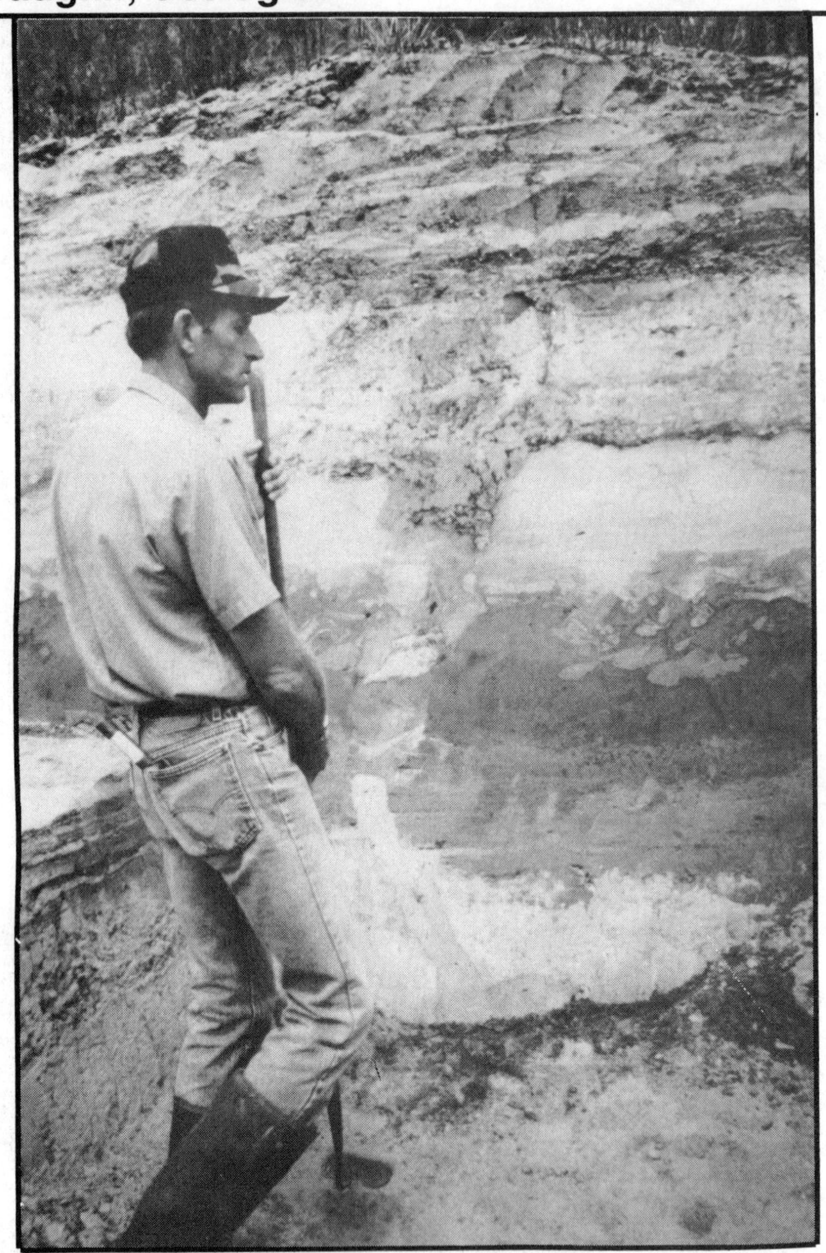

See how the supply vent bores upward through light grey soil, then a dark clay layer, and then through a light yellow layer before it then spreads laterally between a pair of layers. Notice that the material flowing through the vent into the sill deposit is not homogeneous. Several colors of fine material are seen here, as well as bits and pieces of clay, rock and other natural inclusions. The geologist who did all the hard work of excavating the side of this ditch and discovered this seismic sand sill is Jim Vaughn, seen standing here with the hoe. He is a scientist with the Missouri Division of Geology and Land Survey. His research here was by way of a grant from the U.S. Geological Survey (USGS). The man in the two previous slides was a representative of the USGS from Reston, Virginia. This photo, the last two and the next one, were all taken in August of 1991.

## SLIDE #77

LOCATION J

## Sectional View of Seismic Sand Dike In Side of Drainage Ditch Near Dudley, Missouri

On the other side of the ditch viewed in the three previous slides we find a seismic sand dike. This intrusive feature is where a crack below the earth's surface starting breaking vertically with liquefied sand flowing upward as it broke. However, before it cracked all the way to the surface, the earthquake was over. You can see where the top of this intrusion of sand just stops near the top of the photo. Notice that sand is not the only thing carried upward in these features. Chunks of clay, roots, rocks, coal, wood and other natural items are also floated upward with the fluid sand. Some of the organic materials found in these liquefaction features can be used to determine the approximate dates of the earthquakes that caused them. If this sand dike had continued to the surface, then it would have become a supply vent for a sand boil. If it would have separated two horizontal layers and intruded in between them, then it would have become the supply vent for a sand sill. (Slides #7 & #8.) At some future time, another great earthquake could reactivate this feature, causing it to break upward to the surface and form a sand boil or sand fissure. Seismic sand features, once formed, always retain the potential for future liquefaction and reactivation. One wonders how many surface features extruded during the 1811-12 series of earthquakes came from the reactivation of hidden intrusive features of previous strong quakes. It seems that each major earthquake leaves unfinished morphoseismic business to be completed by the next one. The seismic reworking and remolding of the land surface in the NMSZ is never finished. Each new quake adds to the work of previous ones, on and on forever. This sand dike, like the sill seen earlier, was discovered by Jim Vaughn of the Missouri Division of Geology and Land Survey, who also carried out the hard work of excavation to expose it.

**SLIDE #78** LOCATION K

## Witness Tree (300-Year-Old Red Oak) in 1811-12 Sand Boil With Virginia Carlson, Director, New Madrid Historical Museum

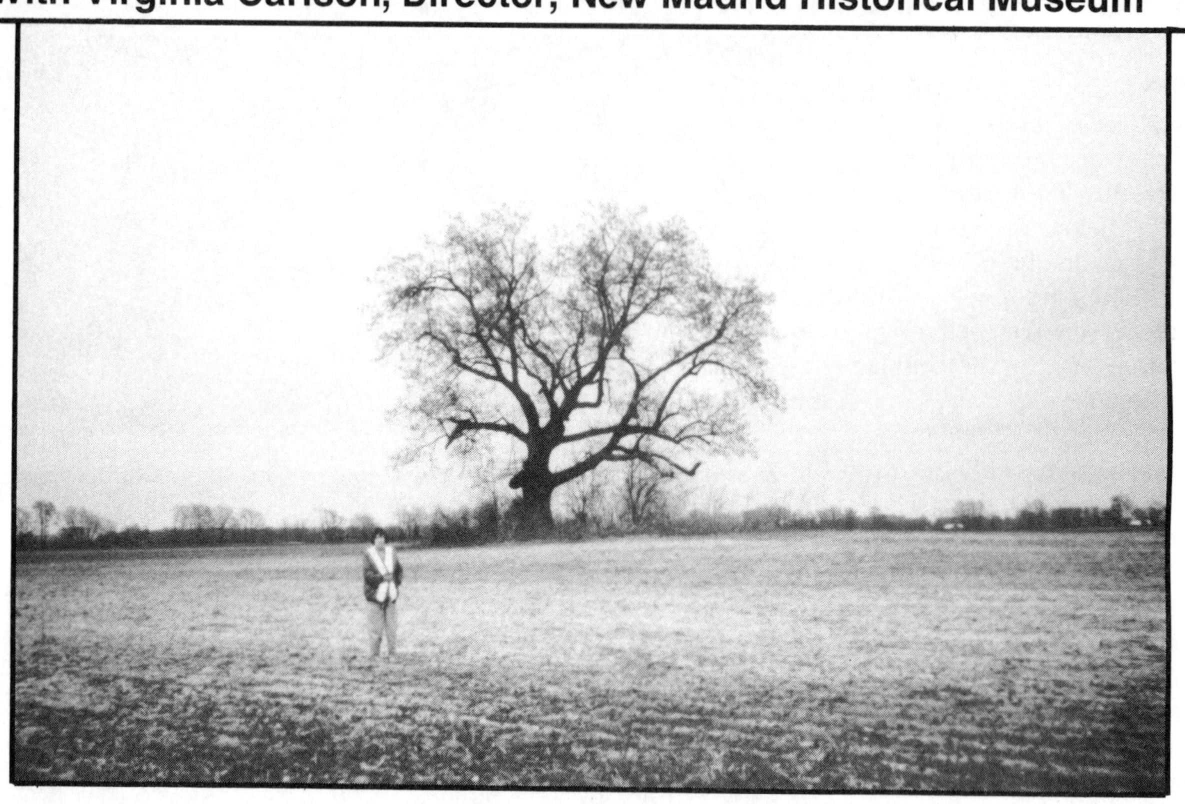

Kewanee, Missouri, is where we are now (about a mile east of the town, actually). New Madrid is about 6 miles south. If you could turn and look to your right, you would see the Associated Electric company smokestack 9 miles away. We are near the northern edge of the epicentral region of the great 8.8 magnitude earthquake of February 7, 1812. We are about to visit a living witness of the great New Madrid earthquakes of 1811-12. "The Witness Tree" is a 300-year-old southern red oak *(Quercus falcata)*. Its diameter at chest height is 5 feet, spreading to more than 7 feet at the ground. What a story this tree could tell if only it could talk. Imagine the experience it must have had. In 1811, it was already over 100 years old, which, for a southern red oak, is about when they reach their maturity and maximum height, as seen here. In human terms, that would be puberty. After this time, in the life of a tree, they don't get any taller, just fatter, not unlike people. After a long peaceful childhood, this arboreal teenager was suddenly jarred into the reality at the peak of its adolescence by the rampages of the New Madrid Fault. Caught in a huge sand boil, sand spewing in the air over its limbs and oozing through the toes of its roots, it is amazing that the tree survived. But it did, only now it tilts slightly to the south, as you can see. Though alive, its subsequent growth was no doubt affected. The person with the red coat in the foreground is Virginia Carlson, Director of the New Madrid Historical Museum. The light colored soil circling the tree is the sand of the boil, mounded slightly higher than the surrounding field. You can spot a couple of white objects in the tree line in the distance to the right of the tree. Those are trucks on Interstate-55, less than a mile to the east. Let's walk closer to the tree.

## SLIDE #79 LOCATION K

## Closer View of Red Oak Witness Tree in Seismic Sand Boil With Students on Earthquake Field Trip

We are joining a class of students visiting the Witness Tree. They are on a field trip as part of a course in earthquakes taught by Dr. Stewart at Southeast Missouri State University. It is about 8:30 in the morning looking east on a cool spring day in early April, 1990. These students got up before 5:30 a.m. to go on this trip. Look at the twisted branches and the elbows in the limbs of this venerable giant. The arms of the tree gesture to us as if to say, "Look what the earthquakes did to me." This monarch of the field is still alive and vigorous. You can sense that when standing silently in its presence, beneath the sheltering cover of its huge branches. When you listen closely, you can almost imagine that it is whispering to you, but what is it trying to say? You can never quite make it out. An inspection of the heavy bark reveals that it has been struck by lightning, at least once, back in the 1950's. But the wound has almost completely healed. What a hardy oak! Surviving the world's greatest earthquakes and lightning, too. Perhaps acorns of this tree could parent a stand of timber that would produce seismically resistant lumber. Would houses built of such wood be earthquake-proof? Or lightning-proof? Just kidding folks! Actually, it was this tree's good fortune to have been caught in a sand boil. Because the soil is so poor and can't produce much of a crop anyhow, the farmers who have tilled this field over more than a hundred years have left this oak standing while cutting down all it neighbors nearby. Hence, while it must have saddened the old tree to witness the felling of its friends and relatives, because of its peculiar situation in the middle of a mound of sterile sand, it was spared. If the old tree had hands it could post a sign at its base saying, "Saved by an earthquake." Who says earthquakes are all bad?

## SLIDE #80 LOCATION K

## Explosion Sand Blow Crater on Old Chartreau Estate With Students on Earthquake Field Trip

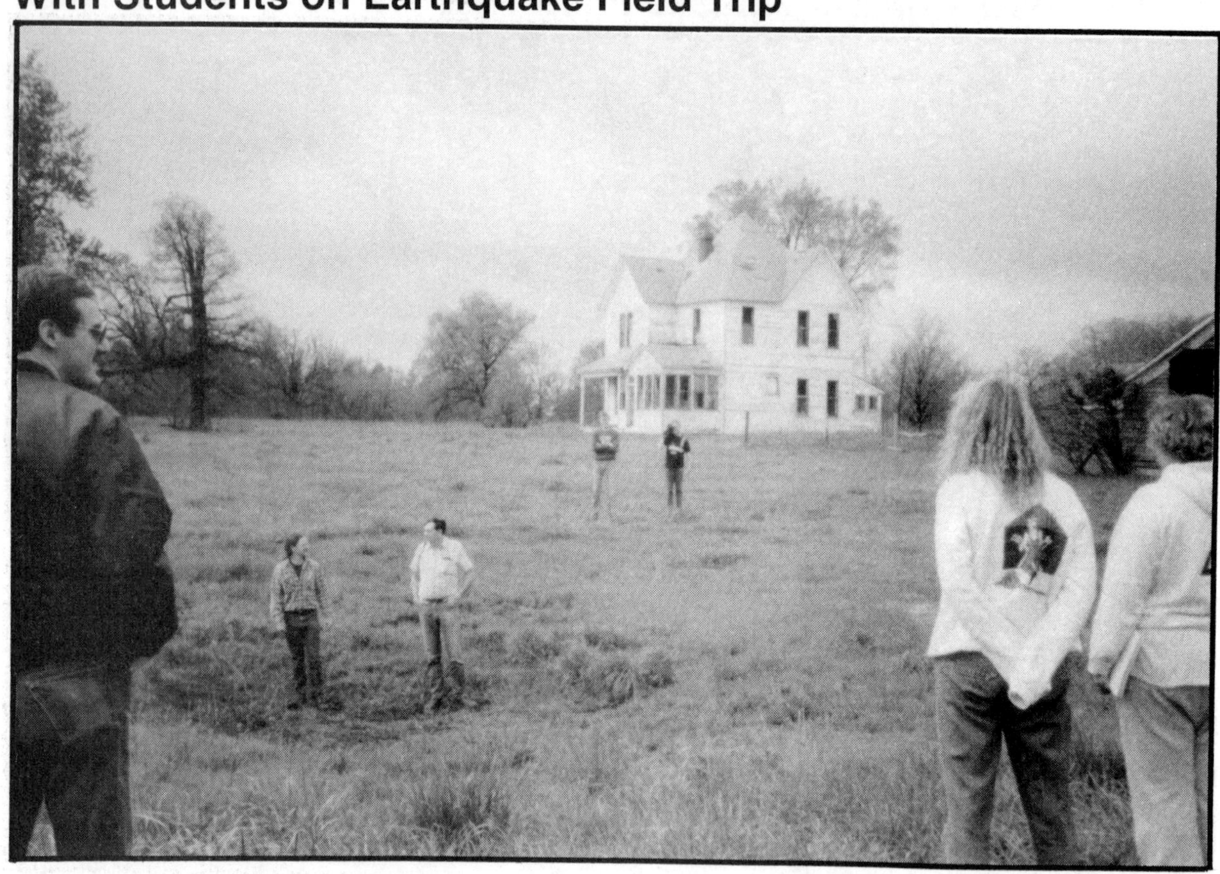

This is an explosion sand blow crater. It is a cone-shaped depression left by the earthquakes of 1811-12 when the earth actually blew-up, blasting sand, soil, water, particles of wood, and bits of coal into the air. At the time of the quakes, there was probably a rim several feet high around this feature while the depth may have been 15-20 feet, as reported by observers of other explosion craters in the NMSZ at the time. Water probably stood in the bottom, boiling and churning from beneath for some time after the quake. It was probably an earthquake pond for a few years until it filled in. The rim has since been leveled, mostly collapsed into the crater, partially filling it up. Settlers living on the property have also thrown brick and other items into the hole. As we view this feature we are still with the same class of earthquake students we joined at the Witness Tree in the previous photo. We are only about a mile or so down Highway 61, right next to Interstate 55 at the north exit and overpass leading to New Madrid (Exit #52). It is about 9:00 a.m. and threatening a little rain. The picturesque old house standing in the background has long been abandoned. It was built by the Chartreau family after the turn of the century and even though they no longer live here, it is still referred to as "The Chartreau Estate." The "Chartreau Explosion Crater" is approximately 75 feet in diameter and 5-6 feet deep. You can get an idea of the scale by the student in the light blue shirt standing in the bottom who is 6 feet 4 inches tall.

## SLIDE #81

LOCATION K

## Low Angle Shot of Explosion Sand Blow Crater With Author, Ray Knox, Standing in Center

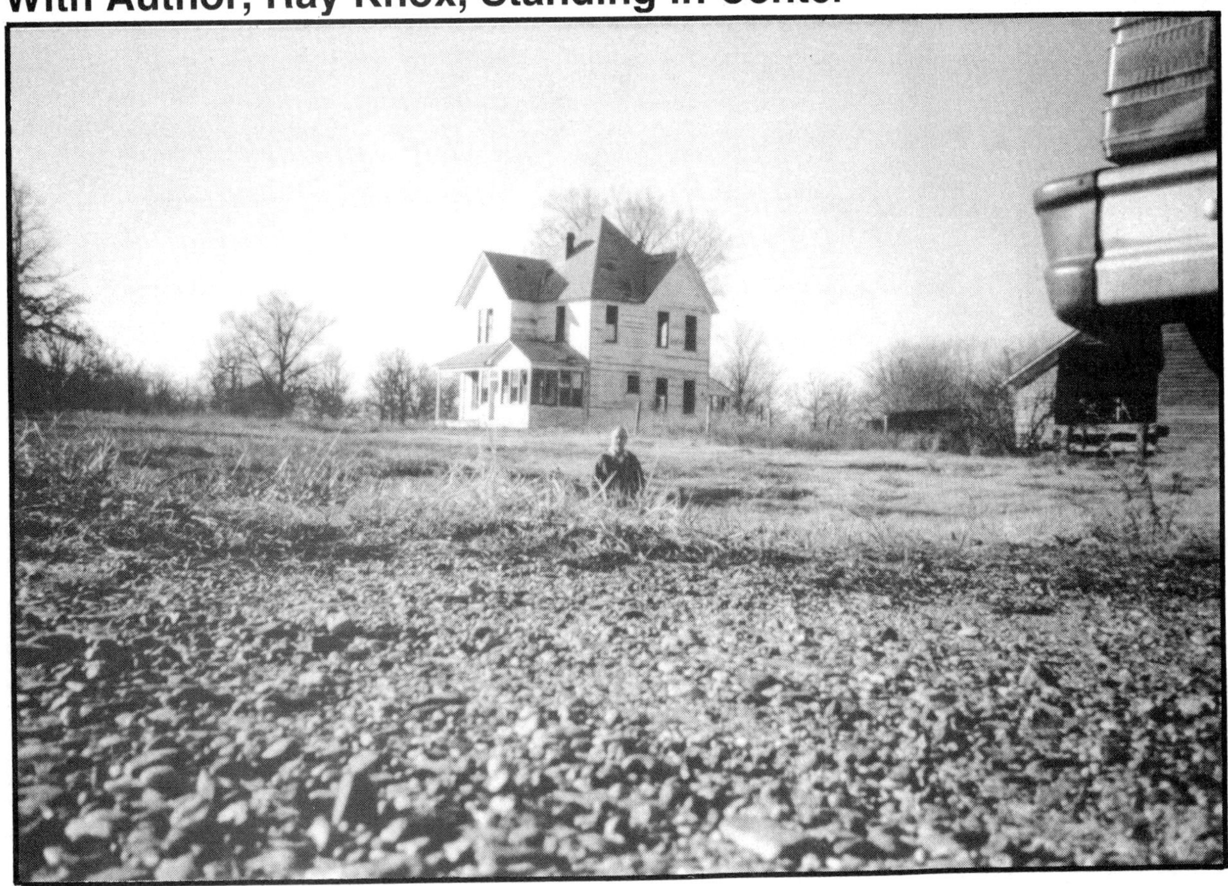

You can get an even better idea of the present depth of the "Chartreau Explosion Crater" from this photograph. To get this picture, Dave Stewart was lying down with the camera, resting his elbows on the ground while, Ray Knox stood in the bottom of the crater. That's the rear bumper of Ray's car in the upper right. Ray is 6 feet 2 inches tall, which can give you some idea of the depth. This would not have been a good time to have a major earthquake since such features tend to explode again, hurling some of their contents into the air while swallowing others.

## SLIDE #82

LOCATION K

## Filled Explosion Sand Blow Crater, Mile Post 53, View Looking East Toward Interstate 55

This is a filled explosion crater next to Interstate Highway 55 at Mile Post #53. The truck reflected in the puddle is speeding south. This feature is perfectly round and is so easy to see that you can spot it at 65 miles per hour as you pass by. Here is an explosion crater now filled with clay and soil, but it has a vent full of sand and other permeable material at its center in direct communication with the water table below. When the water table rises, this area becomes too mushy for farm equipment drive across. Hence, farmers have to till around it or get stuck. Most of the material filling this crater was probably naturally deposited by rainfall erosion, the slumping of the original rim, and wind-blown sand or dust. Some was probably pushed in by land owners who wanted to smooth out the depression and incorporate this area into their field. This never succeeds because of the direct conduit these features have to the water-saturated aquifer below. After vain attempts to bring such spots into tillage, farmers finally give up and just plow around them, but not before getting their tractors mired a few times. The veneer of water you see here is just a shallow puddle held by the impermeable clay soils in the top of the crater. The actual water table is 10-20 feet below, depending on the time of year. This photo was taken in late spring. In early summer this feature will be filled with water-loving (hydrophytic) plants. In late summer this feature dries to a white clay. In the fall it is filled with a distinctive assortment of weeds, peculiar to these features. When flying over the NMSZ at certain times of the year you can spot these filled explosion craters as circular green spots randomly distributed here and there in farmers' fields, bearing no crops.

## SLIDE #83 LOCATION L

## St. Johns Ditch Sunk Land & East Flank of Sikeston Ridge, Aerial Looking South, April 1990

We have now flown about 7 miles north of our last stop. We are looking south toward I-55 Exit #58 (A7-8). This is the Highway 80 Interchange between Matthews and East Prairie. New Madrid County Road #820 crosses the photo just below center line (E1-10) and forms an overpass with I-55 (E5). St. John's Ditch flows toward New Madrid across the upper right corner (D10 – A5). The upper right-hand corner, above St. John's Ditch, is a piece of the Sikeston Ridge, a topographic high about two miles wide and 15-20 feet higher than the lowlands on either side. It runs in a north-south strip for about 25 miles from Haywood City, north of Sikeston, to the Mississippi at New Madrid. Sikeston Ridge is a terrace deposited by the ancient Ohio River many thousands of years ago when the Mississippi River flowed west of Sikeston. The ridge is an erosional remnant of a much wider plateau. When the Mississippi River cut through the Benton Hills between Scott City, Missouri, and Thebes, Illinois, less than 10,000 years ago, it eroded away the east side of the ridge to its present size. The curve in the Interstate (B6-7) is to accomodate the crossing of St. John's Ditch and the incline from the lowland on the east to the higher elevation of Sikeston Ridge on the west. Sikeston Ridge was not caused by earthquakes. However we are looking at several earthquake features here—sand boils, explosion sand blow craters, and a siesmic sunk land. The dark strip parallel to and on the east side of St. John's Ditch (G10-A4) is land that subsided during the earthquakes of 1811-12. At the center of the photo, just east of the Interstate, you can see two yellow dots (D5) while a larger yellow spot is seen on the other side of the highway (D6-7). These are explosion sand blow craters. A large sand boil can be seen cradled in the corner of two fence rows lined by trees at C6 while other sand boils are visible in the field in the lower left corner.

## SLIDE #84



## Large Explosion Sand Blow Crater at Mile Post 60 East Side of Interstate 55, June 1990

Down on the ground now, we are standing at the Interstate 55 fence at Mile Post #60 looking at one of the explosion sand blow craters seen in the last slide. This one is on the east side and is a perfect circle over 100 feet in diameter. Wind has blown a lot of sand into this depression over the decades since it was formed, but it is still 2-3 feet deep and an obvious low spot. Notice how the soybeans have wilted and died out in and around the crater. This is another feature large enough to notice at a glance even while zooming 65 miles per hour down the Interstate. You can find pea gravel, lignite, and chips from Indian arrowheads in this feature. Prickly Pear Cactus grows in abundance on the highway side of the fence here. There is another smaller explosion crater about 200 feet south of this one on the same side of the Interstate. It is only 80 feet in diameter, but imagine if you had been standing there during an earthquake!

## SLIDE #85
## Large Explosion Sand Blow Crater at Mile Post 60 West Side of Interstate 55, June 1990

We have crossed over to the west side of the Interstate and are standing on another large explosion sand blow crater, another one of those visible from the air in Slide #83. You can see that the crater has been partially filled with sand, but is still a 3 foot deep depression. You can see trucks emerging from under the overpass of County Road 820 on the right and thundering southward down the Highway. This particular explosion crater had been used as a dump and contains much broken glass, pieces of rusted metal, and other waste materials. But the debris is mostly covered with sand and has been plowed into the subsurface over the years. I want you to carefully note the overpass because we are going to see it again in the next picture. This is June, 1990. The explosion crater is only a sandy depression in a field of stubble at this time. But that is soon to change.

## SLIDE #86 LOCATION L

## Same Sand Blow Crater as Slide #85, December, 1991, With New 700 Foot Tall Transmission Tower

Here we are standing close to the same spot as the last photo, but now it is December, 1991. You can still see the Interstate running from the center of the picture and off to the right. You can also still see the County Road 820 overpass we saw in the last slide, but now it is partially hidden by an enormous satellite dish. Apparently, a wireless cable company from Oklahoma found this piece of real estate to be a suitable location for a transmitting tower. The tower, equipment building, and receiving dish are all centered over where the explosion crater was seen the year before. They had simply pushed the sand around and leveled it off. The whole complex is built on an earthquake feature which would become extremely unstable in the event of a major earthquake. This transmission tower is 700 feet tall and exerts a downward force of 300,000 pounds at its base which rests on a small concrete pad only 2 feet thick and 14 feet square. An earthquake, or even a high river stage, could cause this area to liquefy and become temporary quicksand.

## SLIDE #87
## View of Richter Dip Stick from Bridge over Interstate 55, February 1992

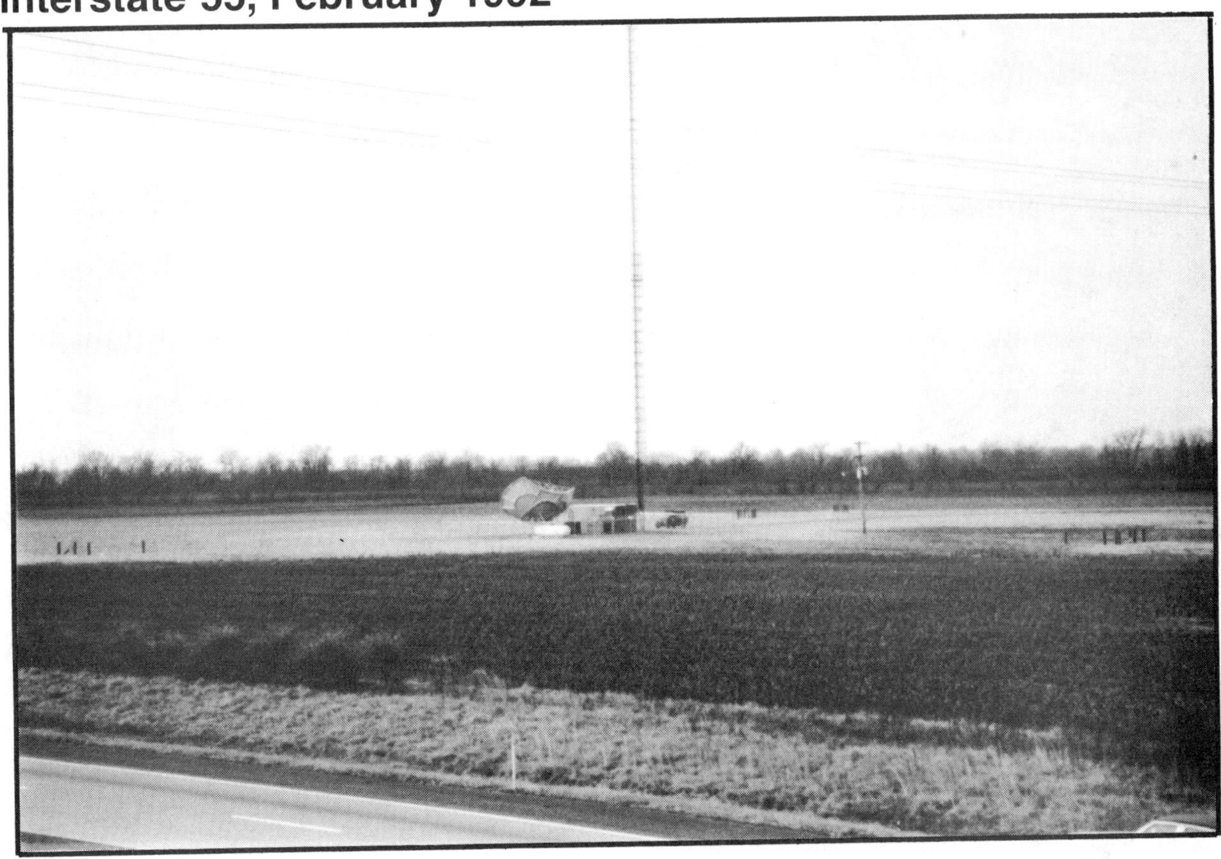

Here we are standing on the overpass spanning Interstate 55 looking down on the wireless cable TV receiving station and transmitting tower. You can clearly see from here that it is centered over a large patch of sand. A seismic patch of sand! In a strong earthquake, we figure the tower will sink. Who knows? You will notice that it is conveniently marked in alternating red and white sections, each 100 feet in length, starting with red at the bottom. For a magnitude 6.0, it should sink about half-way up the first red section. For a magnitude 7.0, it should sink to all the way to the white span. For an 8.0 it the entire red section and half of the first white section should disappear. For an 8.8, like back in 1812, it would just topple over, lying completely across the Interstate. That's why we call it our "Richter Dip Stick*." (We're just kidding, of course.) But really, this tower won't last long in a large earthquake.

* The authors want to thank Mark Winkler, Southeast Missouri Coordinator for the State Emergency Management Agency, for suggesting the name "Richter Dip Stick."

## SLIDE #88 LOCATION L

## Aerial View of Tower at MP 60 Showing Position Relative to Explosion Craters & St. John's Sunk Land

Here we are back in the air again with a low altitude view of the "Richter Dip Stick." You can see all 700 feet of the tower with the red and white alternating sections (3 white and 4 red). You can clearly see the seismic sand blow area around the base of the cable TV tower on the west side of the Highway (D5) and you can see how it extends under I-55 to the east to incorporate the area of the two sand blow craters seen in Slides #83 & #84 (F5-6). Across the upper part of the photo (above a line from C1 to B10) is the Sikeston Ridge, a highland 15-20 feet above the lowland in the foreground. St. John's Ditch runs along the base of the ridge (C1-B10), flowing toward New Madrid on the left. This canal drains what used to be Lake St. John, 12 miles north of Sikeston. (See the Map, Slide #1.) This earthquake lake had about 12 square miles of surface area and lasted for more than 100 years after the New Madrid earthquakes that created it. It was drained between 1918 and 1924 when a system of canals were dug throughout the Bootheel of Missouri to create more land suitable for agriculture. St. John's Ditch connects with St. John's Bayou which empties into the Mississippi at New Madrid. (See Slides #12, #18, & #19.) The dark band of land parallel to the ridge on this side of the ditch is St. John's Sunk Land.

LOCATION L

## SLIDE #89
## Wide Angle Aerial View of Large Sand Ridge, St. John's Ditch Sunk Land, & Sikeston 10 Miles Away

In this higher altitude photo over the same area as the previous slide, you can clearly see the delineation of a large yellow sand deposit with dark green lowlands on either side. This is a sand ridge, but not a seismic sand ridge. Seismic sand boils and seismic explosion sand blow craters are both found on this sand ridge, as seen in the previous slides. Sand boils are extremely common throughout the NMSZ, but explosion craters are not. Explosion craters occur where sand extends from the surface down into the water table with no non-liquefiable soil in between. Sand boils occur when liquefiable sand is overlain by a non-liquefiable layer of soil such as clay or loam. (See Slide #7, page 40.) The fact that this is a sand ridge provided the conditions for explosion craters, as well as boils in some places. This particular slightly elevated body of sand is probably a disconnected remnant of Sikeston Ridge during its wider days, thousand of years ago. (A more detailed discussion of Sikeston Ridge and how it got there is given in the book, *The New Madrid Fault Finders Guide* mentioned on page 216 of this book.) St. John's Seismic Sunk Land is seen here runing along the left (west) side of the sand ridge (DEF1-C5). Interstate 55 runs across the photo north to south (B10-E1). The explosion sand blow craters of the slides just seen are located just right of center (C6-7). The 700-foot-tall "Richter Dip Stick" can just be discerned in the distance (C6-B6) with its three white stripes and four red ones. At top center, on the horizon (A6), you can see a white feature in the distance, approximately 10 miles away. This is the Sikeston Power Plant. But more on that later in Slides #92-#94. While we are on the subject of electric power, let's drop down to Malden to see something interesting.

## SLIDE #90 LOCATION M
## Sand Boil Under Malden Power Substation

One of the benefits we see in a book and slide set like this is that people, including professional seismologists, geologists, and civil engineers, can learn how to recognize seismic features when they see them so that they won't build on them inappropriately. (Like the cable TV tower we just saw in Slides #86-#89.) For example, seismic features abound along Highway 25 from Bernie to Kennett, Missouri, with many buildings and homes constructed over them. Here is a substation just outside of Malden, Missouri, on the Highway 25 bypass, not far from the intersection of Highway 62. Do you see the semicircular exposure of a sand boil partially covered by this electric power installation? There is another boil just to the north of this substation but out of the picture. And this is only what we can see today. There may well be another boil directly under the substation hidden by the gravel surface that covered the enclosure. "Once a boil, always a possible boil," so the saying goes. These should be avoided, if possible, when locating such critical facilities in earthquake zones. Sometimes relocating by even a few tens of feet would provide more stable ground. But substations on sand boils are nothing compared to what you are about to see next. Malden receives its power from several sources, including the New Madrid Associated Electric Plant and the Sikeston Power Plant. In the event of a major earthquake, the Malden substation could be knocked out of operation. But even if it stands, Malden's real problem may not be its substation, but the integrity of its power sources. Let's now take a look at the Sikeston Plant.

## SLIDE #91 LOCATION N

## Sand Boil & Fissure Patterns Around Sikeston Airport

We are flying back to Sikeston now, approaching town from the northeast. We see the Sikeston Airport runway across the photo (C3-D10). Huge seismic liquefaction-prone sand features streak across the foreground of our view. The airport is surrounded by sandy evidence of the great New Madrid earthquakes while a sunk land parallels its length between the runways and Sikeston Ridge (B1-C10). Most of this sunk land is used as a recreational park (BC3-C7) and not for housing. A large part of Sikeston can be seen here, situated mostly on the high ground of the ridge, a safe haven from periodic floods on the Mississippi. The city of Sikeston has found an interesting practical use for sand boils. Ingram Road runs along the east side of town between Sikeston Ridge (B1-C10) and Rodeo Park (BC3-C7). From our airplane view two miles away, you can see a light spot on the flank of the ridge (BC-6) north of where the housing neighborhoods end. This spot is a pair of huge circular sand boils that overlap, each about 250 feet in diameter. Some of the storm drains of the city have been routed to the north of town into a ditch that terminates into these boils. When there is a hard rain, the excess runoff simply flows out of town and into these boils where it disappears into ground. This serves two beneficial purposes. It prevents temporary flooding in the streets of Sikeston and recharges the aquifer from which the city water wells draw their supply. When the city engineers stumbled onto this years ago, they did not know these were seismic features. They only knew that this large patch of sand could absorb a lot of water fast and make it disappear, solving a drainage problem for their streets. So sand boils are not all bad. As direct conduits to the water table, they make excellent drains. At the top center of this view, about three miles away, on the other side of town and the opposite side of the ridge, we see the white plume of the Sikeston Power Plant smokestack (B6).

## SLIDE #92 LOCATION N

## Large Sand Boil in Foreground, Sikeston Power Plant One Mile Away, City of Sikeston in Distance on Ridge

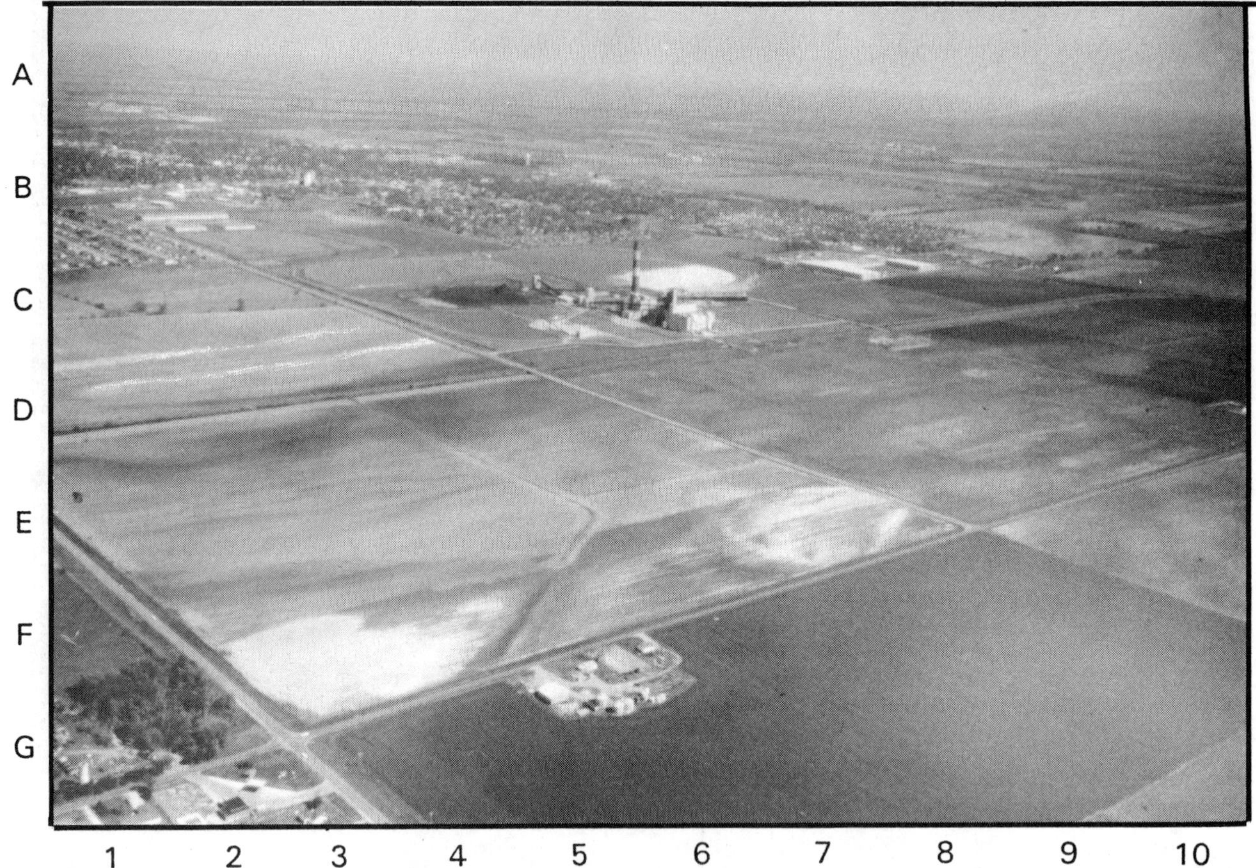


We are now on the west side of Sikeston Ridge and the City of Sikeston. The urbanized portion of the city is almost entirely up on the ridge to avoid occasional floods. Housing developments are built right up to the edge of the ridge and stop near the edge of the dropoff. You can see the linear scarp of the west side of Sikeston Ridge running across the top of the photo (C1-B10). All of the land on this side of that scarp is 15-20 feet lower. Located in this lowland you see a huge sand boil in the lower left (F3) and the Sikeston Power Plant at the center of the photo (C5-6). On the right center area of the photo notice two light streaks extending from the edge of the photo to where they are cut off by Wakefield Road running by the power plant (D1-D4). These are seismic sand fissures. These are lateral spread features where a clayey non-liquefiable soil on the surface was underlaid by liquefiable sand beneath. During the earthquakes the dark upper layers of soil split open allowing the liquid sand to rise up and fill the crack, thus leaving a strip of yellow sand with dark brown loamy clay on both sides. Having split and spread apart at least once before, these sand fissures will liquefy and move again in future major earthquakes.

## SLIDE #93 LOCATION N

## Sikeston Power Plant Sand Fissure, Ground View

Here a group of college students inspect the "Sikeston Power Plant" fissure, an extrusive sand feature formed during the great quakes of 1811-12. It was a college student, in fact, that first discovered this feature back in 1989. Scott Readnour, a senior Geology major at the time, was working on a special project under the supervision of Dr. Stewart when he came across this sandy gash in the landscape and wondered if it might have an earthquake history. Scott brought the authors, Knox and Stewart, to see the feature which did turn out to be seismic. In this photo it is April, 1990, and the sand fissure is completely bare, but on either side you can see the crop stubble in a dark loamy soil that had borne a good yield of cotton in the fall of '89. The sands of the fissure had yielded nothing. You can see how this fissure might affect this power complex during some future major quake. The generating facility containing the turbines is in the buildings on the right. Between the turbine building and the 410-foot tall smokestack are the environmental scrubbers and emission purification equipment to prevent the escape of harmful vapors from the stack. What you see coming out of the top of the smokestack is mostly water and harmless. (The harmful part of industrial emissions is usually invisible.) The problem with this power plant having been situated astride a major seismic sand fissure is this: The rotating shaft of the generator and steam turbines has to remain aligned to within 10 thousandths of an inch or the plant will instantly and automatically shut down. Will Sikeston have power from this plant following a major earthquake? It's not likely. But not to worry. As with all power plants, this one is connected to others that will furnish power in the case of a shut down. In this case, the back-up plant is the Associated Power Plant at New Madrid! (See page 70, Slide #28.)

## SLIDE #94 LOCATION N

## Sikeston Power Plant Seismic Sand Fissure, As Seen from Top of 410-Foot-Tall Power Plant Smoke Stack

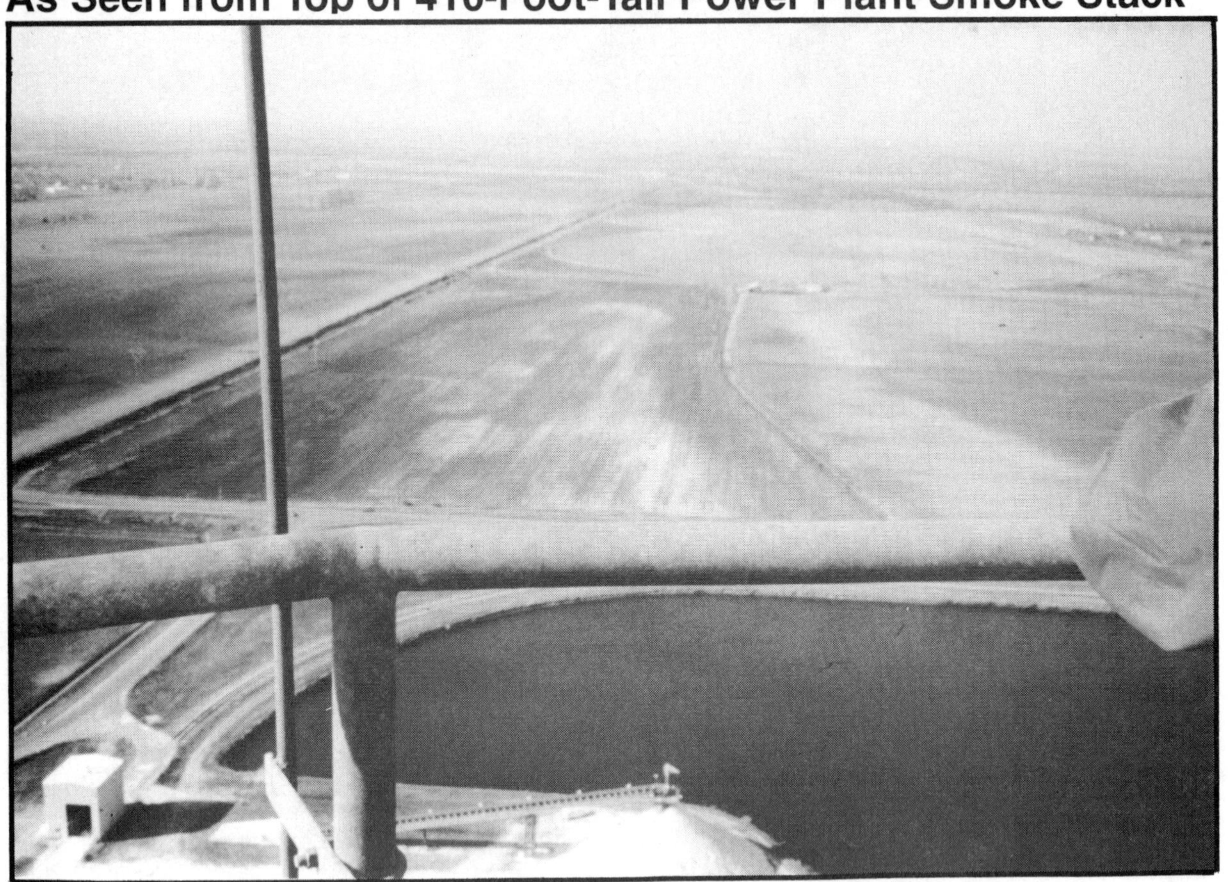

We have reached the top of the Sikeston Power Plant smokestack, 410 feet above ground. It's windy and chilly up here. We hold tightly to the rails. Luckily we did not have to climb a stairway. There is an elevator inside the stack. The plant has been temporarily shut down for an annual maintenance and cleaning operation. Sikeston is receiving its power from the New Madrid Power Plant as we stand on top looking down on the fissures streaking toward the plant property below. You are probably wondering why the planners of the Sikeston Power Plant located their facility over an earthquake fissure. The answer is that they did not know this was an earthquake feature. In fact, back when this plant was built virtually no one knew how to recognize such features nor did anyone realize what their implications might be. Very few professional geologists, civil engineers, or seismologists had experience in this field and it was not taught in the normal course of geoscience training. The field of "morphoseismology," the study of how earthquakes permanently alter landscapes, is so new that even the word "morphoseismology" was not coined until 1992. In fact, this book is the first comprehensive publication on the subject to be made available to the public as well as to most professionals. The fissure property has been farmed for almost a hundred years. No houses were built here for fear of floods. But it has been many years since waters have inundated these lands. The levees and drainage ditches are working well. It has been even longer since a great earthquake has ripped through the region. This photo was taken in 1990. Since then, in late 1992, we learned that there are plans to develop this property for a housing subdivision. Need we say more?

## SLIDE #95
## Blooming Cactus in Deflated Sand Boil with Sand Dune on Fence in Background

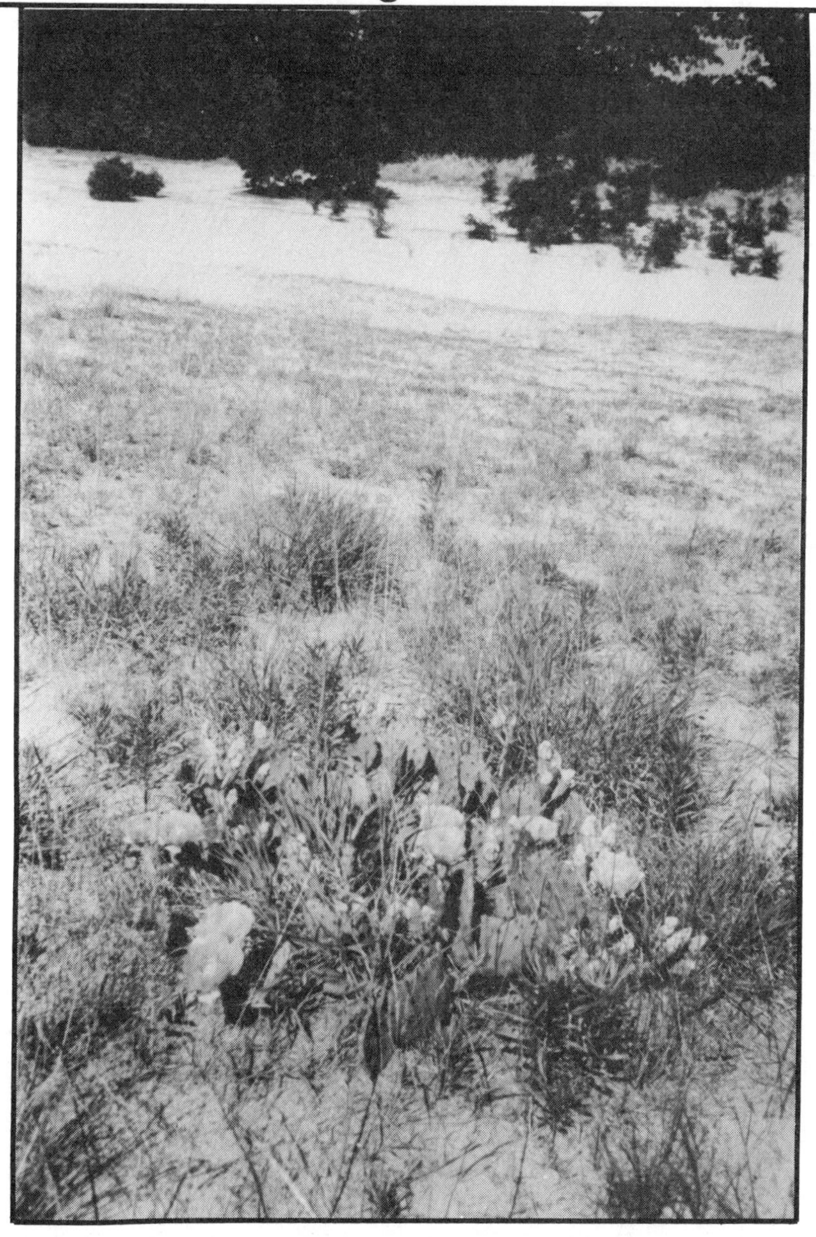

Flowers are beautiful anywhere and at any time. These are bright orange and yellow cactus flowers blooming in June of 1990 on the east side of Sikeston. They are located in a large sand boil deflated by the wind. In the background you can see a sand dune piled up on a fence and tree row. Over the years, the wind has picked up the sand out of this sand boil and redeposited it against the fence. As a result, the boil is now a large shallow depression, but it doesn't hold water because it has a direct connection with the ground water below. When it rains, this sand deposit is not flooded because it is so permeable that runoff simply soaks into the ground as fast as it flows in. If the river rises too high for too long, however, the water table can rise here and temporarily liquefy this spot as well as fill it with water, not from above, but from below.

## SLIDE #96 LOCATION O

## 1811-12 Earthquake Landslide in Benton Hills As Seen from Northbound Lane of Interstate 55, 1.5 Miles Away

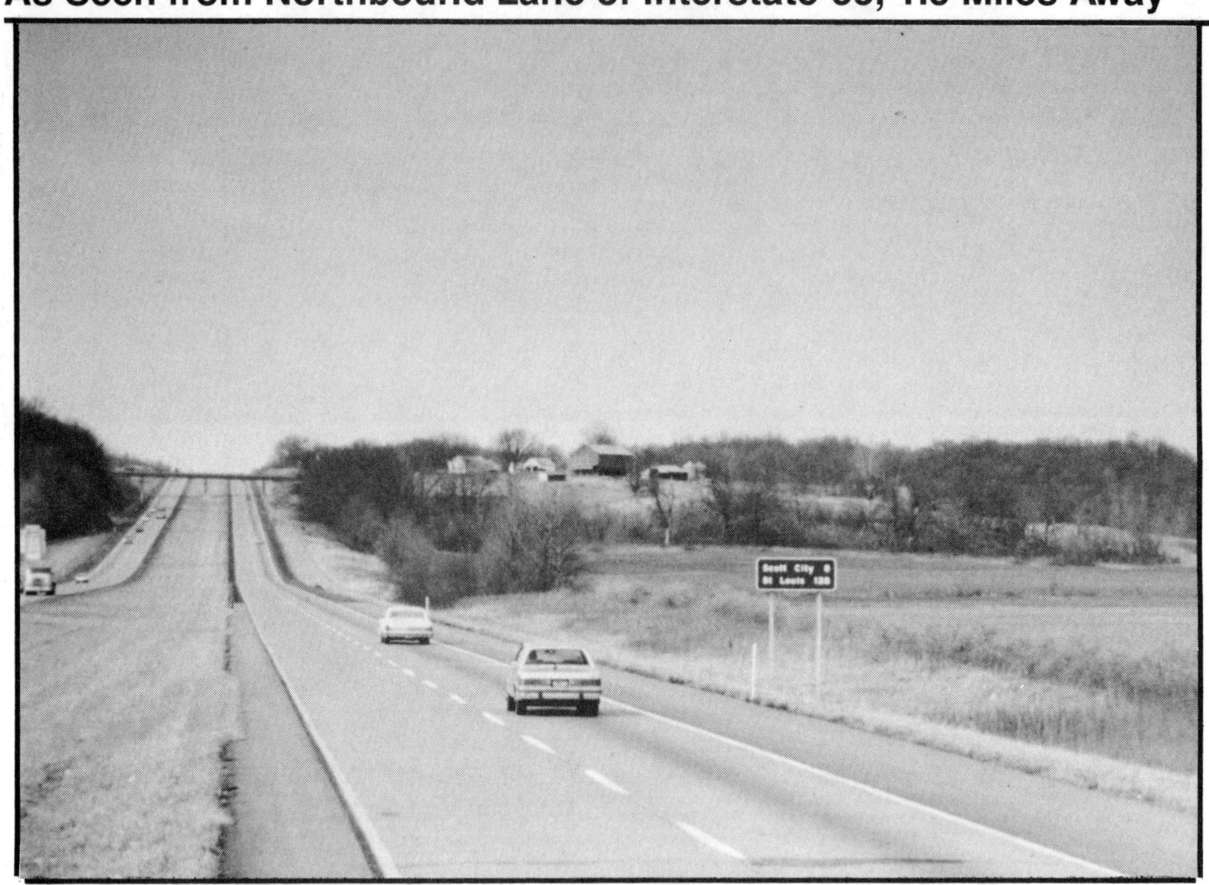

Back on the road again. Now we are on Interstate 55 headed north. The sign says, "Scott City 8, St. Louis 120." We are near Mile Post #81, which means we are 81 miles north of the Arkansas Line. We are also at the northern fringe of the New Madrid Fault Zone, where the flatlands end and the Hills begin. We are looking at the Benton Hills, about a mile and a half away. We see two large seismic features here. You will notice that before the highway bends upward to climb the Benton Hills, it is dipping down. At the base of these hills is a sunk land from the quakes of 1811-12. A former course of the Ohio River once ran through here thousands of years ago, eroding the base of these hills. Old stream channels are especially susceptible to morphoseismic alteration, which is probably why a sunk land formed here in 1811-12. Looking to the large grey barn on the hilltop you can see a massive landslide, also the probable result of the 1811-12 earthquakes. Another strong earthquake struck this area after 1812. This was the Charleston, Missouri, earthquake of October 31, 1895, centered about 35 miles southeast of this point. Once a slope has been destabilized by an earthquake, it will move again and again when shaken by subsequent quakes. So this landslide probably moved some in 1895 too. Let's take a closer look and walk up the slide.

## SLIDE #97 LOCATION O

## View of Earthquake Landslide on Proctor Property with Seep Springs at Toe of Slump

We are standing at the base of the slide now. You can see the barn at the top. Along the toe of the slide you see moist brown earth, seepage springs from the rain runoff that flows into the cracks between the blocks of earth that make up this slide. You see, when a slope breaks up into blocks during a landslide, water can't flow down its surface like before. Instead, it flows to the first crack, disappears into the ground, seeps under the broken blocks of soil, and comes out at the toe. This is one of the things you look for to identify an old landslide feature.

## SLIDE #98 LOCATION O

## View of Earthquake Landslide from Point Halfway Up the Slope Showing Signs of Current Creep

We have walked half-way up the slide to where one of the slumped blocks has broken. You can tell by the exposed, dangling grass roots that this slide is still actively creeping downslope. The earthquake that caused it happened almost two centuries ago, but it hasn't stopped moving yet. This property is owned by Roy and Elaine Proctor, which is why we call this the "Proctor Landslide."

## SLIDE #99 LOCATION O

## Seven Acre Sand Boil in Proctor Field as Seen From Top of Proctor Landslide 1 Mile Away

We now stand on the crest of the hill to the side of the Proctor's barn looking out across the New Madrid Seismic Zone. This is where the NMSZ starts. There are three seismic features to see from here. We are looking down the earthquake landslide we saw before in the three previous slides. Across the base of the hill below us is the seismic sunk land from 1811-12 that we saw from the highway in Slide #96 (E1 – D8). But there is something else. Notice that bright yellow spot near the center of the picture (D6). That is a 7-acre sand boil in Proctor's field. We call it "The Proctor Sand Boil." The Proctor Landslide, Sunk Land, and Sand Boil are the closest seismic features of the 1811-12 earthquakes to the city of Cape Girardeau, only 9 miles to the north. Cape Girardeau and Jackson, Missouri, form a metropolitan area of about 60,000 population. Cape is the largest city in southeast Missouri and the home of Southeast Missouri State University. Now let's walk down the landslide, across the sunk land, and take a look at the sand boil close-up.

## SLIDE #100 LOCATION O

## Proctor Sand Boil (7 Acres) Viewed from Ground With Benton Hills and Interstate 55 in Distance

We are looking at seven acres of pure sand, an elliptic shaped sand boil about 700 feet long by 400 feet wide. This is the "Proctor Sand Boil." Quarter of a mile in the distance you can see a couple of trucks speeding along Interstate 55. You can sometimes see this sand boil from the Interstate when the sun reflects just right in the morning but usually not in the afternoon. Roy Proctor tells a story of one time when he and his father were harvesting soybeans with a large heavy combine across this boil. It was 1973. The Mississippi River had been in flood stage for months, one of its highest and longest floods of this century. Even though the river is 5 miles away to the east and the levee had kept the river within its channel, the high water level had raised the levels of the ground water for miles inland. The Proctor Sand Boil had become a bit mushy (HIL), "like a bowl of jelly," says Roy. As they drove over the boil the vibrations of their tractor helped induce further liquefaction (MIL). "Suddenly, the front right wheel of the combine completely disappeared into the ground," said Roy. They tried to pull it out with another tractor to no avail. A second tractor was brought to help. After several hours of effort and almost getting the other tractors stuck, too, they were still unable to extract the combine caught in the quicksand. Finally, they laid two 8-foot railroad ties on the boil for the combine to roll out on. As the combine finally began to free up, suddenly the ties completely disappeared into the ground. The combine was rescued. But the ties have never been seen since. They are still there buried in the boil. Perhaps during some future earthquake the boil will liquefy again (SIL) and the long buried ties will float to the surface again. And who knows what else may surface at the same time?

## SLIDE #101 — LOCATION O

## Proctor Sand Boil & Earthquake Sunk Land As Seen from Air Looking West Toward Benton

Lets take one last look at the "Proctor Sand Boil" before we fly south again. The boil is in the center of the photo (D5-6). Interstate 55 runs from north to south (D10 to D1). The base of the Benton Hills where it meets the southeast Missouri lowlands runs diagonally across the top (D10 to B1). The seismic sunk land mentioned before runs parallel to the hills and underneath the Interstate Highway (E10 to C3). The Proctor barn is just off the picture on the right (D10). Mr. Proctor tells us that the 7-acre boil we have identified here is the biggest boil he has, but it is not the only one where his equipment has sunk in over its wheels. The "Proctor Sand Boil" is truly a monster boil by world standards. But it is nothing compared to what we are going to see next.

## SLIDE #102 LOCATION P

## World's Largest Sand Boil, "The Beach," 136 Acres, Aerial View Looking West from 2 Miles Distance

Peering from beneath our airplane wing, we see a large yellow streak over a mile away to the west (D1-D7). Could that be a sand boil or seismic fissure of some kind? Whatever it is, it is huge, at least a mile long. And why does that road below us head straight toward the feature (G4-D5) and then make an abrupt left turn when it gets there (DE1-DE5) as it to avoid this place. We notice that the road continues westward on the far side (D5-B5) but does not cross the feature. Why would this be? At this time we are located about 6 miles west of Hayti, Missouri, flying just south of Highway 84.

## SLIDE #103 LOCATION P

### "The Beach Boil" (Length, 1.4 Miles; Width 500-1000 Feet)
### Aerial View Looking South from 1 Mile North

We circle to the north looking south down Pemiscott County Road 415 (G4-EF4). There is a row of houses along the road below us (F4-G4), but why does the road abruptly angle off to the west right beyond the last house (EF-4)? The large sand feature we saw before is still easily visible from this angle (E3-D5), even though we are still a mile away. It appears that the roads of the area are trying to avoid this feature for some reason. Why? All around beneath us, to the right, to the left, in front and behind, we see the distinctive rippled and stripped appearance of land that has undergone liquefaction during past earthquakes. But this large sandy feature has our curiosity up. Let's fly lower and closer to get a better look.

## SLIDE #104 LOCATION P

## Close Up Aerial View of "The Beach" Looking North With Homestead on Southern End in Foreground

From the south we can see the whole thing. This is a linear, compound sand boil, the largest in the world. It is 1.4 miles long, 500-1000 feet wide, and 136 acres in area. Now you can understand why the area's roads avoid crossing this patch of liquefiable earth. Unfortunately, the planners of a major gas pipeline did not recognize what this feature was. A branch of the Associated Natural Gas Pipeline completely crosses one of the widest portions of this monster sand boil from east to west (E10-1). In the foreground is a homestead built on the southernmost edge of the huge boil. The five rows of bushy vegetation to the west are autumn olive trees *(Elaeagnus umbellata),* planted by the tenant as a wind break to keep sand from continually blowing into his house and yard. Dr. Stewart's earthquake students from Southeast Missouri State University have named this feature "The Beach." The location of the gas pipeline crossing The Beach is seen as an east-west dark streak across the sand at C4-6.

## SLIDE #105 LOCATION P

## Scientists & Engineers from 15 Countries Exploring World's Largest Sand Boil

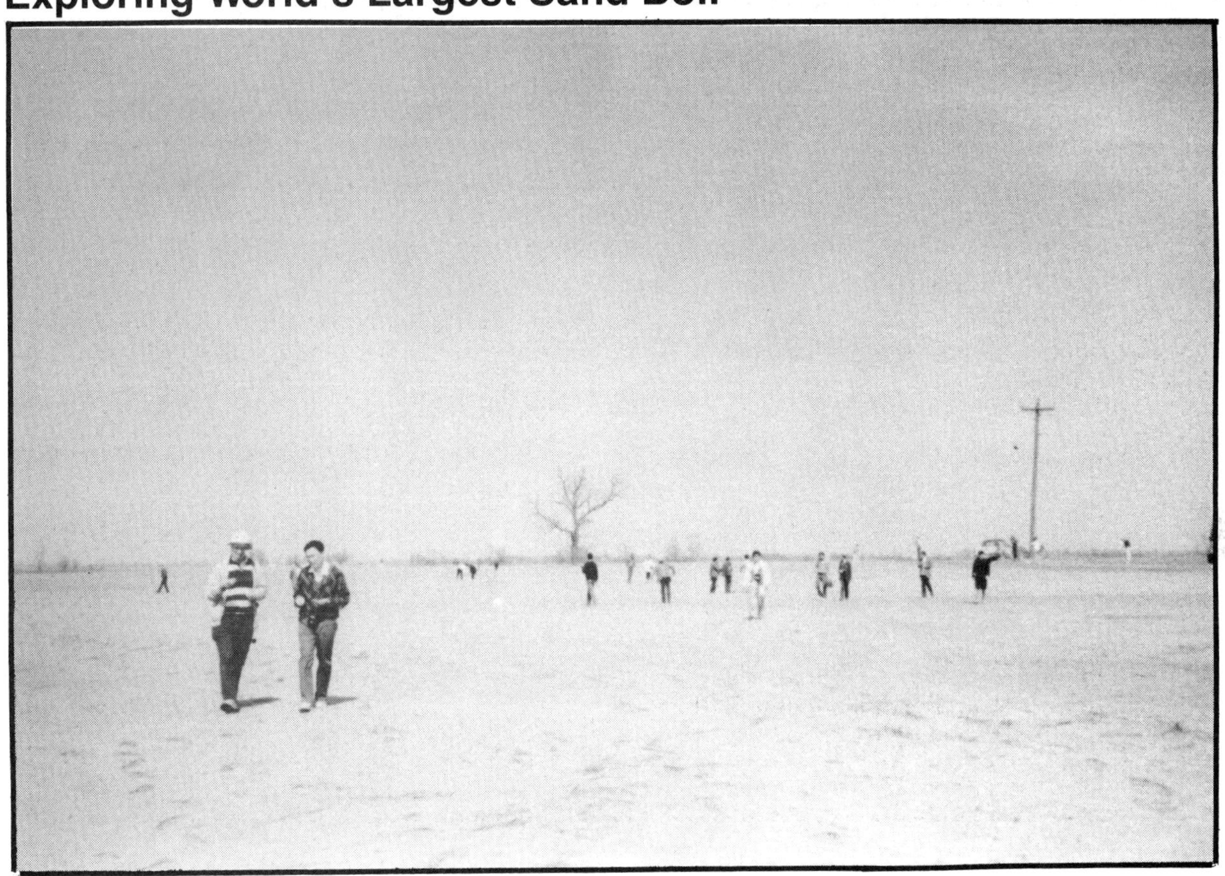

Now we are on the ground exploring the world's largest sand boil. You can see why Dr. Stewart's students called this "The Beach." Only the north quarter of the boil is visible here. The people you see are a group of 40 scientists and engineers, experts in various aspects of earthquakes and liquefaction, from 15 countries around the world. One Japanese scientist was seen shaking his head. When asked why, he replied that he had published a paper in a technical journal on a sand boil from a recent Japanese quake measuring 30 meters (100 feet) in diameter. To him and his colleagues at that time, a 100 foot sand boil was truly huge, something to write about. "I feel very humbled," he said as he surveyed the sea of sand around him, sand that boiled up in the great New Madrid earthquakes. You can find many interesting things on "The Beach:" Coal, lignite, petroliferous nodules, arrowhead chips, stone Indian tools, Native American potshards, and pea gravel as well as occasional bits of broken glass and rusted metal from more recent times. This feature is linear, which is more apparent in the previous three slides. It strikes approximately northeast to southwest. This is a portion of the "Bootheel Lineament" mentioned in the text. This lineament was first noticed in 1988 on satellite photographs by graduate student Ron Marple at Memphis State University. It is still under intensive investigation. It stretches for at least 80 miles from Marked Tree, Arkansas, to a point 12 miles west of New Madrid and possibly northward another 20 miles to an area near Matthews, Missouri, across Sikeston Ridge. It appears to be a right-lateral strike-slip fault. Whether it is primary or secondary remains to be determined. The Bootheel Lineament is the largest visible earthquake feature in the NMSZ. Hence, it is only appropriate that the largest sand boil in the world lies along its stride.

## SLIDE #106 LOCATION P

## Fissures & Liquefaction Features Just West of Bootheel Lineament at Deering, Missouri

This is an aerial view, from the south, of the little town of Deering, Missouri (B4-B9). The town is situated on the north bank of the Little River seen winding across the photo (C10-C1). We are less than two miles south of "The Beach." The "Bootheel Lineament" runs just out of the picture on the right. Notice the numerous signs of past liquefaction that surround this town seen as light colored streaks and blemishes in the landscape. Also notice the dark "canoe-shaped" feature in the lower right (F9-E10). This is a depressed area, probably a seismic sag feature. Notice how the farmers have plowed around this feature, avoiding it with their equipment.

# SLIDE #107 LOCATION P

## Six Mile View of Bootheel Lineament Looking North From Braggadocio Big Boils to The Beach

This is an excellent long view of the Bootheel Lineament. We are six miles south of "The Beach," which you can actually see in this photo in the distance (A6). Draw an imaginary line from the lower left corner (G1) to The Beach and you have the location of the Bootheel Lineament in this area. In the extreme distance, about 4 miles beyond The Beach you can see a tiny white spot. This is the town of Pascola through which the lineament passes. Deering is about 5 miles away just to the left of The Beach (between A5 & B5). But what is this in the foreground under our airplane? These huge sand boils all start at the lineament and extend to the east. The proud town of Braggadocio, Missouri, lies two miles to the east of these boils (off the right side of the photo). That's why we call them "The Braggadocio Big Boils." Something to brag about, for sure. Some of these are 200-300 feet in diameter. Notice the high tension power line with one tower visible on the west side of the lineament and a line of other towers leading off to the right (D3-B9). This carries 161,000 volts of electricity generated by the Associated Electric Plant at New Madrid.

## SLIDE #108 LOCATION P

## "Braggadocio Big Boils" and Bootheel Lineament with Electric Power Line Crossing

Here we are at a lower altitude looking at the same electric line tower we saw in the last slide. Notice how sharp the contrast is between the sandy boil and the clayey soil. Bright green winter wheat has sprouted thickly on the soil but none on the boil. The lineament is quite clear here (G9 to A3). If it is a right-lateral strike-slip fault, as many scientists now believe, the boil side has moved toward the lower right corner while the dark green side has moved toward the upper left.

LOCATION P

## SLIDE #109
## Abrupt Change in Vegetation Along Bootheel Lineament, Braggadocio Big Boils on East

This zoomed-in view shows the sharpness of the contrast between sand and soil even more strikingly. Notice that the electric transmission tower rests on the west side of the lineament which certainly provides a more solid foundation than that seen on the east, a former bog of seismic quicksand. Less than half a mile south of here the Associated Natural Gas Pipeline crosses the Bootheel Lineament. If the Lineament turns out to be an active fault and moves in a right-lateral direction again during some future earthquake, what will happen to the gas pipeline and this 161KV high voltage power line? And what will happen to the towns and rural areas whose power or gas is supplied by these lines, some of which are more than 100 miles away?

## SLIDE #110 LOCATION Q

## Thousand Foot Graben Fissure, Interstate-55 Mile Post 50, Aerial View Looking North

We are back in the New Madrid area again. This time we are 4 miles north of town over Interstate 55 looking north. We are 2 miles east of Kewanee. Notice how the Interstate Highway comes into the picture at the top (A6) and then veers to the west (B6). A curve in a highway is not usually anything unusual. But in this case it tells a story. From this curve northward, the Interstate extends in a perfect north-south line for 40 miles, from here to Kelso, Missouri, with the exception of the one bend near Matthews where it crosses St. John's Ditch and ascends upward onto the Sikeston Ridge, which we saw in Slide #83. At Matthews there was a ditch to cross and a hill to climb, so the Highway curved to accomodate the topography of the land. But what led the highway engineers to design a curve here? You will notice that if the highway had contined its due south course, it would have come right through a small linear body of water (D5). This is an earthquake graben crevasse. (See Slide #10 for a drawing of a graben and a normal fault.) This is a lateral spread feature. Liquefied sand moved beneath the top layer of soil, which did not liquefy. It was stretched from the pulling of the moving sand beneath and a pair of parallel normal faults formed letting a keystone slice of soil drop down between the two cracks. The result is a flat-bottomed depression with sloping sides, a graben in the soil. The water filled portion is only about 1/3 of the total length of this feature which is actually shaped like a long canoe in map view and extends for over 1,000 feet (C5-G5). It gradually pinches out on both ends (C5 & G5) so that the farmer has been able to plow and plant the upper and lower portions of the graben fissure but not the deepest portion whose flat bottom is about 15 feet below the surrounding land surface. According to a 1982 Energy Resources Map published by the Missouri Department of Natural Resources, a buried natural gas pipeline completely crosses the foreground of this photo (F1-10), including the southern portion of the graben fissure (F5).

## SLIDE #111
## Inside "Mile Post 50 Graben Fissure," Ground View Looking South with Author, David Stewart

Standing down in the north end of the graben fissure, you can see the flat bottom key-stone block of soil that dropped down along a pair of normal faults sloping into the depression on either side. The graben is about 100 feet wide at this point. This is the largest graben fissure known in the NMSZ. We call it the "Mile Post 50 Graben Fissure" because that's where it lies along the east side of the Interstate. As you walk into this huge crevasse from the higher ground above, you can see the Associated Electric 812-foot-tall smokestack 8 miles to the south. That puts us near the northern edge of the epicentral area of the greatest of the New Madrid quakes, the magnitude 8.8 event of February 7, 1812. The "Witness Tree" seen in Slides #78 and #79 is only a mile and a half to the northeast on the other side of the freeway. Myron Fuller, a geologist who spent several years between 1900 and 1905 mapping the features of the NMSZ, said that at that time there were many such features to be seen. Most were less than 30 feet wide and ranged in length from tens of feet to hundreds. (See Fuller, 1912.) During that horrible five-month period of the Great New Madrid Earthquakes, thousands of tremors occurred, dozens of which were strong enough to cause crevasses and fissures.

## SLIDE #112 LOCATION Q

## Inside "Mile Post 50 Graben Fissure," Ground View Looking North with Visiting Scientists, March 1991

Here is the Mile Post 50 Graben Fissure as seen from inside looking north. It is reported that back in 1811-12 the people's greatest fear was that they would be swallowed by the earth and be buried alive. Thousands of fissures and crevasses fractured the earth during these cataclysms, but no one died because of them. But several people did fall into them. Some were injured. Some needed assistance in climbing out. Some cattle were lost, however, unable to be rescued or to rescue themselves. The people soon realized that the crevasses tended to always open up in the same directions, depending on the locality. Often this was in a north-south direction, like the Mile Post 50 Graben Fissure seen here. Shortly after the quakes began their five-month siege in 1811-12, the pioneers felled trees in a direction perpendicular to the trend of the crevasses, east-west in this case. Then when the ground would commence shaking, they and their families would all run to the tree trunk lying on the ground and ride out the earthquake. In this way, if the ground opened up beneath them, they would already have a bridge in place. It is reported that during 1811-12, several people saved themselves from falling into these features by such devices. The men and women you see in this photo are an international group of scientists and engineers who have come from all over the world to experience what it is like to "fall into an earthquake crevasse."

LOCATION Q

## SLIDE #113
## "The Grinnel Hole," an Earthquake Pond in a Seismic Sand Slough Near LaForge, Missouri

This is an interesting place. We are standing on a seismic sand ridge looking across a seismic sand slough (E1-10) to a parallel sand ridge on the other side seen as a thin light yellow strip all across the photo (E1-10). (See Slide #9 for a sectional diagram of a sand slough.) Here sand has been extruded along two fissures forming a pair of parallel ridges with a sagged area in between, the slough. This one holds water when it rains and is wet much of the year. The round body of blue water in the foreground (F3-8) is just a puddle from recent rain, but the circular patch of water just beyond the two people in the distance is a partially filled in earthquake pond. The pond was pretty big, more than 100 feet in diameter. Ernest Carpenter, owner of this property, has lived here and farmed this land since 1936. He says that when he first came it was a body of clear spring water with a name: "The Grinnel Hole." A grinnel is a type of fish, *Amia calva*. In Missouri it is also called "Bugle Bass" and "Bowfin." It is an odd species dating back more than 100,000,000 years, predating the great dinosaurs. They are a type of lungfish who can breath either air or water. They have a long fin that extends the entire length of their backs, which certainly gives them a prehistoric appearance. Mr. Carpenter said that years ago grinnel could be seen lying on the bottom of the pond. Some years, during the dry summer months, the water table would fall and the pond would almost dry up, leaving mostly wet mud. These fish would burrow into the mud, go into suspended animation, and survive until the water rose again. Now you can understand why this species has survived for millions of years through conditions both favorable and harsh.

## SLIDE #114

LOCATION Q

## Another View of Carpenter Sand Slough With Students on Class Field Trip

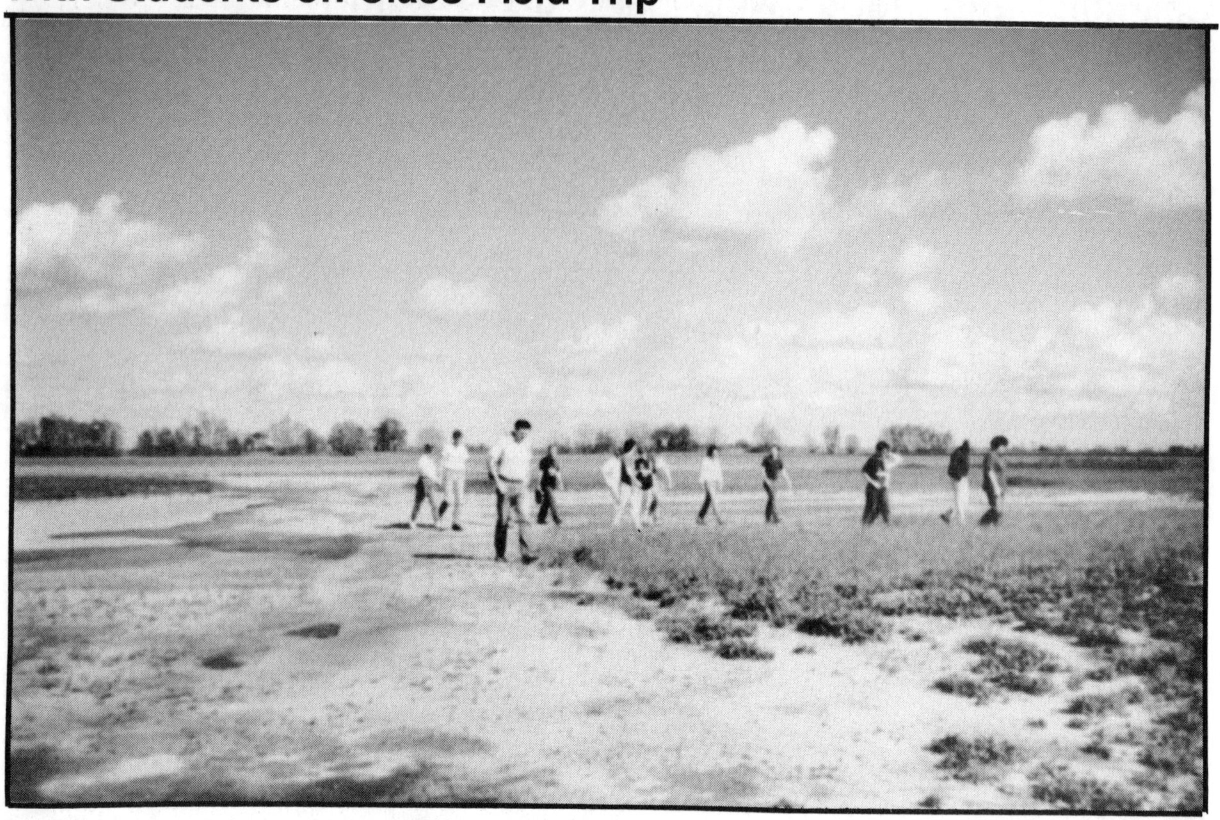

This is another view of the Carpenter Sand Slough. We are standing on the east sand ridge with the northern part of the slough, containing water, visible on the left. The Grinnel Hole is slightly behind us to the left. These are students on a field trip from Southeast Missouri State University. Seismic sand sloughs and ridges are not good farm land. You can't grow much in sand, but if you leave it bare, the sand blows and cuts off the crops in adjacent good soil. Mr. Carpenter has solved the problem on his ridge, for the most part. He never plows it. Instead, he plants wheat, harvests the wheat, and plants soybeans between the wheat stubble without tilling the land. This rotation of crops by "no-till" farming yields him marketable crops and keeps the sand as stable as possible. Mr. Carpenter has been a pioneer in this methodology, having practiced no-till methods in his sandy acreage for more than 40 years.

## SLIDE #115 LOCATION Q

## Carpenter Sand Slough & Sand Ridges, Aerial View Looking South, New Madrid Bend Six Miles Away in Distance

You can see the pair of parallel sand ridges of the Carpenter Sand Slough best from the air (G1 – C7 for the east ridge; G4 to D8 for the west ridge). The slough or seismic sagged area is in between the ridges (F4 – D7). The blacktop highway that cuts across these features is New Madrid County Road P (F1 – E10). According to Myron Fuller, a geologist who mapped many seismic features in the NMSZ between 1900 and 1905, there were many of these sloughs, "like finger lakes," he said. (See Fuller, 1912.)The Grinnel Hole is at the south end of the slough (D7). The pond has long disappeared, however. Mr. Carpenter has gradually filled it with excess soil, sand, rocks, limbs and cotton scraps from the cotton gin (called "cotton trash." His idea was to fill it up so he could farm the area. But he said no matter what he did, he was still never able to plow the spot and farm it because it stayed too "mushy." He did not know it was an earthquake feature. He tells a story about once leaving his diesel tractor to idle on the edge of the Grinnel Hole while he took a lunch break and went back to his barn to get some tools. When he returned, the tractor was buried up to its hubs. The vibrations had mechanically induced liquefaction (MIL). He brought another tractor to pull the first one out, and it, too, became mired in the liquefiable sand. It finally took a third tractor with a long steel cable to winch them out from a safe distance. The little settlement of LaForge is just off the photo at the lower left corner (G1). The town of New Madrid can be seen 4 miles in the distance (A6-10) where the sun reflects off of the surface the Mississippi River at the top of New Madrid Bend (A6-10).

## SLIDE #116 LOCATION R

## Earthquake Pond in North End of Quarter Mile Long Seismic Sand Slough, 2 Miles North of Charleston, Missouri

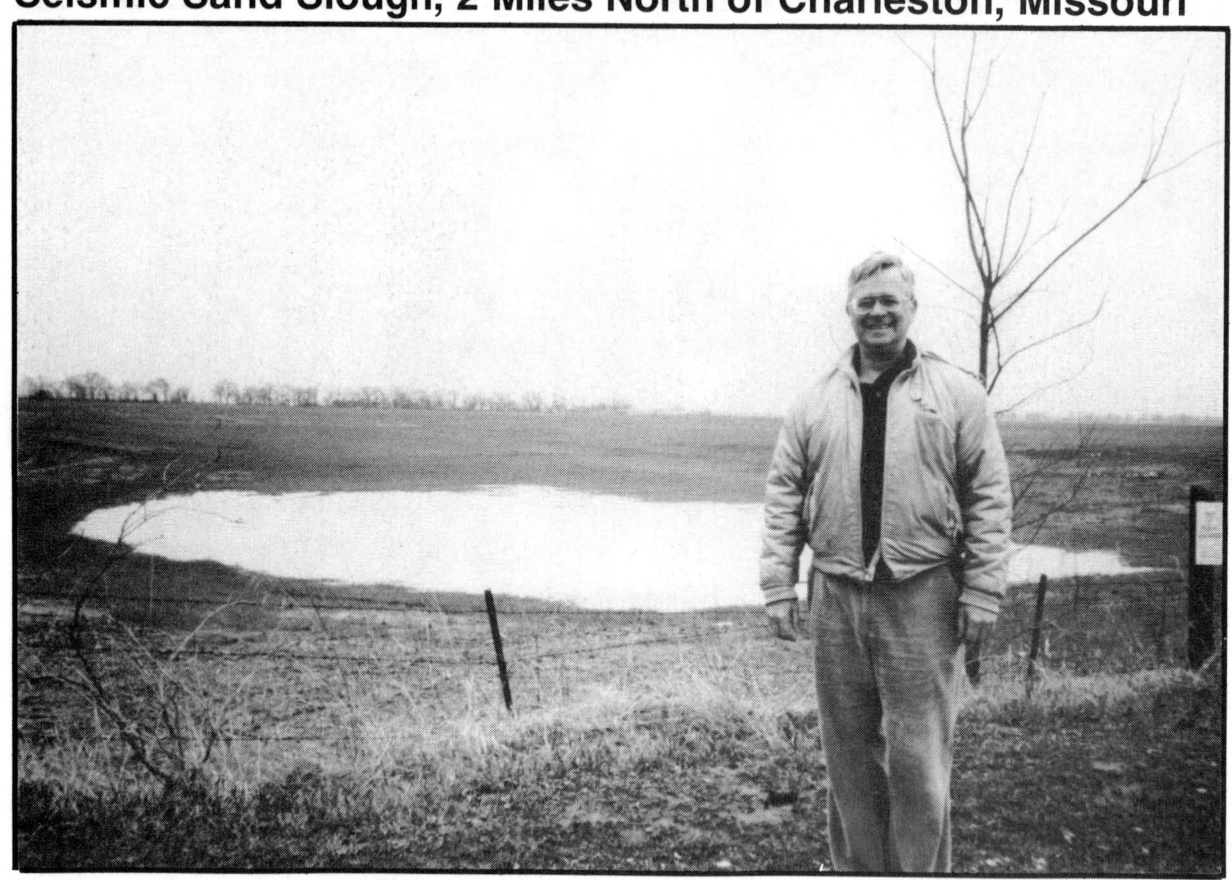

Here is an earthquake pond that still exists near Charleston, Missouri. Like the Grinnel Hole in the Carpenter Sand Slough seen in Slides #113-#115, this earthquake pond is also in the end of a large seismic sand slough. Notice how the shape is a nearly perfect circle. We are standing at the north end the 1,000-foot-long slough where some fill has been emplaced for a parking lot. (The smiling gentlemen is David Stewart. The unseen photographer was Mike Coe, a former director of the Center for Earthquake Studies at Southeast Missouri State University.)

## SLIDE #117 LOCATION R

## Earthquake Pond North of Charleston, Missouri, Looking Northeast Across End of Slough

This is another view of the same earthquake pond in the end of a sand slough as seen in the previous photo. Since a magnitude 6.5 earthquake occurred near here on October 31, 1895, (Halloween) we cannot say if this feature is due to the great New Madrid earthquakes of 1811-12 or the Charleston, Missouri, earthquake of 1895, or both. You can see the author's car parked behind the trees on the left. The trees in the distance on the other side of the road are along the edge of Big Lake. Don't confuse this with Big Lake on the Arkansas-Missouri state line, the earthquake lake created on December 16, 1811, during the first New Madrid quake. The "Big Lake" here, north of Charleston, is a remnant of an old Mississippi River Channel, an oxbow lake and has nothing to do with earthquakes so far as we know. The Charleston, Missouri, earthquake did create an earthquake lake, but it wasn't Big Lake. It was Henson Lake, a few miles south of south of Charleston. There was already a small lake there before 1895, but the quake enlarged it considerably. The level of water in this earthquake pond reflects the rise and fall of the water in Big Lake, not because there is any surface connection, but via the water table.

## SLIDE #118 LOCATION S

## Hydrologically Induced Liquefaction (HIL), Sand Boil Volcano Near Drainage Ditch, February 1991

This is a sand boil cone or sand volcano. It is a liquefaction feature. This is how sand boils often look while they are boiling during and following earthquakes. They form temporary cones or rims about their vents. Later they slump down and flatten into round sandy spots. This one is not due to an earthquake or seismically induced liquefaction (SIL). However, it looks exactly like the ones that seismic forces can cause. This one is due to an unusually high stage on the Ohio River on the other side of the levee less than a mile from here. It is an example of hydrologically induced liquefaction (HIL). This particular sand volcano was active in February of 1991 and continued to be active for another month or so. It was located in a small suburb north of Cairo, Illinois, called Future City. Cairo and Future City are located within the northern portion of the New Madrid Seismic Zone. When a major earthquake does occur in the NMSZ, you will see lots of seismically induced sand volcanoes like these all over the area ranging in diameter from less than 10 feet to more than 50. This one is only 3-4 feet in diameter. It has extruded so much water that it has incised through its cone. This was one of dozens of such sand boil cones in the Cairo area at that time. The largest one we saw was 15-20 feet in diameter. We should mention that the term "sand volcano" is descriptive of the shape of these features but does not imply any associated thermal phenomena. No steam, lava, or hot rock comes from these. They emit no heat of any kind other than the normal temperature of the groundwater which, in this area, is about 65 degrees Fahrenheit (18 degrees Celsius). We use the term "volcano" to caption this photo because it is so descript. In general, however, as a geologist and seismologist, we usually avoid the term because to some people the word connotes molten rock, which we do not wish to imply. We have to admit, though, that they do look exactly like miniature volcanos. This appearance does not last long. They soon smooth out into gentle mounds of sand.

## SLIDE #119 LOCATION S
## HIL Sand Boil Volcano Next to Highway 51 North of Cairo, Illinois, February 1991

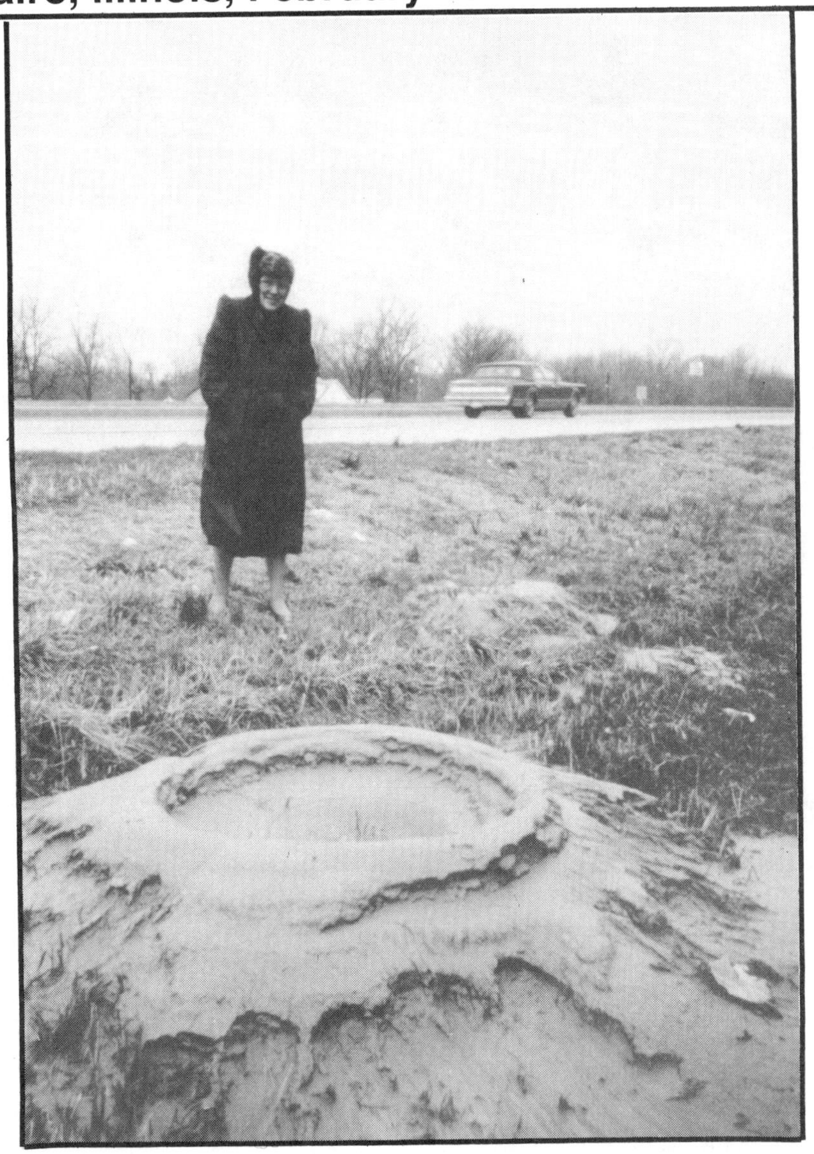

Here's another sand volcano at the same location and time as the previous slide. It is larger, being 6-8 feet in diameter. It is located in the shoulder of Highway 51 just north of Cairo. The person standing in the background for scale is Ms. Linda Dillman, Associate Director of the Center for Earthquake Studies, Southeast Missouri State University, in Cape Girardeau. It was a cold and windy February day when this photo was taken. The wind chill factor was below zero, Fahrenheit (20 below zero, Celsius). The sand boil cone in the picture was actually frozen at the time. These can boil even in freezing weather, however, because the water and sand that issue through these vents originates below ground where it remains a constant 65 degrees Fahrenheit (18 degrees Celsius) level regardless of surface temperatures.

## SLIDE #120

LOCATION S

## Multiple Small Sand Boils Coalescing in Ditch East of Highway 51, Near Cairo, Illinois

Coalescent sand boils like these can grow and merge into huge compound sand boils. They are all small, less than 6 feet in diameter (note the soda bottles for scale). Here, again we are on the side of Highway 51 north of Cairo, Illinois, in February of 1991. These are hydrologically induced liquefaction (HIL) features, but seismically induced liquefaction (SIL) boils look exactly the same. Some compound boils in the New Madrid Seismic Zone cover many acres with their blankets of sand. Most notably are "The Beach," covering 136 acres, (Slides #102 – #105) and the Howardville Sand Boil, covering 25 acres, (Slides #39 – #42).

## SLIDE #121 LOCATION S

## Hydrologically Active Sand Boils with Associated Flooding, Future City, IL, March 1991

Here, again, we are looking at hydrologically induced liquefaction (HIL) near Cairo, Illinois. As you see here, when the boils form, depositing sand on the ground surface, they also extrude copious quantities of water which can eventually flood the boils, submerging them in a temporary body of water. These sand boils have a pink tint to them. When actually standing there by the water's edge, you can see the round pink outlines of many boils completely under the water, many of them still extruding water with some sand. This photo was taken in late March, 1991. They had been boiling slowly for more than a month at the time of the picture. The same thing happens in earthquakes. Your front yard could not only receive a large amount of unwanted sand, but your house and property could also be visited by a seismically induced flood from the large quantities of extruded ground water. Seismically induced (SIL) sand boiling doesn't last for weeks and months, like these hydrologically induced (HIL) boils from the Ohio River. But SIL boils can bubble and flow for up to a week after the quake, and often do with major earthquakes. Some sand boils form under water, like some of those seen here. For example, during the New Madrid earthquakes of 1811-12 many boatmen reported seeing the surface of the river boiling from masses of water and sand erupting from the bottom. In some cases, they even witnessed explosions beneath the river's surface that caused the river to spout fountains of liquid sand and mud high into the air. Some small boats, back in 1811-12, were capsized by these phenomena. You can also find circular sand boil deposits on the beds of earthquake lakes now drained for agriculture. These include Lake Nicormy between Hayti and Kennett, as well as Lost Lake near Bell City and Lake St. John north of Sikeston, Missouri. All of these lakes were formed during the New Madrid earthquake but were permanently drained after 1918.

## SLIDE #122 LOCATION S

## Liquefaction Damage to City Street, Cairo, Illinois, March 1991

This is what liquefaction can do to a city street. When the subsurface turns to quicksand, highways, houses, buildings, and whatever is above them can sink and crumble. During February and March, 1991, this city street in front of the Cairo, Illinois, Public Utility building turned into a quagmire of boiling sand and river water, leaving a destroyed section of pavement almost half a block long. A block away you can see a multi-storied apartment building. This liquefaction was caused by a high water level on the Ohio. Cairo is situated in the NMSZ on a peninsula between the Mississippi and Ohio Rivers. It is surrounded with levees. The city has to deal with this problem every time either one of these rivers gets high. Such repairs are a routine part of the city budget. Can you imagine what would happen here if a major earthquake occurred in the NMSZ while either or both of the rivers were high? Towns have been known to disappear completely due to liquefaction following earthquakes. Cairo was not there in 1811-12. It was founded in the 1850's. There was liquefaction and considerable damage in Cairo during the 1895 earthquake centered a few miles west near Charleston, Missouri. But that quake was only a magnitude 6.5 and the town survived. The river was not usually high at that time, either. They were lucky in 1895. What will happen to Cairo in the event of a magnitude 7.5 or greater?

LOCATION T

## SLIDE #123
## Sand Fissures at End of Runway At the Marston-New Madrid Airport

We are back at the New Madrid Airport now, just outside of the town of Marston, Missouri. We are flying over the epicentral region of the greatest of the New Madrid earthquakes, the 8.8 magnitude event of February 7, 1812. As we circled the field we couldn't help noticing the seismic sand fissures extending from beneath the runway below. The end of the runway is framed by the pilot's small window (EFG-1,2,3) The seismic sand fissures extend from the end of the runway (F1-2) behind the strut of the airplane (EF-4,5) and into the field (E6-7 to D8). In the event of a major earthquake centered in the NMSZ, you can assume that this airport will not be useable because all of the fissures and sand boils in the area would probably be reactivated. There really isn't any place around Marston and New Madrid, Missouri, where you could build anything as long as a runway without crossing numerous earthquake features.

## SLIDE #124 LOCATION T

## Boat-Shaped Crevasse, Linear String of Sand Boils And Sunk Land on Farm West of Marston, Missouri

Here we are not far from Marston and we see a number of seismic features on the ground. Along the left upper corner (E1-A4) we see a string of small sand boils extending under a cluster of farm buildings and a house (C2). In the center (D5) we seen a canoe or banana shaped depression, probably a small graben fissure. And along the right lower corner we see a sunk land.

# SLIDE #125

LOCATION T

## Stressed Vegetation & Disturbed Tree Growth Reflecting Patterns of Seismic Liquefaction, 1811-12

Still in the Marston, Missouri, area, we notice this striking seismic feature, a scar in the landscape that gashes like a huge spear point across fence lines, plowed fields, and disrupts the growth of trees in a small patch of woodland. Can you see it? It extends as a dark green area from the bottom of the photo (G4-6) that narrows to a point at the center of the picture (C7). The light yellow patches on either side are compound sand boils. The dark green "scar" is probably a low spot, a sagged area representing the location of the source of the sands that boiled to either side. The mottled appearance of the soil surface throughout the photo is evidence of liquefaction from previous earthquakes.

## SLIDE #126 LOCATION U

## Parallel Seismic Sand Fissures East of Blytheville, Arkansas

We have now flown down to the Blytheville, Arkansas, airport on the east side of town. The airport is behind us and to the right. The city of Blytheville can be seen in the distance (B1-6). Interstate Highway 55 crosses the photograph from left (B1) to right (B10). Look at the alternating dark and white stripes in the foreground. These are a sequence of parallel sand fissures that opened up in 1811-12 and filled with quicksand. Earthquake features from the great New Madrid sequence abound throughout the Blytheville area. For northbound travelers there should be a billboard a few miles south of Blytheville that says, "You Have Just Entered the New Madrid Seismic Zone." The stretch of Interstate 55 from near Blytheville to the Benton Hills of Missouri (see Slide #96) is lined with innumerable fissures, sand boils, and other seismic landforms for more than a hundred miles. This passage of the Interstate also lies over some of the most active portions of the New Madrid Fault today, which some seismologists consider as the most likely source areas for the next big NMSZ earthquakes. Between Blytheville and Hayti, Missouri, gas pipelines and 161-kilovolt power transmission lines cross the Interstate in six places.

## SLIDE #127 LOCATION V

## Fissures & Boils, Missouri Welcome Station & Rest Area On Interstate 55, 2.5 Miles North of Arkansas-Missouri State Line

Now we have flown along Interstate 55 from Blytheville, Arkansas, into Missouri where we see the Missouri State Welcome Station and Rest Stop (D4-7) only 2.5 miles north of the State Line. We are less than 10 miles from Blytheville. We wonder if people coming into this Welcome Station realize the awesome history of what surrounds them. You can see liquefaction features all around this location on both sides of the freeway. When people drive through this portion of I-55 there ought to be a billboard that says "This is Earthquake Alley." This stretch of highway, from Blytheville to Hayti, lies over one of the most active parts of the New Madrid Fault today. (See Slide #3.) Tremors, too small to be felt, but big enough to be measured by sensitive seismographs, occur here at least once every week or two. Once or twice a year the residents feel them. On April 27, 1989, a 4.5 magnitude quake occurred near Cooter, Missouri, just north of here. It knocked groceries off shelves in Steele and pictures off the wall at Hayti. It was a Thursday. The quake hit at 12 minutes before noon. One lady in Holland was watching her favorite soap opera when the tremor shook her glass of iced tea off the coffee table and onto her rug. Some sixth grade students at Steele had just listened to their teacher describe the Great New Madrid Earthquakes of 1811-12. It was the hour before lunch. She concluded her talk with the comment, "And you know, some day it could happen again." Just then the quake hit the school. The kids knew exactly what to do, "duck and cover" under their desks. Their teacher had just finished explaining the procedure to them only minutes before. When you live on "Earthquake Alley" you need to be ready at all times. The town in the upper left (B1-3) is Holland, Missouri. The highway interchange in the upper right (B10), one mile up the Interstate from the Rest Stop, is Exit #4 to Holland (on the west side of the freeway) and Cooter (on the east). That's Steele that you see in the distance 4 miles to the north (B8).

## SLIDE #128
## Earthquake Sand Fissures, Steele, Missouri

LOCATION V

This is Steele, Missouri (CD1-7). The town is completely surrounded and underlaid by earthquake features. Notice the fissures in the foreground (EFG-3-8). Interstate Highway 55 runs obliquely along the bottom of the photo (G2-G10). This region, between Steele and Cooter (2.5 miles to the south), is thought to be the epicentral location of the second great New Madrid quake on the morning of December 16, 1811. That event is thought to have been 8.0 on the Richter scale and occurred around 8:00 a.m., following the first great quake which hit at 2:30 a.m. and was centered between Blytheville and Big Lake, Arkansas. (See the Map of Slide #1.)

## SLIDE #129 LOCATION V

# Huge Sand Boil & Parallel Sand Fissures, Bootheel Lineament Crossing Highway F, West of Steele, Missouri

As you drive west from Steele, Missouri, along Highway 162, you see many sand boils along both sides of the road. About 4.5 miles from town you cross Pemiscot County Road F. Just south of the intersection with Highway 162 you encounter this massive compound sand boil on the east side of County Road F with numerous parallel fissures streaking across the fields on the west. (County Road F runs from left to right across the middle of the picture.) Notice the striking change in color from dark brown in the bottom half of the photo to sandy yellow in the top. This line between light and dark marks another place where you can clearly see the "Bootheel Lineament." (See the discussion in the Featured Text as well as the comments with Slides #102-#109.) The dark soil is called "gumbo," a heavy sticky black clay, characteristic of some parts of southeast Missouri and northeast Arkansas. Its adhesive properties are so great that when walking across a field of wet gumbo 10-20 pounds of soil can accumulate and adhere to each boot, making it almost impossible to pick up your feet and move. The large compound boil below was trenched by scientists from the Center for Earthquake Research and Information at Memphis State University in 1989. They were hoping to obtain a sectional view of the 80-mile-long lineament that would ascertain if it is a fault and how one side moves relative to the other. Results from this particular dig were equivocal on that point, but evidence from other sources suggests a right-lateral strike slip motion for this feature. This location is about 5 miles south of the Braggadocio Big Boils see in Slides #107-#109 and about 11 miles south of "The Beach" seen in Slides #102-#105. The Braggadocio Big Boils and The Beach both lie along the Bootheel Lineament.

## SLIDE #130 LOCATION W

## Former Site of Little Prairie (Under River) As Seen Through Caruthersville Boat Landing Welcome Sign

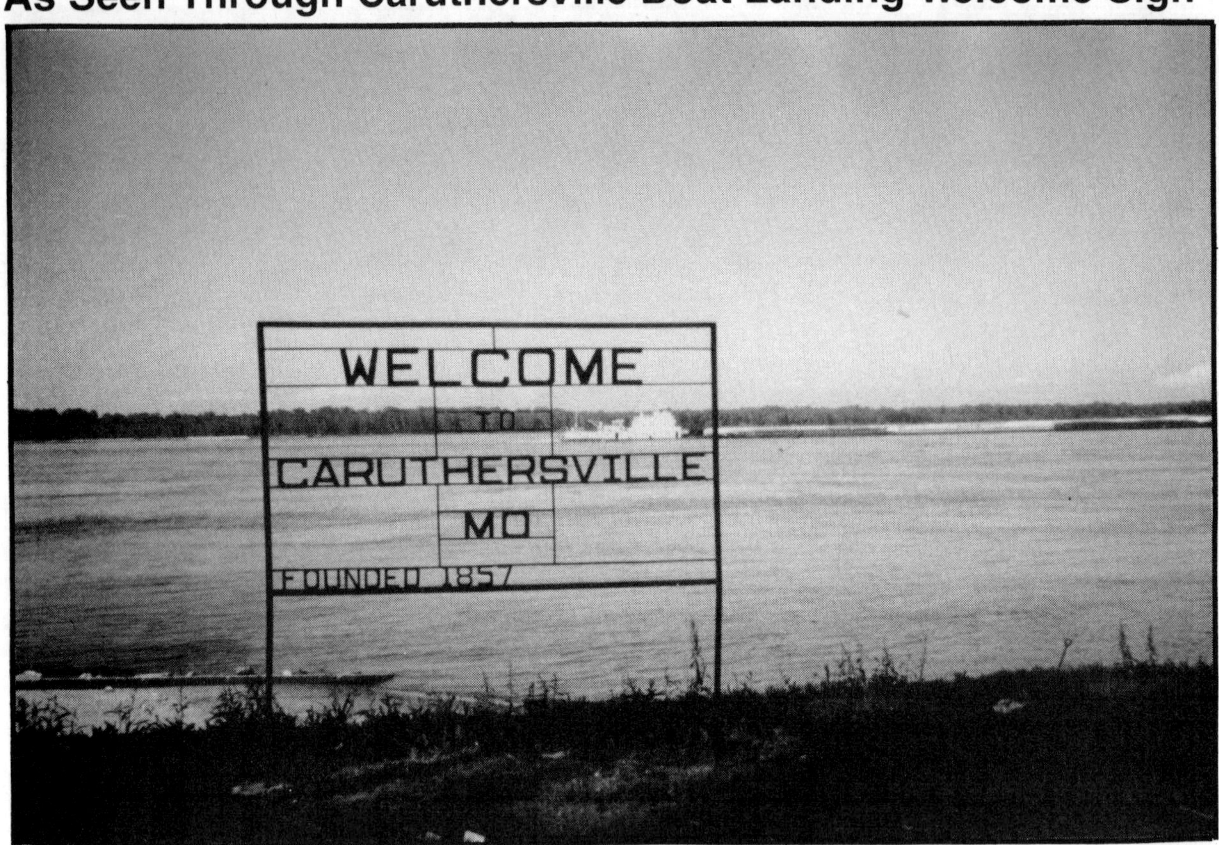


Behind this sign there's a story. It welcomes boatmen and others to the town of Caruthersville today. But before Caruthersville, there was another town here, now lost forever. In 1800 a small village called Little Prairie flourished here. About 2:30 a.m. on December 16, 1811, these people were awakened by a horrendous earthquake. Violently thrown from their beds, some were injured and bleeding. Some were knocked unconscious. The earth continued to rumble through the dark night. About 8:00 a.m. another great shock hit. Others almost as severe shook through the morning. The ground split open. Crevasses were everywhere. Sometimes cracks would open and then slap shut, spouting groundwater over the tops of tall trees. Sometimes the ground would part beneath a large tree, splitting the trunk from the bottom up. Then about noon another great shock hit the town. The ground began to liquefy. The town began to sink. Dark waters oozed from the pores of earth, flooding the town from beneath. There were about 100 people. Imagine them, as they gathered what they could carry in their arms, lifted small children to their shoulders, and headed west. For eight miles they walked through cold waist-deep waters, never knowing from one step to the next if they were going to trip over a buried stump or fall into an unseen crevasse. All the while snakes, opossums, and wolves were swimming for their lives through the murky waters. They finally reached dry ground near present-day Hayti. Later in 1812, a few came back to to the ruins of their log cabins and renamed the town, "Lost Village." But the Mississippi began eroding the banks, claiming the town by bits. By 1820, even Lost Village was no more. Caruthersville was built on this location in 1857. Look through the iron sign where the tow boat is moving downstream. That's Tennessee (a mile away) on the other side. The original site of Little Prairie lies under the river about half way across.

## SLIDE #131 LOCATION W

## Large Lateral Spread/Differential Subsidence Earthquake Feature in Caruthersville

At one point during that horrible December morning when Little Prairie was flooded by the earthquake, the residents said a wide, deep crevasse opened up within the town. The people stood in shock around the yawning abyss as it hissed, seethed, bubbled and gurgled from below, slowly filling with dark muddy waters while vapors, like steam, arose from the pit and permeated the air with the stench of sulfur and rotten vegetation. It was a cold winter day, but some even said the waters rising in that ominous hole were warm. You can imagine what the natives were thinking. God fearing and deeply religious, they thought that the gates of Hell were opening up on their town. To be sure, religious revivals did follow the New Madrid earthquakes. The Methodists and Baptists doubled in membership in the year that followed, while the Shakers and Quakers also considerably increased their numbers. (Really! It's an historical fact.) The deep blue body of water you see here is a lateral spread feature within the city limits of Caruthersville. Ground water rises and falls within its confines. It has no surface inlet nor outlet. We would like to say that this is the abyss that terrified the residents of Little Prairie on December 16, 1811. But it isn't. It's in the wrong place. At the time of the earthquakes this spot would have been about a mile-and-a-half south of the town limits of Little Prairie. Nevertheless, it does give you some idea of the scale of the horrors experienced by those early pioneers.

## SLIDE #132 LOCATION W

## Aerial View of Former Site of Little Prairie In Front of Bunge Grain Elevator, Caruthersville, Missouri

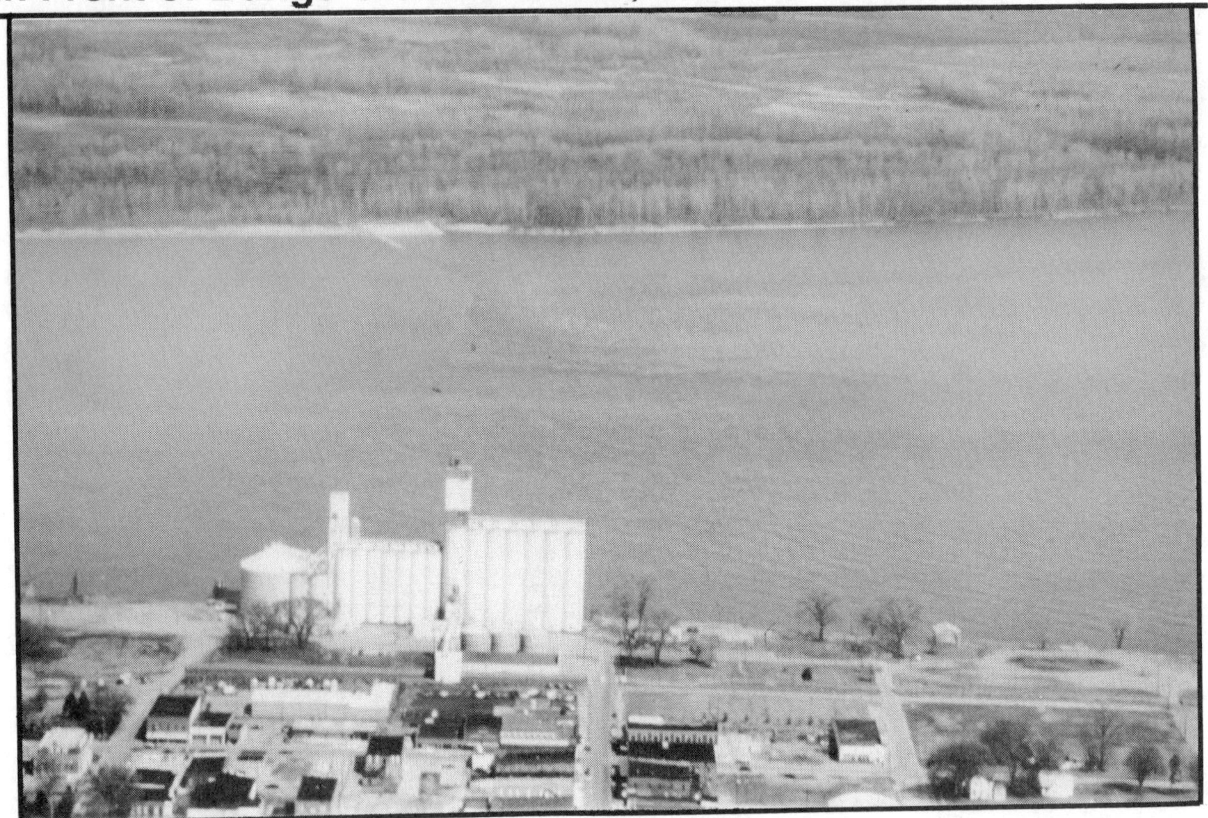

This aerial view of the riverfront at Caruthersville, Missouri, gives you another perspective on the location of the former site of Little Prairie. You see Tennessee on the far side of the river. The Mississippi runs from west to east here, from left to right in the picture. The iron welcome sign you saw in Slide #130 is located on the water's edge just to the right of the grain elevator. The former site of Little Prairie and Lost Village is half way across the river in front of this Bunge Grain Elevator. The structure is 10 stories tall. It can be seen for more than 30 miles on a clear day. When we cross over into Tennessee and stand on the Chickasaw Bluffs during one of our next stops, you will be able to see this elevator in the distance, thus marking the site of Little Prairie. Considering the experience of Little Prairie, one has to wonder what will happen to this riverfront and grain elevator should the New Madrid earthquakes repeat themselves. Hopefully, the magnitude 8.0 events that distinguished those earthquakes won't happen again for at least 200-300 years. But lessor quakes, 6.0-7.5 in magnitude, are likely to occur sooner than that. A 6.0-6.9 event has an average repeat interval of 55-85 years on the New Madrid Fault. The last one this size was the Charleston, Missouri, quake of October 31, 1895. That's more than 85 years ago. What will happen to the Bunge Elevator when the next magnitude 6.5 happens?

## SLIDE #133 — LOCATION W

## January 23, 1812, Epicentral Area, Distant Aerial View Looking 7-8 Miles North from Caruthersville

You can see where the site of Little Prairie lies under the river even better from this higher altitude (D5-6). Across the river is a tongue of Tennessee (C1-10). Beyond the Tennessee strip we see the Mississippi (BC1-B10). This is the great "Caruthersville Bend." Boatmen coming downstream enter the bend from the north B10, turn west for 8 miles, just off to the left (C1) where they turn 180 degrees and head east for another 8 miles (D1-E10). In 1991 Phyllis Steckel, a graduate student working with Dr. Knox at SEMO State University, noticed that the axis of this rather large bend lines up with a tectonic feature in the basement bedrock called "The Pascola Arch." The New Madrid Fault underlies this bend and is highly active today. (See Map of Slide #3.) Pascola lies on the Bootheel Lineament. (See Slide #107.) Could it be that this bend has an earthquake origin like the New Madrid Bend? (See Slide #30.) River experts find this bend to be an anomaly. Perhaps the explanation for its size, shape and orientation lies, not at the surface, but deeply buried in the restless body of the New Madrid Fault. Only future research will tell. Look 7-8 miles in the distance beyond the northern leg of Caruthersville Bend and you'll see a light yellow spot (B6). This is a huge seismic sand feature that marks the approximate location of the 8.4 magnitude earthquake of January 23, 1812. This was the quake credited with beginning the chain of events that created Reelfoot Lake. (See Slide #54.) The January 23 quake is also blamed for the disappearance of the town of Point Pleasant, a few miles up river from the epicenter. The people had already temporarily abandoned the town in December, having gone up to New Madrid for refuge. When they returned in February, the banks on which Point Pleasant had been situated had collapsed into the river and disappeared. There is another town near that site today by the same name, but it is a newer settlement and is prudently located about a mile inland from the river's edge.

## SLIDE #134 LOCATION X

## Aerial View of Campbell Earthflow Landslide Near Lenox At Exit 7 Interchange, Interstate 155 & Highway 186, Tennessee

Now we have followed Interstate 155 from Hayti, Missouri, past Caruthersville and over the Mississippi River to the Chickasaw Bluffs near Lenox, Tennessee. I-155 is a spur that extends between Dyersburg, Tennessee, and Hayti. The bridge over the river on I-155 is seismically designed to resist earthquakes, one of only five seismically designed bridges over the entire course of the Mississippi. The Chickasaw Bluffs extend along the east bank of the Mississippi for 150 miles from Wickliffe, Kentucky, to Memphis, Tennessee. More than 200 landslides have been mapped along these escarpments, most of which are attributed to the earthquakes of 1811-12. (See Jibson & Keefer, 1988, for detailed maps of these landslides.) One of those landslides is seen below. It is huge, more than a mile wide (CD1-9). The highway interchange on the left (CDEF1-2) is Exit #7 where I-155 crosses Tennessee Highway #182. Highway #182 runs north and south along the foot of the bluffs. This interchange and I-155 climb the hills at this point, passing over the northern edge of the earthquake landslide. Because such sites are unstable ground, the highway department has to continually fight the slumping of the soils from above the ramps and lanes. The hillside above the eastbound on ramp (CD2-3) is particularly prone to creep and sliding, sometimes covering the ramp with dirt and rock which the highway department has to periodically remove. If you drive past there, you will see what we mean. If the highway engineers had only located this highway a quarter of a mile to the north, these problems could have been avoided. The right end of the landslide has been deforested CD6-7). There is a gravel mining operation on the hillside (C6) and a cluster of homes at the base of the slump DE6-8). This is the Campbell property and homestead. The earthquake feature is called the "Campbell Landslide." It is an earthflow type slope failure.

## SLIDE #135 LOCATION X

## Upper Portion of Campbell Landslide at Two-Thirds Of the Way Up Looking North, Parallel to Loess Bluff

We are now standing about two-thirds of the way up the slope of the slide, about 130 feet up the 200-foot-high bluff. Here you can see the structure of the Chickasaw Bluffs. The top layer is loess, a windblown soil from 50-100 feet thick. It was deposited 8,000 – 20,000 years ago during the last Ice Age. A darker layer is seen beneath, especially visible on the left side of the photo beyond the students standing there. This is the Lafayette Gravel, a glacial outwash deposit from the Ice Age. Gravel deposits are rare along the Mississippi River south of Cape Girardeau. Hence, this gravel is a valuable resource mined by the Campbell family. The scientific community is grateful to William and Floy Campbell for their hospitality in permitting groups of students and scientists to visit their landslide. Groups from Universities at both Memphis and Cape Girardeau come see this outstanding feature on a regular basis. If you wish to visit this site, please check with Mr. or Mrs. Campbell, who live at the base of the slide, and receive their permission. If you come here you will find some very interesting rocks of many colors in the Lafayette gravel. Some of these stones and cobbles have been moved by the forces of ice and glacial meltwaters from more than 500 miles to the north in Wisconsin. During the deposition of the loess, a variety of extinct snails used to live in abundance on the land where the dust was occasionally heaped up. Hence, you can find white snail shells that probably range in age from 8,000 – 20,000 years in age. You may also find "loess dolls." These are calcareous concretions that accumulate by groundwater action in small holes in the loess. When the loess erodes away, these connected balls of hard gray mineral matter sometimes suggest the figures of dolls. This earthquake landslide was induced by the New Madrid earthquakes of 1811-12. It became relatively stable until the trees were removed some years ago. Now it has been reactivated and moves again with each heavy rain. You can see the dislocated blocks of loess in this photo.

## SLIDE #136 LOCATION X

## Lower Portion of Landslide Showing Active Crevasses In Earthflow, House Roof Tops Visible Below

Here we are standing about halfway down the slide looking down. Although not visible in this picture, you can usually see the Bunge Grain Elevator at Caruthersville 14 miles away, marking the site of Little Prairie. On a clear day, you can also see the tall smokestack of the Associated Electric Company at New Madrid 33 miles to the north, marking the epicentral region of the 8.8 magnitude quake of February 7, 1812. In the foreground you see a highly disturbed earth, filled with small cracks and crevasses, and no vegetation. This loessal soil is slowly flowing or creeping downslope. When saturated with precipitation, it is in a semi-plastic state, a sort of liquefaction. An earthquake during any such time would set this whole hillside into motion. The roof of the Campbell home can be seen on the left below. Another characteristic of loess bluffs that contributes to their proneness to seismic slope failure is a phenomenon called "piping." When water soaks into loess soils, it can form vertical vents or "pipes" straight down into the ground. In this case, the pipes extend down into the Lafayette gravel contributing to the groundwater that flows through that formation and under the loess. In exploring the loess bluff and head scarp of this landslide, be careful that you don't fall into a pipe. Some of them are several feet in diameter and could easily swallow a person. As another footnote, we mentioned "loess dolls" on the previous page. These oddities go by a variety of other names including "loess puppies," "loess kinchen," "loess kindern," and "potato rocks." Some of the local people paint faces on these to look like real figures.

## SLIDE #137

LOCATION X

### Base of Slide with Helter Skelter Fence Posts as Evidence of Currently Active Earthflow Creep

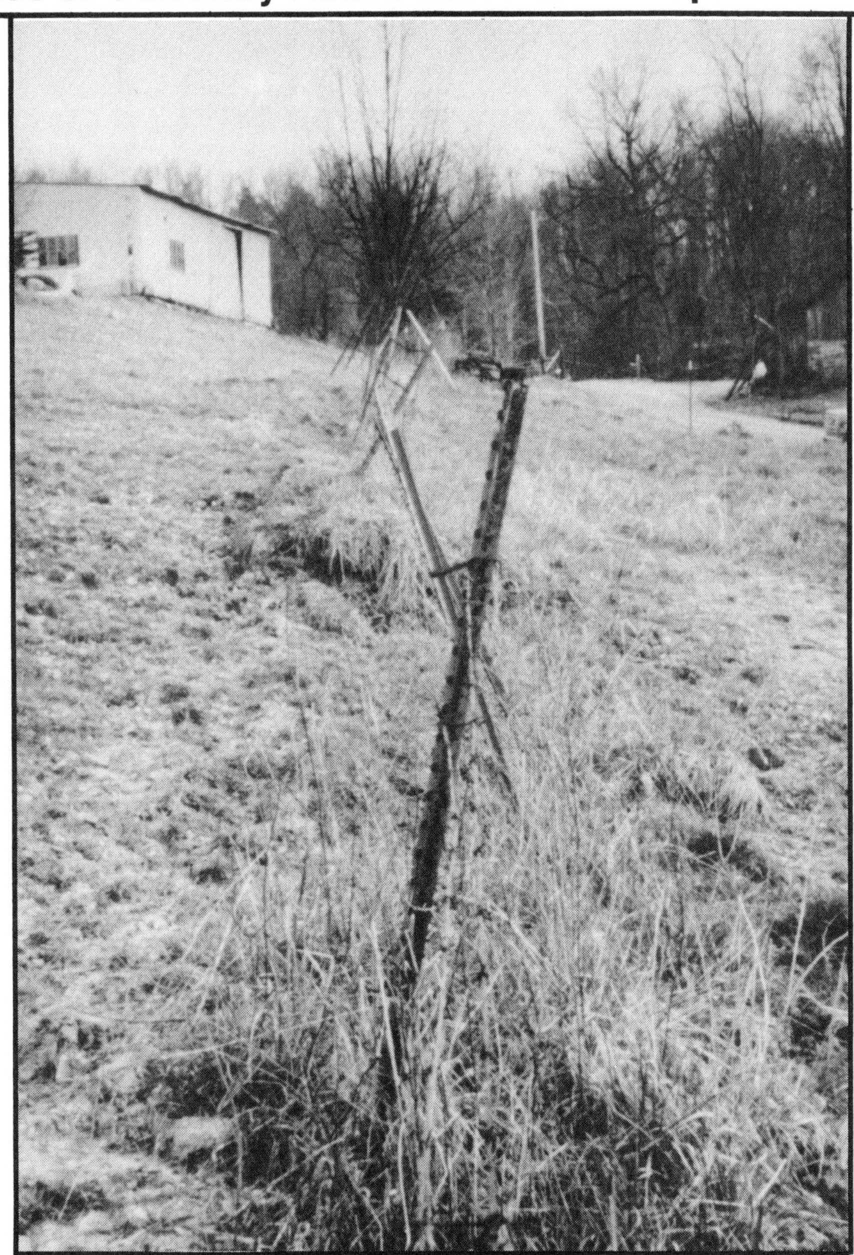

Near the bottom of the Campbell Landslide this fence has been strung, transverse to the slope. It was originally straight, but look at it now. The red metal posts are leaning in just about every direction except vertically. You don't have to be a geologist to figure out that the slope is slowly moving downwards, from the left to the right, taking the fence with it. The yellow metal building above is a tool shed and equipment storage shelter. An old wooden house can be seen on the right across from the metal shed. The brick homes of the Campbell family are down the hill, out of the picture on the right.

LOCATION Y

## SLIDE #138
## Graben Portion of Translational Block Slide Near Obion, Tennessee, Caused by 1811-12 Quakes

This is the graben portion of a translational block slide. (See Diagrams in Slides #10 and #11.) Before the New Madrid earthquakes of 1811-12, the block of earth in the middle of this photo was at least 20-30 feet higher, forming part of a continuous slope from left to right. During the quakes a pair of near vertical breaks formed so that the block of land you now see on the right broke away from the bluff and slid out horizontally more than 150 feet, while this middle portion dropped down like a keystone. If you notice in the diagram of Slide #11, starting at the top of the bluff, a translational block slide consists of a head scarp, a graben (a low, flat, dropped-down block), a horst (a higher prism-shaped block with apex on top forming a sharp ridge parallel with the head scarp), and half-graben (another low shelf-like block), with a slope descending the toe of the slide. In this photo, the head scarp is to the left, the horst block to the right. It is difficult to convey the shape and size of a translational block slide in photos. Because of the trees, even an aerial photo would not have done it. You almost have to climb up the half-graben, over the horst, and into the back graben below the head scarp to appreciate the scale of things. But use your imagination. Here's how it would be if you started at the top of the bluff (out of the photo on your left) and climbed down the entire landslide to the flood plain below. First you would descend a steep slope (the head scarp) into a depression and across a relatively horizontal span (the back-graben), then up a steep slope, over a sharp ridge, and continue down another steep side (up and over the horst block), and then walk across a flat terrace-like piece of land (the half-graben), and finally down a slope that meets the flood plain (the toe of the landslide). Notice where the man is standing. Imagine yourself standing there in the graben and turning to your left to look up at the apex of the horst block for the next slide.

## SLIDE #139
## Horst Portion of Translational Block Slide Near Obion, Tennessee, Viewed from Below in Graben

Here is what you would see if standing in the graben looking up at the horst. A very steep incline with a sharp ridge along the top parallel to the head scarp is behind you. Sometimes the back-graben (where we are standing at this moment) traps water in permanent pools. These are called "landslide sag ponds." This particular landslide doesn't have any sag ponds, but others along the Chickasaw Bluffs do. This translational slide has a dense cover of trees which keep it stable. Earthquake landslides will eventually stabilize by vegetative growth if left alone, but if they are deforested (like the Proctor & Campbell Landslides seen in Slides #96-#99 & #134-#137), they become reactivated and unstable and start creeping and moving again. Every heavy rain can bring them down a few inches more while another major earthquake could bring them down precipitously. The people you see are an international group of scientists on a field trip sponsored by the Geological Society of America in November of 1989. Now let's climb the steep slope of the horst to where these people are standing.

## SLIDE #140

LOCATION Y

## Top View of Horst Block Portion of Slide with International Group of Visiting Geologists

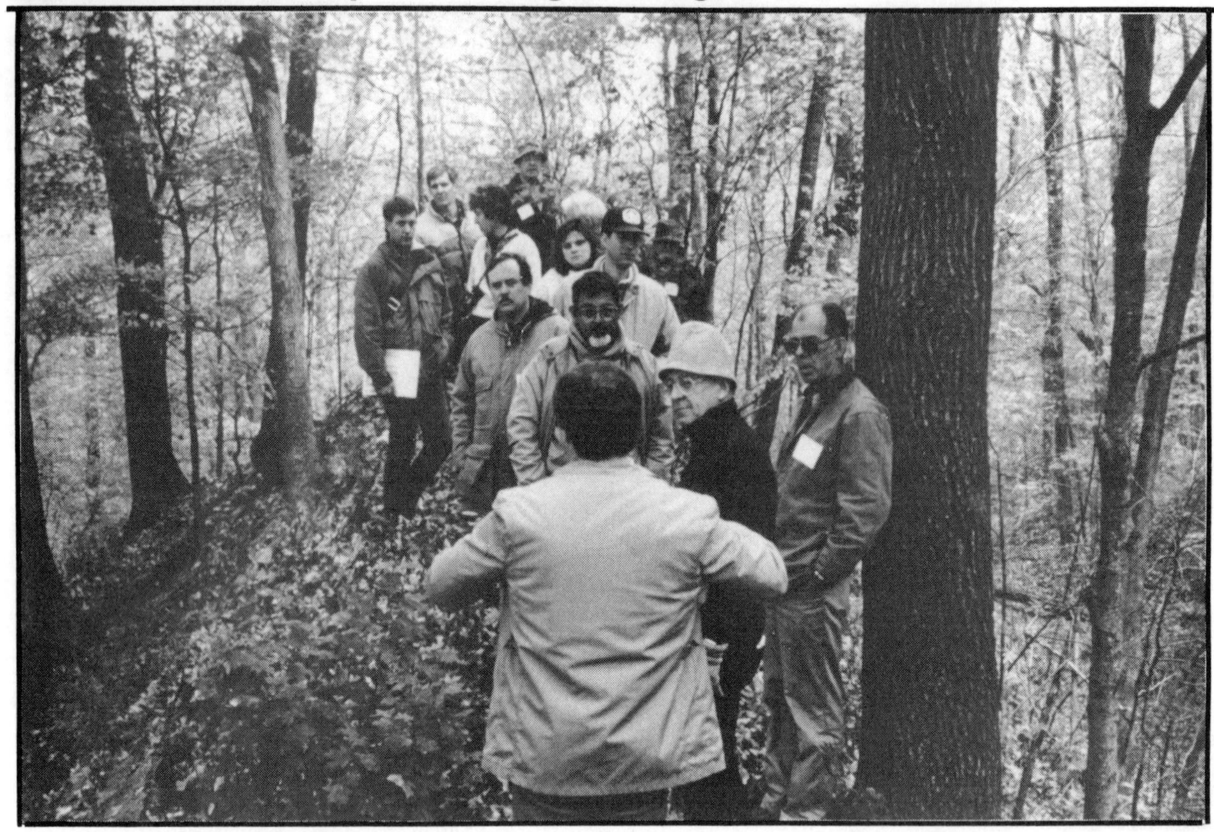

Here you can see a line of geologists standing along the apex of the horst block which slopes off at a steep angle on both sides. The back-graben is to your left, the half-graben and bottom of the landslide is to your right. If you want to visit this impressive graben and horst slide, it is straight up the steep hill (a virtual bluff, actually) above the little community of Gratio, Tennessee, at the intersection of South Bluff Road and Gratio Levee Road.

## SLIDE #141 LOCATION Z

## Rotational Slump Viewed from Bluff on Alleghany Street Involving Several City Blocks in Hickman, Kentucky

Hickman, Kentucky. County Seat of Fulton County. A settlement on the Mississippi River with an interesting history and some of the most spectacular views in the Midwest. Originally settled in 1819 as "Mills Point," it changed its name to "Hickman" in 1845. It sits atop a narrow promontory of highland, a piece of the Chickasaw Bluffs. The Indians called it "Chicken Point," because so many birds roosted there. John Audubon, the famous naturalist and bird authority, was in this area during the earthquakes of 1811-12. On a clear day you can see for more than 30 miles. The castle-like structure perched on the knoll on your left (C1-2) is the Fulton County Courthouse built in 1903. It was renovated in 1990-92 as a historic monument. The previous court house on that spot had been built in 1845. A light blue ribbon of the Mississippi can be seen across the photo (C10-4), flowing south from right to left. The blue-grey strip of land on the far side of the river is Missouri (C4-10). Island #6 (D4-10) shelters the town's waterfront from the swift currents of the river, forming a natural still-water harbor (D6-8), an asset that has contributed to the growth and importance of Hickman in river commerce. You can't see it today because of the haze, but in the distance just to the right of the Court House you can often see the Associated Electric smokestack at New Madrid, 20 miles to the west. We are standing at the corner of of Alleghany and Magnolia Streets on the edge of a stable part of the bluff (stable as of today, that is). Below is a section of town, about 8 city blocks, that sits entirely on an old rotational slump from the New Madrid earthquakes (G2-10 to D4-8). This is June and the vegetative cover is dense, but in the winter months you can see the stair-step terraces that distinguish such a landslide but which also make it attractive for urban development. Carrol Street runs below (G2-D5). Let's go down and take a look.

## SLIDE #142 LOCATION Z

## Leaning Trees & Telephone Poles on Carrol Street (Bus. Hwy. 94) on 1811-12 Slump in Hickman, Kentucky

Here we are looking west along Carrol Street in Hickman Kentucky. We are standing on a massive rotational slump from the New Madrid earthquakes. The saying goes, "Once a landslide, always a landslide." Once a slope has failed, it will never be permanently stable again. It may temporarily stabilize if trees are allowed to take root, but if the trees are removed and/or urbanization takes place, the slope will move again. Here we see that trees on the left and telephone poles on the right of Carrol Street are leaning. This is because the slope is creeping from left to right. Look down Carrol Street as far as you can see. That's where we shall go next.

## SLIDE #143 LOCATION Z
## Curved Tree Trunks and Pavement Separated from Curb, Carrol Street, Hickman, Kentucky

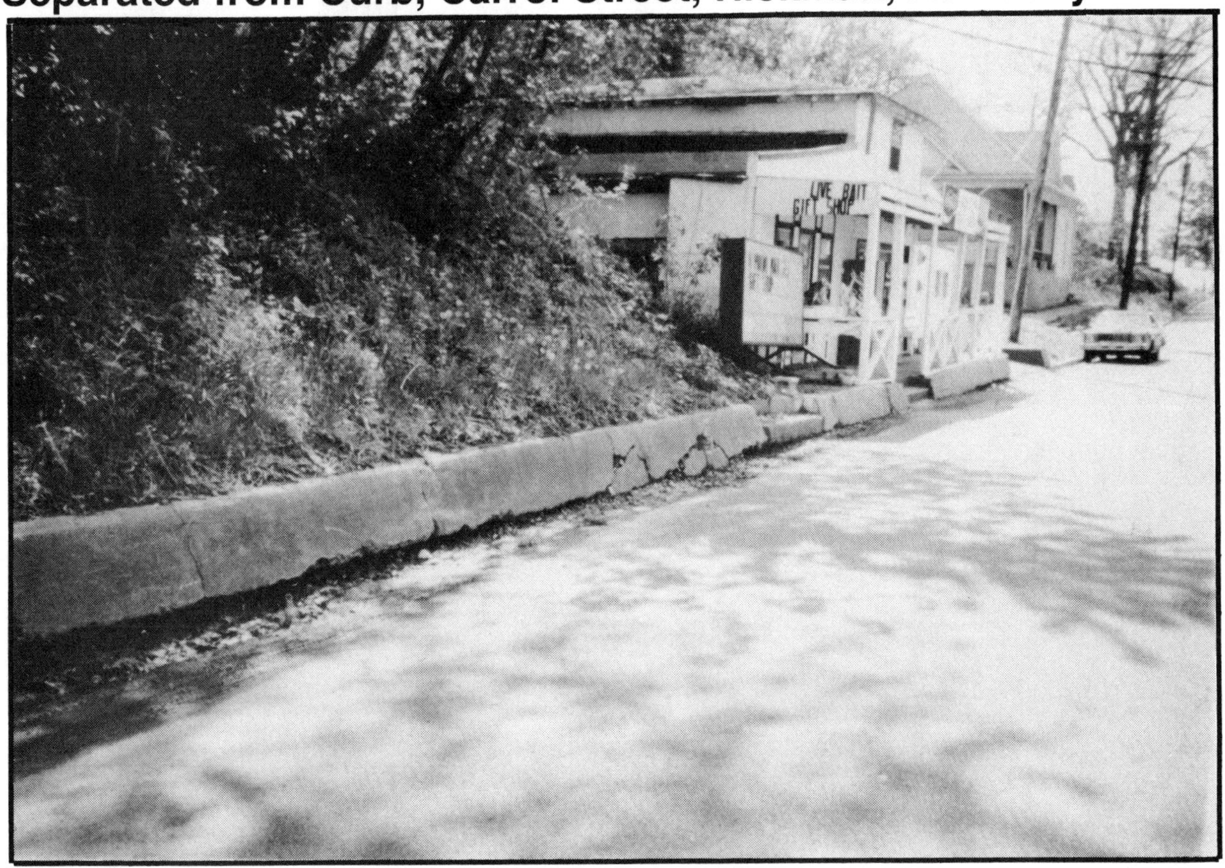


We are now standing in the middle of Carroll Street at the location indicated in the previous photo. Note the trees leaning down the slope on the left. Trees don't grow at such angles. They have been turned this way because the hillside in which they are rooted is slowly creeping downslope. See how this movement has torn the curb away from the street. Also notice the leaning telephone poles further down the street. If you could walk closer to the white concrete block store (The Bait Shop) and the green house beyond on the left, you would see that these buildings are full of cracks. The porch of the house has been repeatedly repaired as the house is pushed from left to right by the inexorable movement of the unstable hillside. Back in the mid-1980's during a period of heavy rain the slump behind The Bait Shop pushed in the back wall filling the rear of the building with dirt and mud. The owner eventually shoveled it out, replaced the collapsed wall, and reoccupied the place. Such is life on an old earthquake landslide. You could spend a full day in Hickman just driving around and looking at these kinds of damages to homes, streets, sidewalks, and buildings. It's too bad we only have space for a few photos here. What you can see is almost unbelievable. And consider the potential for future earthquake damage on such topography. Slopes that creep under normal conditions could lurch into a gallop during the next big quake. To realize that people are living on a hillside in constant slow motion in an earthquake zone would give most people a creepy feeling. Wouldn't you agree?

## SLIDE #144 LOCATION Z

## Faulted Landing on Concrete Stairway Down 1811-12 Rotational Slump Above Carrol Street

We are standing on a rotational slump, an earthquake landslide from 1811-12. This concrete stairway starts across the street from the Fulton County Courthouse and descends more than 100 feet down the bluff and across the slide, down to Carrol Street between the white store and green house we saw in the last slide. From this view on one of the stairway landings the store and house are directly below, but out of sight because of the steepness and height of the slope. An excellent way to appreciate how this old landslide feature is currently creeping is to walk down these steps and notice the cracks, the bent railings, the leaning trees, the crumbling retaining walls, and the precariously perched houses above that could some day tumble down on top of the buildings and streets below during the next strong earthquake. At our feet we see that two adjacent concrete slabs in this landing have shifted relative to one another. It is like a miniature right-lateral strike slip fault. There is no way a photograph can convey the magnitude of this massive earthquake slump and the profound instability of its slope. You'll just have to visit Hickman some day and walk down these steps yourself. When we lead field trips into the NMSZ, we always try to include a walk down these steps. It's an education and an experience.

## SLIDE #145 LOCATION Z

## House Porch Foundation with Non-Parallel Brick, Lower Part of Slump, Union Street, Hickman, Kentucky

We call this "The House with the Non-Parallel Brick." This old house on Union Street in Hickman is situated on the lower part of a rotational earthquake slump, a block below Carrol Street. The whole hillside is gradually moving from left to right. Over the years the right end of the house keeps tipping downward. To keep the house level, the owners have periodically jacked it up and laid a course of brick from right to left until they meet the floor supports. Focus on the top course of brick at the steps on your right and follow it with your eye from right to left. See? It does not go all the way across. The bricks are not parallel to the porch. This photo was taken in 1990. During a 1992 visit, the corner by the steps on the right had cracked and slumped again. It looks like another partial course of brick will be needed soon to reinstate the level of the house. We have taken dozens of interesting photos in Hickman like this, but limited space allows only a fraction to be displayed in this book and slide set. However, many of the pictures omitted here are shown in our other books, *The New Madrid Fault Finders Guide* and *The Earthquake America Forgot.* The founders of Hickman had not forgotten the earthquake when it was first settled in 1819. The courthouse built in 1845 and the one there now built in 1903 were not situated on a landslide, but a solid, undisturbed portion of bluff. The first settlers in Hickman did not build on the old earthquake landslides. They remembered the 1811-12 earthquakes and knew which slopes were stable and which were not. But two generations later, by the late 1800's, this knowledge was forgotten. And the result today is a town with one-third of its buildings and homes constructed on slopes that are slowly failing and which could fail cataclysmically during a future earthquake.

## SLIDE #146 LOCATION Z

## Scenic View from Hickman Bluff On Edge of Reactivated Landslide, East End of Magnolia Street

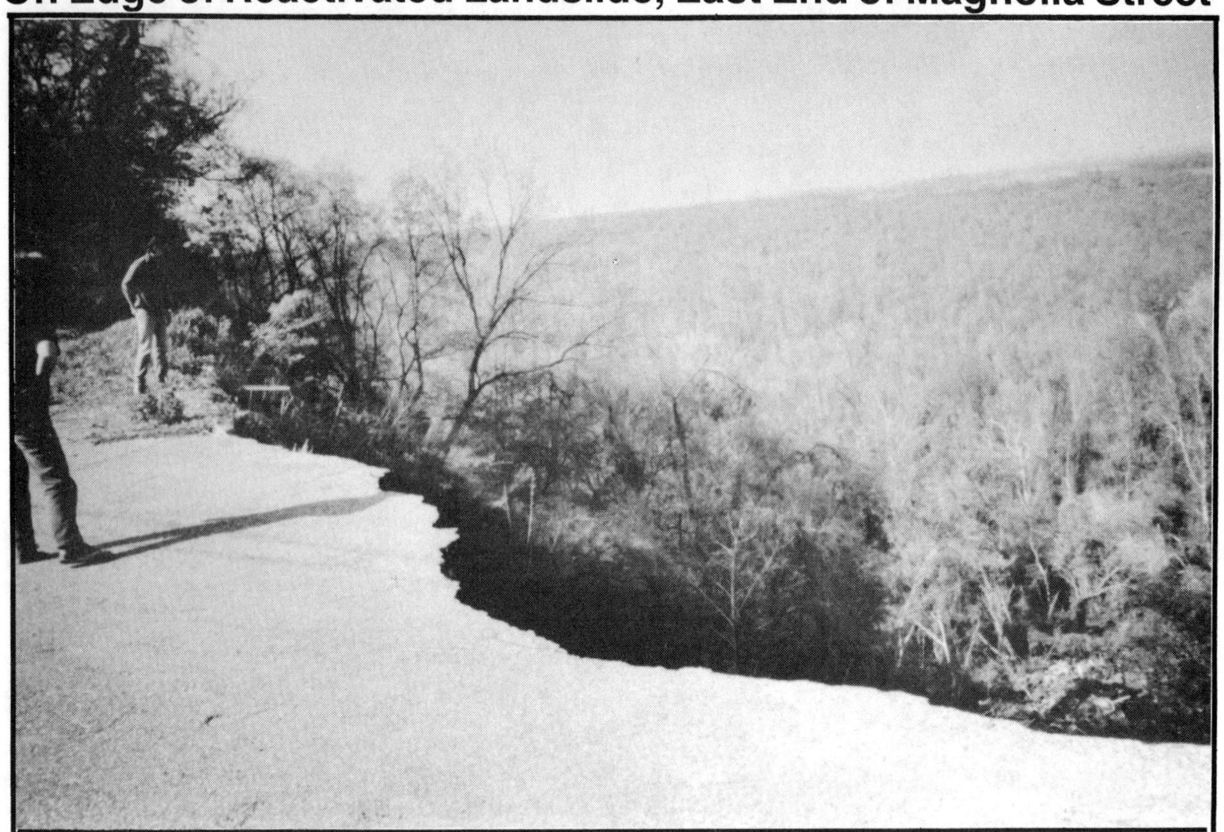

We are on Magnolia Street (or what's left of it) looking north. The precipice gaping before you used to be a scenic overlook, a municipal parking lot atop a 200 foot tall bluff, the pride of Hickman. On a clear day you can see all the way to Wickliffe, Kentucky, and see the plume of the smokestack at the Westvaco Company, more than 30 miles up the river to the north. The scenery is still as spectacular as ever, as you can see, but the parking lot is gone. So is a portion of Magnolia Street. Just over the jagged edge of the pavement is an 80-foot vertical drop-off with an incoherent debris slide from there down to the flood plain another 120 feet below. The original slope below the parking lot for this overlook was an earthquake landslide from 1811-12. The slump had been stable for more than a century, since the trees had reestablished their roots after 1812. It seems that these trees were getting too tall and obstructing the view. Sometime during the late 1970's the city decided to clear the slope. That was a mistake. Removing the vegetation from an old landslide will almost always cause it to slide again, either slowly or quickly, depending on circumstances. At first, the clearance of the trees seemed to have been a good idea. The view was improved. However, within a year or two, the slope below the parking lot began to bulge and move. The parking lot started cracking away in pieces. The city moved Magnolia Street a little further from the bluff and reestablished a new area from which visitors could stand and enjoy the view, but that area eventually disappeared, too, falling down the cliff into the Mississippi bottoms below. It seemed that every time there was a prolonged period of rainfall or a storm of unusual intensity, more of the bluff would break loose and fall away. This picture was taken in 1989.

## SLIDE #147 — LOCATION Z

## Reactivated Earthquake Slump on Magnolia Street, Street Partly Intact, Photo Taken 1989

From this angle you can gain a better perspective of the ragged upper lip of the head scarp above the abyss that yawns below. This is still 1989, the same afternoon as the previous photograph. Notice the buildings in the background toward which direction this slope failure is headed. Starting on the left behind the large leaning tree are two enormous white storage tanks, each containing 500,000 gallons of water, the Hickman city water supply. Next to the tanks is a historic two-story building the city had hoped to turn into a museum or library. Closer to the brink of the bluff is a single story structure, the Fulton County Clinic and Health Department. Behind that you see the rooftops of the Police Station, Fire Station, Ambulance Service, and the Board of Education Building. This is not to mention the brick house behind the telephone pole on the right, as well as another house just off the picture on the right. All of these structures are in jeopardy from this aggressive, progressive monster menacing inch-by-inch in their direction.

## SLIDE #148 LOCATION Z

## Reactivated Earthquake Slump on Magnolia Street, Street Missing, Sidewalk Intact, Photo 1990

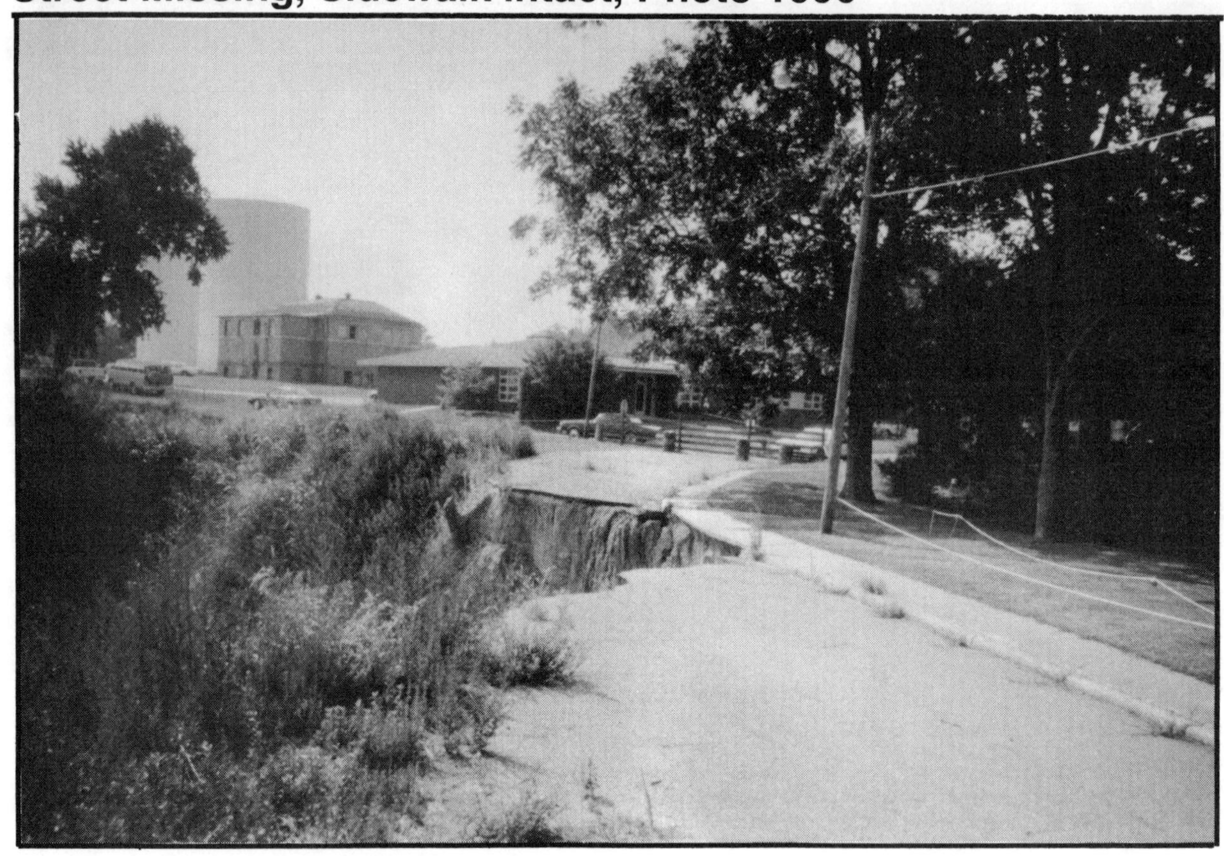

One year later, in June of 1990, we took this photo. Notice how the slide has now taken all of Magnolia Street, but the sidewalk is still intact. Take note of the telephone pole.

## SLIDE #149 LOCATION Z

## Reactivated Earthquake Slump on Magnolia Street, Sidewalk & Telephone Pole Missing, 1991

It is March of 1991, and look at what we see. The sidewalk is now gone, as is the telephone pole. The wires it held are now temporarily draped over the limbs of the elm tree on the right while the pole, itself, has joined the debris scattered below the precipice. If you go there and look down over the edge, you will see thousands of rubber tires scattered in the mud below. We don't know where it is written, but somewhere there must be a scripture that says that old tires can stop erosion. Unfortunately, this scripture is false, as the citizens of Hickman can tell you. The tires thrown over the edge have not arrested the inexorable creep of this failing hilltop. An engineering firm has estimated that it would cost more than $6 million to halt the growth of this creeping disaster and stabilize the slope. Can the town afford it? No. Can the town afford to purchase the row of houses and abandon the buildings now at risk? Probably not. It is a tragedy. No one's fault, really. Hindsight says it would have been better not to have cut the trees below the overlook, but no one knew that then. In the 1970's how was anyone to know that this was an earthquake landslide? The early founders of the city would have known back in 1819 and survivors of the earthquakes might remember such things through the late 1800's. But by the 20th century, this knowledge was lost and forgotten. In 1975 no geologist had yet identified and mapped this as an earthquake slide. Who could have known, then, that the slide would be so dramatically reactivated by the simple clearance of a few trees? The conclusion of this tragedy is yet to come. A major earthquake tomorrow could bring it to an abrupt climax. But the rain that falls year after year will accomplish much the same end, only gradually, an inch or two at a time. We can blame the New Madrid earthquakes of 1811-12. Without them, this would not have happened. When will the impact of these historically distant cataclysms go away? Probably never.

## SLIDE #150 TABLE

## Approximate Recurrence Intervals for Destructive Earthquakes in the Central United States

**APPROXIMATE RECURRENCE INTERVALS FOR DESTRUCTIVE EARTHQUAKES IN THE CENTRAL UNITED STATES**

| Surface Wave Magnitude (Richter) | Mean Repeat Intervals (In Years) |
|---|---|
| 6.3 | 55 - 85 years |
| 7.1 | 170-230 years |
| 7.6 | 200-300 years |
| 8.3 | 450-650 years |

**Modified from Hamilton & Johnston (1990). Preparing for the Next New Madrid Earthquake. U.S.G.S. Circular 1066**

The big question is when will the next "Big One" hit? Every Midwestern earthquake specialist knows that future damaging earthquakes on the New Madrid fault are inevitable. The only questions are: When? How many? How big? How much damage will there be? And how large an area will be affected? Detailed, quantitative answers to the last two questions are given in a book by David Stewart (available for small shipping fee only) entitled, *Damages & Losses from Future New Madrid Earthquakes.* (See the back of this book for details.) Answers to the first three questions are not so easy. Reliable methods of predicting earthquakes have not yet been devised. At best, only probabilities can be estimated. This table is based on historical records that go back a few centuries, on geologic evidence that goes back a few thousand years, and on recent seismographic instrumentation in the NMSZ since 1974. As you can see, we are overdue for a 6.3 event. It was a 6.3 quake that devastated Long Beach, California, in 1933, destroying three-fourths of the school buildings in the city. You can see that we are also at high risk of another 7.1 magnitude quake happening soon. It was a 7.1 magnitude quake that rattled the San Francisco Bay Area in 1989, doing more than $6 billion in damages and killing 67 people. The low death rate was due to California's high level of preparedness and the fact that California has been building to seismic standards for more than 50 years (since the Long Beach disaster). The table indicates that even a major 7.6 is not out of the question in the near future. Such a quake is potentially the greatest disaster in American history, spreading destruction through a 22 state area. Are we ready? There is one good thing in the table. The massive 8.0 magnitude quakes of 1811-12 do not happen often. If we our scientific facts and interpretations of the New Madrid Fault are right, we can let our great-great-grandchildren worry about these in a couple of centuries. As for us now, we only have to worry about the 7.0 and 6.0 quakes, which could happen at any time.

# GLOSSARY

**ALLUVIUM** A general term for clay, silt, sand, and gravel deposited by a stream. Most of the deposits seen throughout lowland regions of the New Madrid Seismic Zone are alluvium. The term may also be used in its adjective form, such as "alluvial sand".

**AQUIFER** A body of rock or sediment that is sufficiently permeable to conduct ground water and to yield significant quantities of water to wells and/or springs.

**ARTIFICIAL LEVEE** An embankment along one or both sides of a stream channel constructed by humans for the purpose of controlling the stream, especially to reduce the frequency of floods. See "natural levee".

**BOOTHEEL** The extreme southeast portion of Missouri that extends south of 36.5 degrees latitude which, on a map, has the shape of a bootheel. It is bounded on the east by the Mississippi River, on the west by the St. Francis River, and on the south by the 36th parallel. See Maps in Slides #1 & # 3.

**BOOTHEEL LINEAMENT** A line visible from high resolution satellite imagery extending from southwest of Blytheville, Arkansas, to west of New Madrid characterized by differences in sand boil appearances, sizes, and distributions on either side and by intermittently distributed massive sand boils along the lineament. It has the appearance of a strike-slip surface fault. It is currently under study to determine if it is an extension from depth of one of the branches of the deeply buried New Madrid fault. See Slides #1, #102-#109, and #129. See "fault" and "New Madrid fault".

**BORROW** Earth material taken from one location to be used for fill at another location.

**BORROW PIT** An excavated area where borrow has been obtained to build up the level of the highway road bed to avoid flooding or to create fill for approaches to highway overpasses. Construction of Interstate 55 required a lot of these. There are usually one or more borrow pits near any highway overpass, exit or interchange that required fill.

**BRAIDED BAR ISLAND** Islands within the branching channels of a braided stream. They are usually quite temporary as long as the stream is active, shifting as the stream "braids." The term may also be applied to a landform that was formed this way, even though the stream that created it is no longer active in that location. There are some braided bar islands along the east side of Interstate 55 between Sikeston and Matthews, Missouri, created by the Ohio River thousands of years ago when it braided there. Today they are gentle hills.

**BRAIDED STREAMS** A stream that divides into an interlacing network of several branching and reuniting channels. Streams tend to braid when their gradients are steep and when there is plenty of sediment available to the stream. In the bootheel, these conditions were more likely when climates were dry during the last glacial epoch between 6,000 and 20,000 years ago. This is because during dry periods the sparse vegetative cover does not protect sediment from erosion as well as during more moist climates. At this time, the mouth of the Mississippi River in Louisiana is braided, but between there and New Madrid it meanders. See "meandering streams."

**CARBONIZED WOOD** Pieces of what was once wood, now altered by time and burial into lignite or near-lignite. Streams have originally deposited most of this, sometimes later removing it and redepositing it. Of special interest to the bootheel are the black or dark brown fragments often found in sand that has been ejected by seismically-induced liquefaction. Sizes found range from granules less than 1/8-inch diameter to pieces two or more inches in size. One can usually find this material when investigating a sand boil, sand fissure or sand blow up close. See "coal" and "lignite".

**COAL** A combustible rock formed from compaction and hardening of plant remains. This ancient organic material has become hardened and modified into material having a high carbon content. Pieces of coal may be found in the sand boils and other liquefaction features of the New Madrid Seismic Zone, some almost fist size. Some of these came from deposits hundreds of miles away, washed here by streams over long periods of time. The age of much of this coal is Eocene, in geologic terms, which makes them 36 million to 58 million years in age. See "carbonized wood" and "lignite".

**DAL** Abbreviation for book entitled, *Damages And Losses from Future New Madrid Earthquakes.* See back of book for details of how to obtain your free copy.

**DS** Abbreviation for "dry sand." See Slide #7.

**DIFFERENTIAL SUBSIDENCE** Subsidence produced by unequal settling of earth materials, leaving the ground lower in some places than

---

**NOTE:** Every earthquake feature seen in the photos and/or diagrams of this book is defined on pages 27 through 51 in the "Featured Text" of this book in the order given in the table of Slides #4, #5 #6. Therefore, most of these terms are not repeated in this glossary.

others. In the New Madrid Seismic Zone, earthquake ground motion may be stronger in some places than others, and certain earth materials may react to it differently in some places than others, causing differential subsidence. Foundations of buildings will crack if underlain by soils that differentially subside during an earthquake, a very common cause of damage. Differential subsidence during earthquakes can also disrupt the flow of streams, temporarily or permanently reversing their gradients. See "gradient."

**EAF** Abbreviation for book, *The Earthquake America Forgot. See back of book for details.*

**EARTHQUAKE** The sudden release of strain energy when rocks beneath the earth's surface are stressed to the breaking point and suddenly shift along a deep fault zone. Sometimes the break or fault motion intersects the surface with a visible trace. Most of the time, the earthquake faults do not break the surface, but the seismic vibrations caused by the catastrophic, brittle fracture of the rocks deep below can travel thousands of miles through the earth and along the earth's surface. Relatively few people happen to be directly over a faulted region during an earthquake. What most people experience from a quake are seismic waves traveling to them from the source, which can be many miles away. The New Madrid Fault or Seismic Zone is confined to southeast Missouri, southern Illinois, northeastern Arkansas, and western Kentucky and Tennessee. Two to twenty miles below the surface of this area lies the fault that moves and the brittle bedrock that breaks. However, the ripples from the New Madrid Fault events have been felt for hundreds of miles and in 1811-12 were felt from Canada to Mexico, from the Rockies to the East Coast. See "epicenter" and "focus".

**EPICENTER** The point on the earth's surface directly above the focus or actual rupture point in the rocks that caused an earthquake. The epicenter is the closest point on the earth's surface to the source zone, but is not necessarily the location of greatest damage. See "earthquake" and "focus".

**ESCARPMENT** A long, more or less continuous steep slope facing in one general direction, breaking the continuity of the land by separating two relatively level surfaces such that one surface lies higher than the other. North and west of Reelfoot Lake is an escarpment called the "Reelfoot Scarp" which is several miles long facing mostly toward the east from the Mississippi River southward to the south side of the lake. The flat land west of Reelfoot Scarp lies 10-20 feet higher than the land to the east. (See Slides #44-#48.) Other notable escarpments in the New Madrid Seismic Zone include the flanks of the Sikeston Ridge (See Slides #83-#89, #91-#92.); slopes of Benton Hills (Slides #96-#101); Crowley's Ridge, which runs from Bell City, Missouri, to south of Jonesboro, Arkansas; and the Chickasaw Bluffs along the east side of the Mississippi stretching from Wickliffe, Kentucky, to Memphis, Tennessee. (Slides #1, #134-#149.)

**FAULT** A break in earth materials (rock or soil) with relative displacement on both sides. (A break without displacement is sometimes called a "joint" or a "crack".) In regard to earthquakes, there are two basic kinds of faults: One, those that cause earthquakes when they move: and Two, those that are caused by earthquakes. The causative faults are called "primary" faults, while those that are the consequences of earth ground motion are called "secondary" faults. Faults may be quite small, measured in feet, or very large, measured in miles. The New Madrid Fault is a complex of many faults spanning parts of Arkansas, Illinois, Kentucky, Missouri, and Tennessee. It is a zone thought to be some fifty miles wide and 120-150 miles long along a portion of the Mississippi River valley. See "Bootheel Lineament", "earthquake", and "New Madrid Seismic Zone". Also see "graben," "horst," "normal fault," "reverse fault," "strike slip fault," "thrust fault," and Slide #10.

**FFG** Abbreviation for book entitled, *The New Madrid Fault Finders Guide. See back for details.*

**FLOOD PLAIN** The nearly flat lowland that borders a stream and that may be covered by its waters at flood stages.

**FOCUS** The actual source zone or region below land surface where rocks suddenly rupture to create an earthquake. Earthquake foci (plural) may be shallow or deep, the shallowest being 2-20 miles deep, the deepest being 350-400 miles below land surface. The most destructive earthquakes are shallow. The source zone of the New Madrid Fault is 2-20 miles deep and, therefore, shallow. See "earthquake" and "epicenter".

**GEOMORPHOLOGY** The branch of geology that specializes in the nature, origin, and development of landforms and their relationships to underlying structures, and the history of geologic changes as recorded by these surface features. See "landform" and "morphoseismology).

**GRABEN** An elongate, relatively depressed series of sediment or rock units that is bounded by faults on its long sides. Technically, it is a structural form, which may or may not be expressed as a surface feature. The word comes from German and means "grave." Grabens caused by seismically induced liquefaction from the great New Madrid earthquakes will have surface expression. They will usually be canoe-shaped, banana shaped, or slightly curved, tapering at both ends. At least some have formed where intense ground motion has modified a former drainage channel, an extreme variety of differential subsidence. See "fault," "horst," and Slides #10, #110-#112, & #138-#140.

**GRADIENT** When referring to streams, gradient is the slope of the stream down its valley. A measure of vertical drop in a horizontal distance. Most geologists express gradient in units of feet per mile. Gradients range from more than 200 feet/mile in some mountain streams to less than half-a-foot/mile in lowlands, such as the Bootheel. The gradient of the Mississippi River at New Madrid is slightly less than 0.4 feet/mile.

**GREAT EARTHQUAKE** Richter magnitude of 8.0 or more. See "magnitude."

**GROUND WATER** Water below the surface of the earth that saturates the pores of the soil, alluvium, or rock. Normally, ground water moves down gradient by the pull of gravity. When earthquakes occur, excess pore pressure can build up in the ground water by the successive compressions of a seismic wave over a period of time. This excess ground water pressure can separate the grains of sand, silt or clay, causing temporary quick conditions or liquefaction. See "ground water table," "liquefaction" or "quick conditions".

**GROUND WATER TABLE** The top of the unconfined, saturated zone beneath ground surface. Below this level, all the interconnected spaces between sand and silt grains are full of water. In the bootheel, the ground water table is not far beneath the surface, ranging from maximum depths of 30 feet to areas where it is above the land surface. Saturated sediment and soil allows ground motion to create "liquefaction" during earthquakes. When the ground water table is above land surface, swamps and certain kinds of lakes or ponds result.

**GROUND MOTION** A general term for the various kinds of ground movements caused by earthquakes. Movements may be up and down, side to side, torsions, rotations, compressions and expansions, or combinations of all of these during an earthquake. Damage during a quake depends on the maximum amplitudes, durations, and frequencies of ground motion as well as soil conditions. When saturated with ground water, clay amplifies ground motion as much as 20-40 times the amplitudes of bedrock, while sand liquefies. For minimal earthquake damage, the safest foundation earth material for a building is rock or hard, dry soil well above the water table.

**HIL** See "hydrologically induced liquefaction."

**HORST** An elongate, uplifted rock unit or block of soil that is bounded by normal faults on its long sides. It is a structural form and may or may not be expressed at the surface. A horst is sort of opposite to a graben. The word is from the German language and means "high" or "raised up." In the New Madrid area, the Tiptonville "Horst" is a surface feature that is part of the larger Tiptonville "Dome." (See Slides #1 & #45-#48.) See "fault," "graben," and Slides #10 & #138-#140.

**HYDRAULIC HEAD** This is water pressure caused by a water level in one location being higher than at another. Water tries to "seek its own level," i.e., move from a higher head to a lower one (viz. flow downhill). Water to a faucet in a city flows under pressure because the water tanks are higher than the faucet. In much the same way, water standing higher in a flooded river will produce upward pressure on water on the "protected" side of a levee which is lower than the river. This produces Hydrologically Induced Li quefaction (HIL). See "HIL" and Slides #118-#122.

**HYDROGEOLOGY** See "hydrology."

**HYDROLOGICALLY INDUCED LIQUEFACTION** Abbreviated: HIL. Liquefaction primarily caused by ground water movements, especially vertically moving ground water, such as water seeking its own level behind levees during times of high stream levels. Towns along the river surrounded by levees, such as Cairo, Illinois, experience hydrologically induced liquefaction almost every year as the Ohio and Mississippi Rivers reach their peaks during winter and spring. Such liquefaction periodically damages streets and foundations in such towns. (See Slides #118-#122.) Areas that liquefy due to hydrologic forces will also liquefy when stimulated by dynamic loads of earthquake forces and vice versa. That is, seismically induced liquefaction (SIL) features will also respond to the hydrologic loads of ground water. See "SIL," "MIL," and "liquefaction."

**HYDROLOGY** A branch of geology and/or civil engineering that deals with the occurrence and movements of water in our environment. This includes ground water, soil water, surface water, rivers, lakes, and even the oceans. The term, "hydrogeology," is coming more into usage as a preferred term for "hydrology."

**HYPOCENTER** The same as "focus."

**INTENSITY** A measure of an earthquake's ground motion as indicated by damages to human constructions or disturbances to the land by way of liquefaction, landslides, subsidences, etc. The Mercalli scale, from I to XII, is used to gauge earthquake intensity. The Mercalli scale, thus, measures the "effects" of an earthquake, but not its "cause". The Richter scale is a measure of energy release at the source and is a measure of the "cause" of an earthquake, but not its effects. The effects of an earthquake at your location have to do with the distance from the epicenter and the soil conditions where you are. In general, the closer you are to the epicenter, the more intense the shaking, but not necessarily. Saturated clay soils amplify earthquake vibrations while saturated sand liquefies, both of which can magnify the intensity of the effects of an earthquake. A house on bedrock close to an epicenter may fare better than a house on sand or clay 100 miles away. See "Mercalli scale," "magnitude," and "Richter scale."

**LANDFORM** A component of the Earth's surface. One of the multitudinous features that taken together make up the surface of the earth. It may include broad features, such as mountains or plateaus, or minor features, such as valleys or levees. Seismic landforms, such as found in the New Madrid Seismic Zone, include surface faults, fissures, sand boils, landslides, earthquake lakes, and other features of the landscape partly or wholly formed by earthquake forces. See "polygenetic" and Slides #4-#11.

**LIGNITE** A low-grade coal, usually brown in color. Some of the lignite found in the seismic liquefaction features of the New Madrid Seismic Zone was carried there by rivers from hundreds of miles north or east, and can be many thousands of years old. See "carbonized wood" and "coal".

**LIMONITE** A term for a group of brown to rust-colored amorphous hydrous ferric oxides. It is a common secondary mineral formed by weathering of iron-bearing minerals. It may also occur as a precipitate in bogs or lakes. It occurs as coatings, nodules, earthy masses, and in a variety of other forms, and is the coloring material of yellow clays and soils. Some pea-sized nodules of limonite are ejected by extrusive sand features during seismically-induced liquefaction.

**LIQUEFACTION** The transformation of loosely packed, saturated sand, silt, clay or gravel into a fluid mass due to the excessive build up of pressure in the ground water. Also referred to as "quick conditions" which can give rise to "quicksand" and "quick clay." The excess pore pressure in the ground that produces quick conditions can be caused by hydraulic heads from hydrologic conditions (high river stages or flooding conditions), from mechanically induced vibrations in the ground (trains, tractors, etc.), or from earthquakes. See "seismically induced liquefaction (SIL)," "hydrologically induced liquefaction (HIL)," and "mechanically induced liquefaction (MIL)."

**LOESS** Wind deposits, primarily silt-size particles of dust. A lot of this material in the NMSZ was derived from glacial outwash to the north, 6,000-20,000 years ago when the climatic conditions of the region were more arid than today. The tops of the Benton Hills (See Slides #96-#101) and the Chickasaw Bluffs (See Slides #134-#149) are covered with deposits of loess, more than 100 feet thick in some cases. When saturated, loess can liquefy during earthquakes and produce catastrophic landslides. During seasons of heavy rainfall, loess can form earthflows and creep. (See Slides #134-#137 & #141-#149.)

**LOESS DOLL** Small spherical concretions of calcareous minerals formed when loess deposits contain small void pockets through which ground water can percolate and deposit calcium carbonate and calcium magnesium carbonate. The sizes of these nodules or concretions range from less than half an inch to an inch and a half. When little grey balls these weather out during the erosion of the loess, they are often found cemented together in forms that suggest a children's doll. See commentary with Slides #135-#136.

**LSS** Abbreviation for "liquefiable saturated sand." See Slides #7-#9.

**MAGNITUDE** The energy released by, or "size" of an earthquake. The term, magnitude, refers to the source of cause of the earthquake. It is expressed in Arabic numerals to one decimal place in terms of the Richter scale. Seismologists use a set of adjectives to represent ranges of magnitude on the Richter scale as follows: "Great" = 8.0 or more; "Major" = 7.0-7.9; "Strong" = 6.0-6.9; "Moderate" = 5.0-5.9; "Light" = 4.0-4.9; "Minor" = 3.0-3.9; (Very Minor" = 2.0-2.9; and "Tiny" = 1.9 or less. See "intensity," "Richter scale," and "Mercalli scale."

**MAJOR EARTHQUAKE** Richter magnitude in the range 7.0-7.9. See "magnitude."

**MEANDER** A sinuous or serpentine curve or loop in the course of a stream produced as the stream shifts its course from side to side as it flows across its floodplain. The largest meander bend or loop on the Mississippi River is New Madrid Bend. See Slides #1, #29, #30.

**MEANDER BELT** The zone along a floodplain across which a meandering stream shifts its channel from time to time. Reelfoot Lake is within the meander belt of the Mississippi River.

**MEANDERING STREAM** A stream that flows in a meandering pattern, as opposed to a braided pattern. Meandering streams are more likely when their gradients are gentle, and where sediment supplied to the stream does not exceed the ability of the stream to handle it without braiding. Below Commerce, Missouri, the Mississippi meanders. There have been times in the past when it has braided.

**MECHANICALLY INDUCED LIQUEFACTION** Abbreviation: (MIL). Liquefaction induced by ground motion caused by vibrating vehicles, locomotives, or other heavy machinery. We know of one instance where a farmer very nearly lost a tractor which was parked over a liquefiable area and left running during a lunch break. It nearly buried itself before the situation was realized and the tractor rescued. See "HIL," "SIL," "liquefaction," and Slides #23, #99-#102, & #113-#115.

**MERCALLI SCALE** A measure of the intensity or effects of an earthquake at different locations on ground surface. The scale is a subjective methodology whereby Roman numerals are assigned to an area from I to XII. Where I = a level almost no one feels but is measurable by sensitive instruments. VI = a level of ground motion that everyone feels and minor damage occurs. VIII = the level where serious damage can occurs, including the threshold of building collapsing. XII = total destruction. Theoretically a specific quake can have but one Richter magnitude, but can have many Mercalli intensities from some maximum to zero. The Richter scale says how much energy was released at the source, but the Mercalli scale tells what happened at each location. Some receive lots of shaking, some a little, some none. The Richter scale is a measure of the cause of the quake. The Mercalli scale is a measure of the effects. See "intensity,] "magnitude," and "Richter scale".

**MODERATE EARTHQUAKE** Richter magnitude in the range of 5.0-5.9. See "magnitude."

**MORPHOSEISMIC** Refers to a landforms that were created by earthquakes or pre-existing landforms that were extensively modified by earthquakes.

**MORPHOSEISMOLOGY** A field of scientific endeavor that combines the knowledge and methods of of geology, geomorphology, seismology, hydrology, soil science (a branch of agricultural science) and soil mechanics (a branch of civil engineering) to identify and explain landforms caused by or modified by earthquakes. Because of the multidisciplinary nature of the subject matter and the approaches necessary to study seismic landforms, morphoseismologists work best in teams whose aggregate of experiences encompass all of these disciplines. The research and field work that produced this book was carried out by Ray Knox, a geologist and geomorphologist, and David Stewart, a seismologist and hydrologist. Both have some knowledge and experience in civil engineering, but consulted with experts in soils and soil mechanics when writing this book.

**NATURAL LEVEE** A ridge or embankment of sand and silt, built by a stream on its flood plain along both banks of its channel, especially in times of flood when water overflowing the normal banks is forced to deposit the coarsest part of its load. The term also applies to a sand and silt deposit that was produced this way in a former time.

**NEW MADRID FAULT** Also called "New Madrid Fault Zone." A complex of faults considered to be approximately 150 miles long by 50 miles wide extending in a northeasterly trend from near Marked Tree, Arkansas; through Blytheville, Arkansas; Steele, Caruthersville, New Madrid, and Charleston, Missouri; to Cairo and Metropolis, Illinois. It joins with the Wabash Valley Fault and the Ste. Genevieve Fault near Metropolis. The zone also includes portions of western Kentucky and Tennessee, including the Tiptonville and Reelfoot Lake, Tennessee, areas. The portion of the New Madrid Fault complex from which more than 200 earthquakes a year originate lies from 2 to 20 miles deep. The presently active northern and southern legs of the fault are right-lateral strike-slip faults. The center portion of the fault, from Dyersburg, Tennessee, to New Madrid, Missouri, is a thrust fault. The largest earthquake on the New Madrid Fault during the 20th century was a moderate magnitude 5.0 in 1976 near Marked Tree, Arkansas. The second largest was a 4.7 in 1991 near Risco, Missouri. No direct surface expression of the fault has yet been discovered and proven, although many secondary surface faults can be found throughout the zone. See "fault," "Bootheel Lineament," "Ste. Genevieve Fault," "Wabash Valley Fault," and "New Madrid Seismic Zone".

**NEW MADRID SEISMIC ZONE** Abbreviation: (NMSZ). See subsection entitled "Defining the NMSZ" in the Featured Text portion of this book. Also see Slide #3 and "New Madrid Fault" in this glossary.

**NLS** Abbreviation for "non-liquefiable soil." See Slides #7-#9.

**NMSZ** See "New Madrid Seismic Zone."

**NORMAL FAULT** A fault whose relative motion is parallel with the direction of the angle of dip. Normal faults mainly produce vertical motions, with only a small component of horizontal movement. In sectional view, the downward moving side of a normal fault appears to be sliding down the incline of the fault plane. See "fault," "strike-slip fault," "reverse fault," "thrust fault," and Slide #10.

**NWA** Abbreviation for book entitled, *The Earthquake that Never Went Away.*

**OXBOW LAKE** An oxbow is a closely looping stream meander, having an extreme curvature such that only a neck of land is left between two parts of the stream. If and when this meander is cut off, a horseshoe-shaped lake is formed. Maybe we should call these kinds of lakes "horseshoe lakes", because the younger generations have never seen an oxbow. On the other hand, they probably haven't seen a horseshoe either!

**PERMEABILITY** The property or capacity of earth material for transmitting a fluid, such as ground water. High permeability means that the water can move through the material with ease. Low permeability means that the water can move, but with difficulty. Impermeable, or nonpermeablé, means that the water cannot pass through the material at all. Hydrologists also refer to permeability as "hydraulic conductivity."

**PETROLIFEROUS NODULE** Black nodules found in several of the extrusive sand features in the NMSZ ranging from "pea-sized" to an inch in diameter. When scratched, they smell like petroleum. They burn with a bright yellow flame. Their origin has not been satisfactorily explained.

**POLYGENETIC** Literally means "many geneses" or origins. The term is applied when more than one agent or process has been important in producing a landform. Virtually all of the features photographed for this book were "polygenetic." They all had something to do with earthquakes, but seismic forces were not the only forces that molded and made them into what is seen today. Among the variety of forces that helped sculpture and create landscape of the NMSZ are oceans, rivers, lakes, rain, wind, ice, glaciers, gravity, animals, and people. Every earthquake feature in the NMSZ was made of something there before the quake and which has been modified by the forces of humans and nature since.

**POTSHARD** See "shard."

**QUICK CONDITIONS** See "liquefaction."

**RICHTER SCALE** A measure of earthquake magnitude or energy released at the focus or causative source. A seismograph is usually needed in order to measure the numerical value of the scale to be assigned to any given earthquake. However, estimates of Richter magnitude can be made by analyzing intensity data and damage levels. The magnitude of the New Madrid earthquakes of 1811-12 were all estimated from damage and liquefaction data. See subsection at the end of the Introduction entitled, "How Richter Magnitudes and Epicentral Locations Were Assigned to These Events." The Richter scale is logarithmic to base 32. That is, for each unit increase (say from a 5.0 to a 6.0) the energy released at the source is by a factor of 32 times. Hence, a magnitude 8.6 is 32 times bigger than a 7.6. It would take 32 earthquakes of magnitude 4.1 to equal the energy released by a single event of Richter 5.1. Every two units on the Richter scale represents a thousand-fold difference while every two tenths of a unit represents a two-fold difference. Hence, a 6.4 releases as much energy as 1,000 small quakes 4.4 in size while a 6.4 quake is double the size of a 6.2. See "intensity" and "magnitude."

**SAND BLANKET** A layer of sand, from a few inches to several feet thick, extruded onto ground surface through a central vent or linear fissure by a sand boil. See Slide #7.

**SAND DUNE** A low mound, ridge, bank, or hill of loose, windblown sand. Most of the sand in the bootheel dunes was derived from "reworking" the braided streams in the area during dry swings of climate. However, some dunes have formed by the sand brought to the surface by extrusive seismic features later lifted by the wind and redeposited. (See Slide #95.)

**SCARP** See "escarpment".

**SEDIMENT** A general term for material carried by streams or other erosion agents and deposited as loose fragments. In the New Madrid Seismic Area, most sediment has been deposited by streams, but considerable wind-deposited sediments exist.

**SEICHE** (Pronounced "saysh"). An oscillation of a body of water in an enclosed or semi-enclosed basin. Earthquake induced ground motion can cause a seiche if the frequencies of the seismic wave strike a resonance with the water body. If the natural period of vibration is in harmonic phase with the periodicity of the ground motion, a seiche may form in lakes, bays, or segments of a stream. We suggest this factor as a possible contributor to the destruction of the great forest upstream from New Madrid on February 7, 1812. (See Slides #32-#35.)

**SEISMIC** Pertaining to earthquakes. See "earthquake," "seismic wave," and "seismology."

**SEISMIC WAVE** Vibratory waves that travel within and along the surface of the earth. They can be caused by natural sources like earthquakes or by human sources such as explosions. The four basic types are P-waves, S-waves, Rayleigh waves, and Love waves. A P-wave is a compressional wave like the waves in air we call sound waves. An S-wave is a shear wave that does not exist in gaseous or liquid matter, but only in solids. P- and S-waves are called "body waves" because they can propagate through the body of a solid in any direction. Earthquakes can send P- and S-waves through the earth, from one side to the other. Rayleigh and Love waves are called "surface waves" because they only travel parallel to the earth's surface and cannot propagate through the body of a medium. Rayleigh waves cause the earth to rise and fall in an elliptic motion much like the motions at the crests of water waves on the ocean. Love waves cause a horizontal shear motion perpendicular to the direction the wave is traveling. Rarely would you be situated at or near the epicenter of an earthquake, the point directly over the source of the disturbance and rarely would one directly experience the motions of a fault rupture as it produces a quake. When we say we have experienced an earthquake, we are almost always talking about experiencing the passage of the seismic waves as they ripple through our location. The origin of the quake can be hundreds of miles away. If an earthquake is 100 miles away, the fault rupture that caused it would have happened 20-25 seconds before you would feel it at your location. Among the various types of seismic waves, P-waves are the fastest, traveling 4-5 miles per second. They are the first to inform you that an earthquake is on the way. That's why they are called "Primary" or "P-waves". S-waves are the second fastest, traveling 2.5-3 miles per second. They are the second waves to arrive when the train of seismic waves from a distant quake has begun to shake the ground where you are located. The slowest waves, and the ones with the lowest frequencies (slow vibrations), are the surface waves which travel at different speeds ranging from 1.8-2.0 miles per second. Seismic waves can be very destructive and ultimately account for every earthquake features seen in the photos of this book. See "earthquake" and "seismology."

**SEISMICALLY INDUCED LIQUEFACTION** Abbreviated: SIL. Liquefaction which is caused by ground motion during earthquakes. Sand boils or sand fissures which are instances of SIL can also respond to ground water pressures and the vibrations of vehicles, trains, or machinery subsequent to the earthquake that formed them. Thus, a SIL can also, from time to time, be a HIL or a

MIL. See "hydrologically induced liquefaction (HIL) and mechanically induced liquefaction (MIL).

**SEISMOLOGY** A branch of geology or geophysics dealing with the causes, consequences and interpretations of seismic waves in the earth. Earthquake seismologists study seismic waves caused by earthquakes. Measurement and interpretation of these natural waves has enabled scientists to deduce the internal structure of the earth. Exploration seismologists study seismic waves caused by planned explosions. Measurement and interpretation of these artificially-induced seismic waves have enabled geologists to find oil and other valuable mineral deposits. Every petroleum deposit found since 1940 has been discovered this way. See "seismic waves."

**SHARD** A piece or fragment of pottery. American Indians have lived in the NMSZ for more than 20,000 years. It is not uncommon to find pieces of Indian potshard in extrusive seismic sand features throughout the region.

**SIL** See "seismically induced liquefaction".

**SPOIL BANK** An embankment of earth material dredged from a channel and dumped beside it. The spoil may also serve as an artificial levee in some cases.

**STE. GENEVIEVE FAULT** A large fault zone extending for 100 miles from west of Bloomsdale, Missouri, across the Mississippi River at Grand Towers, and terminating at the conjunction of the Wabash Valley Fault and the New Madrid Fault near Metropolis, Illinois. The Ste. Genevieve Fault has produced no large earthquakes in historic times. See "Wabash Valley Fault" and "New Madrid Fault."

**STRIKE-SLIP FAULT** A fault on which the movement is horizontal, parallel to the compass direction (strike) of the fault trend. In other words, it's major movement is, for example, north-south instead of up-down (dip). In fault line looking down of a strike-slip fault, if the relative motion has been such that the right side has moved toward you then that is a "right lateral strike-slip fault. If it was the left side that moved toward you, we call that "left-lateral" motion. The Bootheel Lineament seems to be a right-lateral strike-slip fault. The northern and southern branches of the New Madrid Fault, as defined by seismic instruments, are also right-lateral strike-slip faults. See "fault," "normal fault," "reverse fault," "thrust fault," and Slide #10.

**STRONG EARTHQUAKE** Richter magnitude in the range of 6.0-6.9. See "magnitude."

**STRUCTURE** The orientations and relative positions of the rock masses of an area. Structural features result from such processes as faulting, folding, or other deformation. Geologists would call the Tiptonville Dome a "structure". See "tectonic."

**TECTONIC** Referring to geologic processes involving faulting, folding and other deformations due to regional stresses in the earth's crust. The Tiptonville Dome and Bootheel Lineament are probably tectonic features. See "structure" and "fault."

**TECTONICS** A branch of geology dealing with deformational features of the outer part of the earth, and their relations, origins, and historical evolution. See "tectonic."

**THRUST FAULT** A reverse fault whose plane of fracture is nearly horizontal. Such faults result from horizontal compressional forces, like those in the NMSZ. The center portion of the New Madrid Fault is a thrust fault. Thrust faults tend to produce larger magnitude earthquakes than normal or strike-slip faults. See "fault" and Slide #10.

**USGS** Abbreviation for "United States Geologi- cal Survey," a division of the U.S. Department of the Interior.

**WABASH VALLEY FAULT** An active fault zone roughly paralleling the Wabash River valley in southwestern Indiana and southeastern Illinois. The Wabash Valley Fault appears to be colinear with the New Madrid Fault and perpendicular to the Ste. Genevieve Fault. All three of these major faults connect near Metropolis, Illinois. The Wabash Valley Fault has produced the two largest earthquakes in the Midwest during the 20th century: A magnitude 5.4 near Eldorado, Illinois, in 1968 and a magnitude 5.2 near Lawrenceville, Illinois, in 1987. By comparison, the largest earthquake on the New Madrid Fault since 1895 was a 5.0 in 1976 while the Ste. Genevieve Fault has not produced anything larger than 3.0 in recent history. See "New Madrid Fault" and "Ste. Genevieve Fault."

**WASHOUT** The washing-out or away of earth materials as a result of a flood or a sudden and concentrated downpour, often causing extensive scouring and bank caving; also, a place where such an event has occurred. In the New Madrid area, water ejected during SIL events might well have created washouts, especially along the flanks of escarpments. See the discussion of the feature known as Des Cyprie, Slide #20.

# BIBLIOGRAPHY


Ad Hoc Working Group on Dec. 3, 1990, Earthquake Prediction. (1990) *Evaluation of the December 2-3, 1990. New Madrid Seismic Zone Prediction.* Nat'l Earthquake Prediction Evaluation Panel Report, U.S. Geological Survey, 58 pp.

Algermissen, S.T., and Hopper, Margaret. (1984) *Estimated Maximum Regional Seismic Intensities Associated with an Ensemble of Great Earthquakes that Might Occur Along the New Madrid Seismic Zone.* U.S.Geological Survey, Reston, Virginia, Map MF-1712, (Reprinted 1986)

Amick, D., Maurath, G., and Gelinas, R. (1990) *Characteristics of Seismically Induced Liquefaction Sites and Features Located in the Vicinity of the 1886 Charleston, SC, Earthquake.* Seismological Research Letters, Vol. 61, No. 2, pp. 117-130.

Amick, D., and Gelinas, R. (1991) *The Search for Evidence of Large Prehistoric Earthquakes Along the Atlantic Seaboard.* Science. Vol. 251. pp. 655-658.

Byerly, P. (1956) *The Fallon-Stillwater Earthquakes of July 6, 1954, and august 23, 1954.* Bull. Seis. Soc. Am. Vol. 46, No. 1, pp. 1-33.

Chapman, M.C., Bollinger G.A., Sibol, M.S., and Stephenson, D.E. (1990) *The Influence of the Coastal Plain Sedimentary Wedge on Strong Ground Motion from the 1886 Charleston, SC, Earthquake.* Earthquake Spectra. Vol. 6, No. 4, pp. 617-640.

CMVEB. (1974-91) *Central Mississippi Valley Earthquake Bulletin (CMVEB).* Compilations by Stauder, Himes, and others of current seismicity periodically published from the seismic data recorded by St. Louis University and Memphis State University.

CUSEC. (1992) *Proceedings of Research Summit Workshop.* cosponsored by Federal Emergency Management Agency (FEMA), U.S. Geological Survey (USGS), and the Central U.S. Earthquake Consortium (CUSEC), July 29-30, 1992, Memphis, TN. 158 pp.

Davis, L.L., and West L.R. (1973) *Observed Effects of Topography on Ground Motion.* Bull. Seis. Soc. Am., Vol. 63, No. 1, pp. 281-296.

Ervin, C.P., and McGinnus, L.D. (1975) *The Reelfoot Rift: Reactivated Precursor of the Mississippi Embayment.* Geol. Soc. Am. Bull., Vol. 86, pp. 1287-1295.

Ferguson, J. (1976) *Seismic Wave Attenuation in the Coastal Plain Wedge of South Carolina.* Master's Thesis. University of North Carolina, Chapel Hill. 122 pp.

Fuller, Myron. (1912) *The New Madrid Earthquake.* U.S.G.S. Bulletin 494, Reprinted in 1991 (with Foreword by David Stewart) by Center for Earthquake Studies, SEMO State Univ., Cape Girardeau, MO. 120 pp with fold-out map.

Gomberg, J. (1992) *Tectonic Deformation in the New Madrid Seismic Zone: Inferences from Boundary element Modeling.* Seismological Research Letters, Vol. 63, No. 3, pp. 407-426.

Gori, P., and Hays, W., editors. (1984) *Proceedings of the Symposium on the New Madrid Seismic Zone.* U.S. Geological Survey, Reston, Virginia. Open File Report 84-770, 468 pp.

Guion, W.B. (1850) *Swamp Lands in Missouri and Arkansas.* U.S. Corps of Engineers, Appendix to Congressional Report No. 108, U.S. House of Representatives, 31st Congress, 1st Session, (to accompany Bill H.R. No. 44), pp. 11-14.

Hamilton, R., and Johnston, A. (1990) *Tecumseh's Prophecy: Preparing for the Next New Madrid Earthquake.* U.S. Geological Survey, Reston, Virginia, Circular 1066, 30 pp.

Heaton, T. (1975A) *Tidal Triggering of Earthquakes.* Geophysical Jour. R. Astro. Soc. Vol 43, pp. 307-326.

Heaton, T. (1975B) *Sun and Moon Tidal Forces May Trigger Some Classes of Earthquakes.*Earthquake Information Bulletin, Vol. 7, No. 3, May-June, pp. 14-15.

Hildenbrand, T.G., Kane, M.F., and Stauder, W. (1977) *Magnetic and Gravity Anomalies in the Northern Mississippi Embayment and their Spatial Relation to Seismicity.* U.S. Geol. Survey Misc. Field Studies Map, MF-914.

Jibson, R., and Keefer, D. (1988) *Landslides Triggered by Earthquakes in the Central Mississippi Valley, Tennessee and Kentucky.* U.S. Geological Survey, Denver, Colo., Professional Paper 1336-C, 24 pp. plus maps.

Jibson, R., and Keefer, D. (1992) *Analysis of the Seismic Origin of a Landslide in the New Madrid Seismic Zone.* Seismological Research Letters, Vol. 63, No. 3, pp. 427-438.

Johnston, A.C., and Nava, S. (1985) *Recurrence Rates and Probability Estimates for the New Madrid Seismic Zone.* Jour. Geophysical Research, Vol. 90, No. 87, pp. 6736-6753.

Johnston, A.C., and Shedlock, K.M. (1992) *Overview of Research in the New Madrid Seismic Zone.* Seismological Research Letters, Vol. 63, No. 3, pp. 193-208.

Johnston, A.C., Shedlock, K.M., Herrmann, R.B., and Hopper, M.G., editors, (1992) *The New Madrid Seismic Zone.* Seismological Research Letters, Special Issue, published by Seismological Society of America, Eastern Section, Vol. 63, No. 3, July-Sept, 489 pp.

Kellog, F.H., Mann, O.C., and Howe, W.H. (1974) *Regional Earthquake Risk Study*, Mississippi-Arkansas-Tennessee Council of Governments, Memphis Delta Development District; U.S. Dept. Housing & Urban Development (MATCOG Report), 382 pp.

*Kilston, S., and Knopoff, L. (1963) Lunar-Solar Periodicities of Large Earthquakes in Southern California.* Nature. Vol. 304, July 7, pp. 21-25.

Knox, Ray. (1992) *Geomorphic Evidence of Recent Seismicity on an Extension of the Northwest Branch of the New Madrid Seismic Zone.* Paper given at Annual Meeting of Missouri Academy of Science, Rolla, Missouri, April 1992.

Knox, Ray, and Stewart, David. (1992) *Matching the More Dramatic Contemporary Accounts of the New Madrid Earthquake With Geology* Paper presented at Annual Meeting of Missouri Academy of Science, Rolla, Missouri, April 1992.

Knox, Ray, and Stewart, David. (1993) *A Classification of Morphoseismic Features in the New Madrid Seismic Zone.* Invited paper accepted for presentation at 1993 Meeting of Geological Society of America, North-Central Section, Rolla, MO, to be submitted to the *Bulletin of the GSA* in Spring 1993.

Kokus, M. (1990) *18.6 Year and 19 Year Periods in Southern California and the Upland Earthquakes.* Cycles. March-April, pp. 76-79.

McKeown, F.A., and Pakiser, L.C. (1987) *Investigations of the New Madrid, Missouri, Earthquake Region.* U.S. Geological Survey, Washington, DC, Professional Paper 1236, 102 pp.

Nishenko, S.P., and Bollinger, G.A. (1990) *Forecasting Damaging Earthquakes in the Central and Eastern United States.* Science, Vol. 249, Sept. 21, 1990, pp. 1412-1416.

Mikumo, T., Kato, M., Doi, H., Wada, Y., Tanaka, T., Shichi, R., and Yamamoto, A. (1977) *Possibility of Variations in Earth Tidal Strain Amplitudes Associated with Major Earthquakes.* Jour. Physics of the Earth, Suppl. Issue., Proceedings of Earthquake Precursor Seminar, Japan Scientific Press.

Munson, P.J., Munson, C.A., Bluer, N.K., and Labitzke, M.D. (1992) *Distribution and Dating of Prehistoric Earthquake Liquefaction in the Wabash Valley of the Central U.S.* Seismological Research Letters, Vol. 63, No. 3, pp. 337-342.

Nishenko,S.P., Bollinger, G.A. (1990) *Forecasting Damaging Earthquakes in the Central and Eastern U.S.* Science, Vol. 249, Sept. 21, pp. 1412-1416.

Nuttli, Otto. (1973) *The Mississippi Valley Earthquakes of 1811 & 1812: Intensities, Ground Motion, and Magnitudes.* Bulletin of the Seismological Society of America, Vol. 63, pp. 227-248. (Includes microfiche appendix of numerous newspaper accounts throughout U.S. during time of earthquakes.)

Nuttli, Otto. (1979) *Seismicity of the Central United States.* Geological Society of America, Reviews in Engineering Geology, Vol. IV, 67-93.

Nuttli, Otto. (1989) *Effects of Earthquakes in the Central United States.* Second Edition. (Foreword & Appendices by David Stewart) Center for Earthquake Studies, SEMO State Univ., Cape Girardeau, MO. 50 pp.

Obermeier, S.F. (1984) Liquefaction Potential in the Central Mississippi Valley. U.S. Geological Survey Open File Report. 84-515.

Obermeier, S.F. (1989) *The New Madrid Earthquakes: An Engineering-Geologic Interpretation of Relict Liquefaction Features.* U.S. Geological Survey Professional Paper 1336-B, 114 pp. with maps.

Obermeier, S.F. (1990) *Earthquake-Induced Liquefaction Features in the Coastal Setting of South Carolina and in the Fluvial Setting of the New Madrid Seismic Zone.* U.S. Geological Survey Professional Paper 1504, 44 pp. with maps.

Obermeier, S.F., et al. (1992) *Liquefaction Evidence for Strong Holocene Earthquakes in the Wabash Valley of Indiana-Illinois.* Seismological Research Letters, Vol. 63, No. 3, pp. 321-336.

Palumbo, A. (1989) *Gravitational and Geomagnetic Tidal Source of Earthquake Triggering.* Il Nuovo Cimento. Jour. of Italian Geophysicists. Vol. 12, No. 6, Nov-Dec, pp. 685-693.

Penick, J.L. (1981) *The New Madrid Earthquakes.* Revised Edition. University of Missouri Press, Columbia, MO. 176 pp.

Roosen, R., Harrington, R., Giles, J., and Browning, I. (1976) *Earth Tides, Volcanoes and Climatic Change.* Nature. Vol. 261, June 24, pp. 680-682.

Russ, David. (1979) *Late Holocene Faulting and Earthquake Recurrence in the Reelfoot Lake Region.* Geological Society of America Bulletin, Vol. 90, pp. 1013-1018.

Saucier, R. (1977) *Effects of the New Madrid Earthquake Series in the Mississippi Alluvial Valley.*U.S. Army Engineer Waterways Experiment Station Miscellaneous Paper S-77-5, 10 pp.

Saucier, R. (1989) *Evidence for Episodic Sand Blow Activity During the 1811-12 New Madrid Earthquake Series.* Geology. Vol. 17. pp. 103-106.

Saucier, R. (1991) *Geoarchaeological Evidence of Strong Prehistoric Earthquakes in the New Madrid Seismic Zone.* Geology, Vol. 19, pp. 296-298.

Schweig, E.S., and Jibson, R. (1989) *Surface Effects of the 1811-12 New Madrid Earthquake Sequence.* MO Dept. of Natural Resources, Div. of Geology and Land Survey, Rolla, MO. GSA Field Trip ;6, 20 pp.

Schweig, E.S., and Marple, R.T. (1991) *Bootheel Lineament: A Possible Coseismic Fault of the Great New Madrid Earthquakes.* Geology, vol. 19, pp. 1025-1028.

Schweig, E.S., Shen, F., et al. (1992) *Shallow Seismic Reflection Survey of the Bootheel Lineament Area, Southeastern Missouri.* Seismological Research Letters, Vol. 63, No. 3, pp. 285-296.

Schweig, E.S., Marple, R.T., and Li, Y. (1992) *Update of Studies of the Bootheel Lineament in the New Madrid Seismic Zone, Southwestern Missouri and Northeastern Arkansas.* Seismological Research Letters, Vol. 63, No. 3, pp. 277-284.

Seed, H.B., et al. (1988) *Relationship Between Soil Conditions and Earthquake Ground Motions.* Earthquake Spectra, Jour. EQ Engineering, Vol. 4, No. 4, November, pp. 687-729.

Seed, H.B. (1968) *Landslides During Earthquakes Due to Soil Liquefaction.* Amer. Soc. of Civil Engineers, Jour. Soil Mechanics and Foundation Div., Vol. 94, pp. 1055-1122.

Sexton, J.L., Henson, H., Dial, P., and Shedlock, K. (1992) *Mini-Sosie High Resolution Seismic Reflection Profiles Along the Bootheel Lineament in the New Madrid Seismic Zone.* Seismological Research Letters, Vol. 63, No. 3, pp. 297-308.

Spence, W., Herrmann, R.B., Johnston, A.C., and Reagor, G. (1992) *Scientific Retrospective of Iben Browning's Prediction of a 1990 New Madrid Earthquake.* Proceedings of Research Summit Workshop, July 29-30, 1992, Memphis, TN, cosponsored by Federal Emergency Management Agency (FEMA) & U.S. Geological Survey (USGS), pp. 121-124

Stahle, D.W., VanArsdale, R.B., and Cleaveland, M.K. (1992) *Tectonic Signal in Baldcypress Trees at Reelfoot Lake, Tennessee.* Seismological Research Letters, Vol. 63, No. 3, pp. 439-448.

*Stauder, W., Kramer, M., Fischer, G., Schaeffer, S., and Morrissey, S.T. (1976) Seismic Characteristics of southeast Missouri as Indicated by a Regional Telemetered Microearthquake Array.* Bulletin of the Seismological Society of America, Vol. 66, pp. 1953-1964.

Stauder, W. (1982) *Present-day Seismicity and Identification of Active Faults in the New Madrid Seismic Zone.* In McKeown and Pakiser (1987), op cit., pp. 21-30.

Sterns, R.G., and Wilson, C.W. (1972) *Relationships of Earthquakes and Geology in West Tennessee and Adjacent Areas.* Report to Tenn. Valley Authority, Nashville, TN, Vanderbilt, Univ., 344 pp.

Stewart, David. (1991) *Damages & Losses from Future New Madrid Earthquakes.* Federal Emergency Management Agency & Missouri State Emergency Management Agency, Jefferson City, MO. 65 pp with maps.

Stewart, David, and Knox, Ray. (1991) *Representative Earthquake Features in the New Madrid Seismic Zone.* Second Printing. Center for Earthquake Studies, SEMO State Univ., Cape Girardeau, MO. 62 pp.

Stewart, David, and Steckel, Phyllis. (1991) *Significant Damage at a Distance from Moderate to Minor Earthquakes.* Paper in preparation. SEMO State Univ., Dept. of Geosciences, Cape Girardeau.

Tamrazyan, G.P. (1967) *Tide Forming Forces and Earthquakes.* Icarus. 7:59-65.

Thompson, John, and Stewart, David. (1992) *Landslides Induced by a 4.7 Magnitude Earthquake in the Benton Hills of Missouri.* Paper presented at 1992 Annual Meeting of Missouri Academy of Science, Rolla, MO **Published in MAS Transactions, Vol. 26, pp. 91-104 in 1993.**

U.S. Department of Agriculture. (1977) *Soil Survey of New Madrid County, Missouri.* U.S. Dept. of Agriculture & Missouri Agricultural Experiment Station. 71 pp. with maps.

U.S. House of Representatives. (1850) *Swamp Lands in Missouri and Arkansas.* Report No. 108, 31st Congress, 1st Session, February 20, 1850, (to accompany Bill, H.R. 44), 14 pp.

Weems, R., and Perry, W. (1989) *Strong Correlation of Major Earthquakes with Solid-Earth Tides in Part of the Eastern U.S.* Geology, Vol. 17, pp. 661-664.

Wesnousky, S.G., and Leffler, L.M. (1992A) *Repeat Time of the 1811 & 1812 New Madrid Earthquakes: A Geological Perspective.* Bulletin of the Seismological Society of America, Vol. 82, No. 4, August. pp. 1756-1785.

Wesnousky, S.G., and Leffler, L.M. (1992B) *On the Search for Paleoliquefaction in the New Madrid Seismic Zone.* Seismological Research Letters, Vol. 63, No. 3, pp. 343-348.

Zetler, B.D. (1966) *The Contribution of Earthtides to Earthquakes.* ESSA Symposium on Earthquake Prediction, Feb. 7-9, 1966 Proceedings. pp. 35-37.

Zoback, M.D. (1979) *Recurrent Faulting in the Vicinity of Reelfoot Lake, Northwestern Tennessee.* Geological Society of America Bulletin, Vol. 90, pp. 1019-1024.

Zoback, M.D., Hamilton, R.M., Crone, A.J., Russ, D.P., McKeown, F.A., and Brockman, S.R. (1980) *Recurrent Intraplate Tectonism in the New Madrid Seismic Zone.* Science, Vol. 209, pp. 971-976.

# INDEX

## A



## B



## C

## D



## E



## F



## G

## N



## O



## P

## Q



## R



## S



## T

# ABOUT THE AUTHORS

## DR. RAY KNOX

Burnal Ray Knox was born March 29, 1931, at Whizbang, Missouri, a country store and a post office and not much else. It no longer exists. Whizbang was in the Ozark hills of southwestern Missouri, "Not too far from Cyclone," he likes to say, "and actually not too far from Pineville and Huckleberry Ridge, either." He attended high school and "did most of his growing up" in Bentonville, Arkansas—better known as home of the late Sam Walton, founder of the Walmart Chain.

Dr. Knox is also part Native American. His great grandmother was a full-blooded Indian of the Wyandot Tribe. Her native name was "Missouri."

Presently, Dr. Knox is a Professor of Geosciences at Southeast Missouri State University and former Chairman of that Department. His major research interest is geomorphology, the scientific study of landforms and how they got that way. He earned his bachelors and masters degrees in geology from the University of Arkansas at Fayetteville and his doctorate from the University of Iowa in Iowa City.

In recent years he has become quite interested in morphoseismology—the study of how earthquakes mold and alter the landscape. Prior research had focused on the formation of the Ozark Mountains—especially its streams and caves. He is author of fifteen professional presentations and sixteen professional publications. He is coauthor of four books on the New Madrid Seismic Zone.

Dr. Knox is an avid fisherman and backpacker. He loves to involve his students in hiking trips that usually combine geology with such things as trail building and maintenance, wildflower admiring, bird watching, mountain goat observing, and fishing.

He is married to the former Karen Twell, his "bride" of more than 40 years, with whom he lives in Cape Girardeau, Missouri. Karen and Ray have three kids and two "extraordinary" granddaughters.

## DR. DAVID STEWART

David Mack Stewart was born September 20, 1937, in St. Louis, raised in Crystal City, Missouri, graduated from high school in Jefferson City (1955), attended Central Methodist College in Fayette, Missouri, 1955-58 (majoring in philosophy, religion and English) and went to Los Angeles Trade Technical College, 1959 (to study photography). He was the photographer for Self Realization Fellowship, Inc., 1959-1962. He went to Central Missouri State University in Warrensburg, 1962-63 (majoring in social and life sciences), transferred to the University of

Missouri at Rolla where he worked his way through college as a piano teacher, and received a B.S. in Math and Physics (1965), graduating as Salutatorian of his class. After two years as a hydrologist and hydraulic engineer with the U.S. Geological Survey in Garden Grove, California, he returned to Rolla to earn an M.S. and Ph.D. in Geophysics in 1971.

Former Director of the Central U.S. Earthquake Consortium, Marion, Illinois. Former Director of MacCarthy Geophysics Laboratory and Assistant Professor at the University of North Carolina, Chapel Hill. Founder and former Director, Center for Earthquake Studies and Associate Professor at Southeast Missouri State University, Cape Girardeau. He is an Adjunct Instructor at the Emergency Management Institute, Emmitsburg, Maryland. He is a private consultant on seismic risk and damage assessment to government, insurance, and industry. He has given expert testimony for earthquake legislation on state and federal levels and has been an expert witness in many litigations.

He has given lectures, presented seminars, led field trips, or taught courses to thousands of people on virtually every aspect of earthquake seismology, mitigation and engineering. He has given international seminars on earthquake preparation for hospitals in Lima, Peru, and Bogota, Colombia, at the invitation of the Pan American Health Organization and the United Nations Disaster Relief Organization. He has been invited to conduct tours of the New Madrid Seismic Zone attended by scientists and engineers from many countries.

Dr. Stewart is author or coauthor of more than 200 publications, in ten languages, including thirteen books. Two of his works received the "Books of the Year" Award from the *American Journal of Nursing*. Two of his papers won national awards for clarity in technical writing. Two other publications have sold or circulated over a million copies each. In 1990-93 he served on the Editorial Board of *Earthquake Spectra*—the International Journal of Earthquake Engineering.

Dr. Stewart has been quoted in many journals and magazines, as well as by virtually every newspaper in the United States. He has appeared on national television in forty-four countries.

He and his wife, the former Lee Pomeroy, have five children ages 19 to 32—four sons and a daughter. Two are married. They have three grandchildren. (as of June 1995) David cannot claim any Native American blood, but Lee and his children are all part Cherokee. David and Lee celebrated their thirty-third wedding anniversary on September 1, 1995.

Dr. Stewart is a former licensed United Methodist Pastor who served the Illmo United Methodist Church at Scott City, Missouri, in 1993 and 1994. David and Lee are both members of the First United Methodist Church of Marble Hill, Missouri, where Lee is a choir director. David enjoys playing the piano, loves hiking and raises four-leaf-clovers for a hobby. David and Lee live on a farm in Bollinger County, Missouri.

# THE EARTHQUAKE AMERICA FORGOT

## 2,000 Temblors in Five Months . . . And it Will Happen Again

### by Dr. David Stewart & Dr. Ray Knox

**Cover by Don Greenwood, Illustrations by Anthony Stewart**

You'll be an eye witness. An experience you'll never forget. This book will take you back to the times and places of the greatest sequence of earthquakes in the last 2,000 years of World History—the New Madrid earthquakes of 1811–12. From the safety of your favorite reading chair, you'll encounter River Pirates, Indians, Romance, War, Peace, Good Times, Tough Times, Slavery, Corruption, Heroes, Scoundrels, Bizarre Animal Behavior, Murder, Mystery—Political, Social and Geologic Upheavals all at the same time. Famous people were there—President Thomas Jefferson; Artist and Naturalist, John James Audubon; Explorer and Governor, Meriwether Lewis; Abraham Lincoln (age three at the time); Teddy Roosevelt's Grandfather, the fiery, charismatic Shawnee Chief Tecumseh, and his brother, the Shawnee Prophet Tenskwatawa. This is the most complete account of these earthquakes ever published. Dozens of incredible stories, fascinating first-person accounts, and here-to-fore unpublished facts—plus more than two-hundred photographs, figures, maps and illustrations, including pictures of seismic features still visible in the landscape of the New Madrid Fault Zone today. The definitive work on the Great New Madrid earthquakes. Reads like a novel. But this is not fiction. These fantastic events actually happened. Once you start you won't want to put it down. When you read this book you'll feel like you were there . . . and are glad you survived. If you buy only one book, buy this one.

(EAF) First Edition 1995
376 pages, 8.5x11, 280 photos, maps and illustrations, index, bibliography, hardcover
LCCN 91-91492
ISBN 0-934426-45-7
$29.95

# THE EARTHQUAKE THAT NEVER WENT AWAY

## The Shaking Stopped in 1812 . . . But the Impact Goes On

### by Dr. David Stewart & Dr. Ray Knox

Get comfortable and take an armchair field trip to the greatest display of earthquake features in the world. See how a sequence of massive earthquakes long ago still effect the live and times of people living in and around the New Madrid Fault Zone now. When the shaking is over, the impact of a great earthquake is not. It's lasting effects can reach down through the centuries to touch people today—influencing engineering, agriculture, transportation, and the way people live and think. You will see seismic sand boils formed two centuries ago where farmers still get stuck with their tractors. You'll see 200-year-old seismic sand fissures under railroad tracks that cause train derailments today. You'll see modern houses built over old earthquake landslides whose foundations are cracking up and creeping down hill—a process started by seismic forces long before the town was settled. This book gives you a "vicarious visual tour," complete with the narrative you would hear from two leading world authorities as your personal guides. 138 original photos, 5 figures, and 3 maps of faults, fissures, and scars in the landscape still visible today from the great New Madrid earthquakes of 1811–12. (These same illustrations are also available as 35 mm color slides, see page 217). Carefully researched and scientifically rigorous, yet written with wit and entertainment for the enlightenment of the public. You will be amazed at what you can still see of these earthquakes—evidence permanently impressed upon the landscape of the unbelievable churning, boiling, cracking and splintering of the earth's surface from the unimaginable violence of the cataclysms that caused these lasting landforms that people must still deal with today.

(NWA) First Edition 1993, Second Printing 1996.
222 pages, 8.5xll, 138 photos, 5 figures, 4 tables, 3 maps, index, bibliography, quality paperback
LCCN 92-75133
ISBN 0-934426-54-6

$19.95

# THE NEW MADRID FAULT FINDERS GUIDE

## by Dr. Ray Knox & Dr. David Stewart

Fault finding is fun. And the New Madrid Seismic Zone is the place to do it. This book has maps, road logs, directions and commentary—a set of seven exciting, educational self-guided field trips. Shows you where to visit and see for yourself some of the thousands of faults, fissures, crevasses, sand boils, and other scars in the landscape still seen today—200 years after the great New Madrid earthquakes of 1811–12. Great for teachers and students of earth science classes. Step into an explosion crater. Climb into an earthquake crevasse. Walk barefoot on the world's largest sand boil. Go boating on an earthquake lake. Talk with a living witness —a giant 300-year-old oak caught in a sand boil in 1812. See where the Mississippi River ran backwards and waterfalls formed. See where whole towns disappeared. Visit the epicenter of the largest earthquake (8.8) in the history of the lower 48 states—a place where a factory, a power plant, and an airport are located today. See city streets slowly sinking and cracking because they were built over earthquake landslides from 1811-12. Look out over the Mississippi River where the original site of New Madrid, Missouri, is now under water on the Kentucky side. You will learn how to recognize sand boils, explosion craters and other earthquake features that dot the farm fields and line the highways throughout this fascinating region—features you may have passed many times before, but did not recognize as seismic in origin. Interstate Highway 55, between Blytheville, Arkansas, and Benton, Missouri, is a 101-mile stretch that should be called "Earthquake Alley." There is at least one chance in three that a measurable earthquake will happen on the New Madrid Fault on any day you should drive the Interstate through here. This is the greatest outdoor earthquake laboratory in the world. Great vacation guide. One trip with this book and you'll never look at a landscape the same again. It'll change your outlook on earth.

(FFG) First Edition 1995
181 pages, 8.5x11, 56 maps, photos and figures, index, biblio, quality paperback
LCCN 91-91374
ISBN 0-934426-42-2 $16.95

# 150 EARTHQUAKE SLIDES ON THE NEW MADRID SEISMIC ZONE

## by Dr. David Stewart & Dr. Ray Knox

It has been said that "an expert is someone more than twenty miles from home with a tray of slides." Now you can become an expert on the Great New Madrid Earthquakes of 1811-12—taking friends, civic groups, professional peers, and students of all ages on a fascinating picture-tour of the fault zone and its thousands of earthquake features. The New Madrid Fault Zone is the most extensive and outstanding display of landforms sculptured by earthquakes known on earth. Scientists, engineers, and visitors from all over the world come to see what is there and marvel. There are more sand boils, fissures, landslides, broken stream channels, seismic ponds, explosion craters, and earthquake lakes in this region than anywhere on earth. See the world's largest sand boil—over a mile long and 136 acres in size. (Most sand boils are less than 10 feet in diameter.) These slides will take you and your audience on a tour where you fly over, drive by, and walk on some of the world's greatest morphoseismic features. Step into a graben crevasse. Fly along the Bootheel fault. Climb up an earthquake landslide. Photos from five states—Arkansas, Illinois, Kentucky, Missouri and Tennessee. 150 color slides, 35 mm, two carousel trays full. Complete set of narrative notes, a glossary of definitions, and instructions for a smashing presentation to any group. The New Madrid Seismic Zone has a story to tell and you can be the one to tell it. All you need is this set of slides and the book that accompanies it. You will be awed by what you see—and so will your audiences.

Slide set comes in an attractive 3-D-ring binder with archival plastic sleeves for storage and easy previewing. Delivered shrunk-wrapped and ready to use. Binder contains a 3-hole punched copy of *The Earthquake that Never Went Away* (see p. 215) which serves as the narrative notes for the set.

(SET) First Edition 1993
150 color slides, 35mm, D-ring binder, 222 page book of notes with index, bibliography
ISBN 0-934426-51-1 $180.00 for complete set with book
Slides from set also available individually $4.00 each ppd

# OTHER BOOKS Available from Gutenberg-Richter

## DAMAGE & LOSSES FROM FUTURE NEW MADRID EARTHQUAKES

**Dr. David Stewart**

The New Madrid Fault has the capability of causing damage in 22 states. Do you live in one of them? What will happen in your area when the next major New Madrid quake hits? What is the probability in your lifetime? With this easy-to-use manual you can find out how many buildings will collapse, how many will be injured, how many will die, how many bridges will be out, and a host of other valuable information about the county where you live. Ideal for medical personnel, emergency planners, business owners, insurance personnel, school officials, government leaders, national guard units, Red Cross chapters, or anyone who wants to know what will happen during the next destructive New Madrid earthquake. Published jointly by Missouri State Emergency Management Agency and Federal Emergency Management Agency.

(DAL) Fourth Printing 1994. 74 pp, 8.5x11, 16 maps, softcover
ISBN 0-934426-53-8 FREE ON REQUEST (postage & handling $3.00)

## THE NEW MADRID EARTHQUAKE

**by Myron Fuller (Foreword by Dr. David Stewart)**

This is the book all researchers and serious students start with in studying the great New Madrid earthquakes of 1811-12. Originally released in 1912 as a U.S. Geological Survey publication, Written by a geologist, this is the first serious scientific study of these events to be put into print. Many photos and figures. A "must book" for serious students of Midwestern earthquakes.

(NMF) 1990 edition. 120 pages, 8.5x5.5, quality paperback
ISBN 0-934426-49-X $15.95

## THE NEW MADRID EARTHQUAKES

**by Dr. James Lal Penick Jr. (Foreword by Dr. Otto Nuttli)**

A scholarly and authoritative account of the New Madrid earthquakes written by a historian. Meticulously documented. Photos and line drawings. Well written. Published by University of Missouri Press. See Order Form on p. 223.

(NMP) Revised Edition 1981. 176 pages, 5x7, quality paperback.
ISBN 0-8262-0344-2 $16.95

## EFFECTS OF EARTHQUAKES IN THE CENTRAL UNITED STATES

**by Dr. Otto Nuttli (Foreword by Dr. David Stewart)**

Dr. Nuttli was the leading world authority on this subject in his life-time. This was his last published work. Maps, figures, and photos. Considers all active faults in the Midwest. Clearly articulated. The perfect primer on earthquake risk in the central U.S.

(CUS) 1990 edition. 50 pages, 6x9, quality softcover.
ISBN 0-934426-50-3 $9.95

# OTHER ITEMS Available from Gutenberg-Richter

## NEW MADRID FAULT TOURS

Take a tour of the New Madrid Fault Zone with Dr. David Stewart and/or Dr. Ray Knox. If interested, send name, address and phone number to Dr. Stewart in care of Gutenberg-Richter Publications.

## GUEST LECTURERS

David Stewart is available for a variety of public lectures or seminars suitable for any audience, profession, or age group. Address inquiries to Gutenberg-Richter Publications, address and phone given on page 221.

## T-SHIRTS AVAILABLE WITH EARTHQUAKE ART

Don Greenwood's exquisite artwork displayed on the cover of the book, ***The Earthquake America Forgot,*** is available on a T-shirt. For information on prices and sizes, contact Gutenberg-Richter Publications, address and phone given on page 221. A great gift idea!

## HOW TO MAKE YOUR OWN LIQUEFACTION MODEL

**Free Booklet by Dr. David Stewart**

Complete and simple instructions on how to make an earthquake liquefaction model. Make an earthquake (hit the table or stomp on floor) and watch the soil turn to quicksand. A great science fair project. Copies are free with book order. Otherwise, send $1.00 for postage and handling.

## EARTHQUAKE GUIDE FOR HOME AND OFFICE

**Free Booklet by Maria Dillard and Dr. David Stewart**

Published in 1990 by Southwestern Bell Telephone Company and the Center for Earthquake Studies at Southeast Missouri State University, this excellent illustrated twelve-page booklet summarizes the hazards, what you should expect, and what you should do during an earthquake whether you are at home or at the office, in a vehicle, in an elevator or on the street. Also contains advice on earthquake preparation and what phone numbers you should post prior to an earthquake emergency. Copies are free with book orders. Otherwise send $1.00 for postage and handling. Available in bulk quantities to schools, civic organization, and others for cost of shipping.

GR

GUTENBERG-RICHTER
PUBLICATIONS

# ORDERING INFORMATION

You may order Gutenberg-Richter Publications by directly from the publisher by remitting check or money order. A convenient order form is given at the end of this book on page 223 which may be photocopied, completed, and sent with your order. You may also use your VISA or Master Card, either by mail (see Order Form, p. 223) or by telephone via the toll free number given on the next page. You may also inquire at your local bookstore who can special-order these books for you should they not have them in stock. If your library does not have copies of Gutenberg-Richter publications, encourage them to order copies directly from the publisher. Purchase Orders Welcome.

**MISSOURI SALES TAX:** Missouri residents must pay 6% sales tax on all orders. For non-Missouri residents there is no tax.

# SHIPPING INSTRUCTIONS

**BOOK ORDERS:** Please remit appropriate total for books desired plus shipping and handling as follows: For U.S.A., Mexico and Canada, add $3.00 for first book, plus $1.50 for second book, plus $1.00 per book thereafter. Other countries: Surface Parcel Post is $8.00 for first book, plus $4.00 for second book, plus $2.00 per book thereafter; Air Parcel Post is $15.00 for first book, plus $8.00 for second book, plus $3.00 per book thereafter.

**SLIDE ORDERS:** Complete set of 150 Colored Slides including book of narrative notes, $8.00 for Priority Mail within the U.S.A., $10.00 for Canada, and $35.00 for International Air Parcel Post in all other countries. Individual slides retail for $4.00 each which includes First Class Postage for U.S.A., Mexico, and Canada. All other countries include an additional $1.00 per slide for International Air Mail. Specify slides by numbers given in the book, *The Earthquake that Never Went Away.*

**COMPLETE LIBRARIES:** Books only, $8.00 (N. America), $15.00 (Other countries). Books plus Slide Set, $15.00 (N. America), $50.00 (Other countries)

# ✌ SPECIAL DISCOUNTS ✌

**COMPLETE NEW MADRID EARTHQUAKE LIBRARY at SPECIAL PRICE**
All seven books listed on Order Form on page 223 ($110 value) — Only $90
All seven books plus full set of 150 colored slides ($290 value) — Only $250
**• SAVE $20.00 ON BOOKS • SAVE $40.00 ON BOOKS & SLIDES •**

**Convenient Order Form Provided in Back on Page 223**

(Please Photocopy This Form as Needed)

**PRE-EARTHQUAKE SALE**
Buy Now before the next Major quake in your area and Qualify for a 5% Discount on all Purchases.*

# ORDER FORM

**IF YOU BUY ONLY ONE BOOK, GET *"THE EARTHQUAKE AMERICA FORGOT."***

| ISBN | Code | Title | Author(s) | Price | Qty | Total |
|---|---|---|---|---|---|---|
| **BOOKS:** | | | | | | |
| 0-934426-45-7 | (EAF) | The Earthquake America Forgot | Stewart/Knox | $ 29.95 | ______ | ______ |
| 0-934426-54-6 | (NWA) | The Earthquake that Never Went Away | Stewart/Knox | 19.95 | ______ | ______ |
| 0-934426-42-2 | (FFG) | The New Madrid Fault Finders Guide | Knox/Stewart | 16.95 | ______ | ______ |
| 0-934426-49-X | (NMF) | The New Madrid Earthquake | Fuller | 15.95 | ______ | ______ |
| 0-8262-0344-2 | (NMP) | The New Madrid Earthquakes | Penick | 16.95 | ______ | ______ |
| 0-934426-50-3 | (CUS) | Effects of Earthquakes in Central U.S. | Nuttli | 9.95 | ______ | ______ |
| 0-934426-53-8 | (DAL) | Damages & Losses from Future Quakes | Stewart | FREE* | ______ | ______ |
| | | * The book DAL is FREE, but Please enclose $3.00 shipping. | | | | |
| **35 mm COLOR SLIDES:** | | | | | | |
| 0-934426-51-1 | (SET) | 150 EQ Slides on the New Madrid Fault | Stewart/Knox | $180.00 | ______ | ______ |
| | (SGL) | Single Slides (Specify by numbers given in NWA) | | 4.00 ea | ______ | ______ |
| **OTHER ITEMS:** | | | | | | |
| | (EQG) | Earthquake Guide for Home and Office | Dillard/Stewart | FREE** | ______ | ______ |
| | (LIQ) | How to Make Your Own Liquefaction Model | Stewart | FREE** | ______ | ______ |
| | | **Please enclose $1.00 shipping unless request is accompanied with purchase. | | | | |

**GET A COMPLETE NEW MADRID EARTHQUAKE LIBRARY & SAVE $20–$40**

(CLB) All seven books listed above (A $110 Value) • Save $20 — ONLY $ 90.00 ______ ______

(CLS) All seven books plus full set of 150 slides ($290 Value) • Save $40 — ONLY 250.00 ______ ______

SUBTOTAL ______________

***YES! I WISH TO TAKE THE 5% PRE-EARTHQUAKE SALE DISCOUNT** 95% of Above = ______________

**SHIPPING CHARGES:** (complete international shipping info on p. 360 of EAF)
Books: (for USA , Mexico & Canada) $3 for first book, $1.50 for 2nd book, $1.00 per book thereafter.
150 Slide Set: (for USA) $8.00. (For Mexico & Canada) $10.00 (Other Countries) $35.00 for Air Parcel Post.
Single Slides: (for USA, Mexico & Canada) No additional charge. (Other Countries) Add $1.00 per slide.
Complete Libraries: (for USA, Mexico & Canada) Books only, $8.00. Books and Slide Set, $15.00.

SHIPPING ______________

☞ **MONEY-BACK GUARANTEE** — 6% SALES TAX (MO Residents Only) ______________

***NOTE: Prices Subject to Change Without Notice*** — **TOTAL**

NAME ______________________ COMPANY ______________________

ADDRESS ______________________________________________

CITY ______________________ STATE __________ ZIP __________

COUNTRY (if outside the U.S.A.) ______________________ PHONE ______________

❑ Enclosed is Check, Cash or Money Order in Amount of ____________

❑ Please Charge to my VISA or MASTER CARD

❑ VISA ❑ MASTER CARD Expiration Date ____________ VISA MasterCard

Card Number ______________________ Signature ______________________

**PURCHASE ORDERS OKAY • Standard Discounts to Bookstores • Federal EIN: 43-1165937**

• Please Make Checks or Money Orders to: Gutenberg-Richter. Enclose with Order and Send To: •

**Gutenberg-Richter, Rt. 1, Box 646, Marble Hill, MO 63764 USA**

☎ **For Telephone Orders Use Toll Free Number: 1-800-758-8629** ☎